Making Public Services Management Critical

Routledge Critical Studies in Public Management

EDITED BY STEPHEN OSBORNE

The study and practice of public management has undergone profound changes across the world. Over the last quarter century, we have seen

- increasing criticism of public administration as the over-arching framework for the provision of public services,
- the rise (and critical appraisal) of the 'New Public Management' as an emergent paradigm for the provision of public services,
- the transformation of the 'public sector' into the cross-sectoral provision of public services, and
- the growth of the governance of inter-organizational relationships as an essential element in the provision of public services

In reality these trends have not so much replaced each other as elided or co-existed together – the public policy process has not gone away as a legitimate topic of study, intra-organizational management continues to be essential to the efficient provision of public services, whist the governance of inter-organizational and inter-sectoral relationships is now essential to the effective provision of these services.

Further, whilst the study of public management has been enriched by contribution of a range of insights from the 'mainstream' management literature it has also contributed to this literature in such areas as networks and inter-organizational collaboration, innovation and stakeholder theory.

This series is dedicated to presenting and critiquing this important body of theory and empirical study. It will publish books that both explore and evaluate the emergent and developing nature of public administration, management and governance (in theory and practice) and examine the relationship with and contribution to the over-arching disciplines of management and organizational sociology.

Books in the series will be of interest to academics and researchers in this field, students undertaking advanced studies of it as part of their undergraduate or postgraduate degree and reflective policy makers and practitioners.

1. Unbundled Government
A Critical Analysis of the
Global Trend to Agencies,
Quangos and Contractualisation
Edited by Christopher Pollitt
and Colin Talbot

2. The Study of Public Management in Europe and the US
A Competitive Analysis of National
Distinctiveness
Edited by Walter Kickert

3. Managing Complex Governance Systems
Dynamics, Self-Organization and
Coevolution in Public Investments
Edited by Geert Teisman, Arwin van
Buuren and Lasse Gerrits

4. Making Public Services Management Critical
Edited by Graeme Currie, Jackie Ford,
Nancy Harding and Mark Learmonth

Making Public Services Management Critical

Edited by Graeme Currie, Jackie Ford, Nancy Harding and Mark Learmonth

Routledge
Taylor & Francis Group
New York   London

First published 2010
by Routledge
270 Madison Avenue, New York, NY 10016

Simultaneously published in the UK
by Routledge
2 Park Square, Milton Park, Abingdon, Oxon OX14 4RN

Routledge is an imprint of the Taylor & Francis Group, an informa business

Typeset in Sabon by IBT Global.

Library of Congress Cataloging-in-Publication Data

Making public services management critical / edited by Graeme Currie . . . [et al.].
    p. cm. — (Routledge critical studies in public management ; 4)
    Includes bibliographical references and index.
    1. Public administration—Management.   2. Nonprofit organizations—Management.
3. Social service—Management.   4. Public welfare—Management.   I. Currie, Graeme.
    JF1351.M32 2009
    351—dc22
    2009006695

ISBN10: 0-415-44998-7 (hbk)
ISBN10: 0-203-87261-4 (ebk)

ISBN13: 978-0-415-44998-4 (hbk)
ISBN13: 978-0-203-87261-1 (ebk)

Contents

PART III
Radical Alternatives

Tables

Introduction
Making Public Services Management Critical

Graeme Currie and Mark Learmonth

This volume brings together public services policy and public services management in a novel way that is likely to resonate with academics, policy makers, and practitioners engaged in the organization of public services delivery as it is from a perspective that challenges many received ideas in this field. Starting from the perspective of critical management studies, we embed a critical perspective on policy orthodoxy to present a collection of chapters that cohere around, what we call critical public services policy and management studies (CPSPMS). In so doing we bring together previous disparate fields of public services policy and public services management, but more importantly, debate and present what 'critical' constitutes when applied to public services policy and management.

CRITICAL MANAGEMENT STUDIES

Public services organizations, full of the rhetoric of leadership, quality, evidence, teams (the list can go on and on) can be lonely places for those of us who do not buy the rhetoric—those of us who are skeptics, who might even describe ourselves as 'nonbelievers.' And the trouble is, management rhetoric seems inescapable. It is seemingly in every report you read, every pronouncement by anyone who is anyone; the pressure to appear to be 'on-message' is so strong that it can often seem like you are the only one with reservations.

Those who can identify with this sort of picture of public services are the kind of people at whom *Making Public Services Management Critical* is aimed. The book offers ways to think about managing and organizing public services that are radically critical of the current beliefs underpinning supposedly 'good management' in public services organizations.

The thinking in this book is radically critical because we do not argue that certain management and leadership practices are flawed and should be replaced by something 'better'; rather we believe that in the current climate of public services, any ambition to manage or lead is problematic. Problematic at root, because management and leadership is intrinsically connected to practices associated with the domination and control of some over others—however humanistic and reasonable the latest form of leadership or team working might make it appear. Public services management is not, in the end, about the pursuit of efficiency, but about the pursuit of power.

Although there are exceptions, there is often little hint of this sort of reading of management and leadership in the academic literature concerned with public services. Indeed, though in many ways heterogeneous, there is an important thread of continuity within the dominant theories and ideas propounded by most writers who have written influentially on public services management: a support for those occupying managerial positions, as well as for the wider social structures that maintain and enhance managers' interests. In other words, much of this work (usually unobtrusively) has reinforced managerial power by taking for granted ways of understanding organizational life that coincide with the priorities and interests of top managers, while simultaneously obscuring nonmanagerial ways to understand organizational life.

But the last 10–15 years have witnessed the rise of a subdiscipline within management studies that has come to be known as "critical management studies" (CMS, hereafter; Fournier and Grey, 2000). In contrast to the dominant traditions in management research that are orientated towards finding ways to make management "better" (better as defined by those in charge of organizations), CMS is concerned with nurturing forms of intellectual engagement with management that challenges the interests of the people in charge. In particular, it seeks to question the dominant way in which we tend to think about management and leadership (as a more or less apolitical set of techniques) and to show how these very techniques themselves can act as a cover for managerial power (Alvesson and Willmott, 2003).

CRITICAL PUBLIC SERVICES POLICY STUDIES

Regarding the model that has informed government reforms worldwide since the 1980s, we might identify the following terms as influential: "New Public Management (NPM)" (Hood, 1991), the development of which the United Kingdom has played a central role, and located within the United States, "Reinventing Government" (Osborne and Gaebler, 1992). It is not our intention to detail the characteristics of NPM or Reinventing Government within our introduction. Readers unfamiliar with such terms might consult another edited volume published by Routledge, *New Public Management: Current Trends and Future Prospects* (McLaughlin, Osborne, and Ferlie, 2002) to gain both a historical and comparative perspective upon contemporary government reforms for the delivery of public services. However, readers should note the impact of NPM and Reinventing Government has spread beyond the United Kingdom and

United States, particularly across North America, Australasia, and the Pacific Rim, with both the World Bank and the Organization for Economic Co-operation and Development (OECD) acting as conduits for the diffusion of reform (McLaughlin and Osborne, 2002). This has led Osborne and Gaebler (1992) to claim the rise of entrepreneurial government is a process evident throughout the world. Certainly the broad aims of NPM and Reinventing Government movements of producing more efficient, effective, and responsive public services appear widely shared worldwide, even if a mixture of strategies, priorities, styles, and methods have been adopted by different governments, dependent upon their tradition regarding the role of the state (Pollitt, 2002). Among early adopters, the United Kingdom can be seen as a radical reformer that exemplifies the managerialist assumptions driving government reforms impacting upon the delivery of public services worldwide. Reflecting this, within our volume we draw mainly upon contributions from the United Kingdom, and to a lesser extent from the United States (as well as one contribution drawing upon the Belgian context), but consider their wider transferability worldwide. Our volume might thus be viewed as a critique of Anglo-American government reforms. However, in asking contributors to consider their readership as international, we hope our critique resonates more widely beyond the Anglo-American case. We also highlight that the CMS perspective is particularly strong in the United Kingdom and this has encompassed a more radical critique of public services reforms, so far relatively absent in other countries.

In the United Kingdom, the CMS critique of government policy focused upon the efficiency and effectiveness of public services delivery is exemplified by the work of John Clarke and Janet Newman (Clarke and Newman, 1993; Clarke et al., 2000; Newman, 2001). Their more radical critique has a number of dimensions that should resonate internationally. These are: professional–management relations; the relationship between social and economic ends, including policy desire for distributed governance of public services organizations; aspirations for joined-up public services delivery against a backdrop of hierarchies and markets; tension between centralization and decentralization of government; increased emphasis upon leadership and other managerialist apparatuses, such as human resource management strategies. We detail each of these in turn.

Within radical critiques of NPM, firstly, the managerialism embedded within policy has been viewed as an attempt to curb the powers of overly independent professionals and an opportunity to inject the type of proactive management evident in more vigorous private sector organizations and drive out the old fashioned bureaucratic administration that was unable to deal with powerful professions. These heighten the latent professional–managerial conflict within public services organizations. Of particular note has been the desire to restate and raise the profile of service quality to the level occupied by efficiency, associated with which 'quality management' has been a central mechanism for diluting professional autonomy and self-regulation.

Secondly, the coexistence of social (concerned with inequity) and economic (concerned with efficiency) facets of NPM, now relabeled (and adapted) as "modernization" in the United Kingdom, offers particularly fertile ground for a radically critical appreciation of management within public sector organizations. The interaction of the economic and social agendas of modernization upon the management of a public services organization may be one whereby, "new patterns of accountability for outcomes sit uneasily with organizationally focused inspection and audit regimes that retain a strong focus on more limited conceptions of accountability and that emphasise the need to limit risk-taking behaviour" (Newman, 2002, 89). Connected to social ends of government policy, there is fierce debate regarding the governance of public services—for example, regarding how decisions are made, on whose behalf and for which stakeholders. Policy encourages public service organizations to build relationships with multiple stakeholders and in particular that citizens and users participate in decision-making. However, this has proved difficult to realize. Consequently, the extent to which public services organizations are in practice moving beyond a narrow economic agenda to encompass a broader social agenda and involve users of service in decision-making is unclear.

Thirdly, linked to the previous point, and consistent with the desire to improve the quality of the public services through new forms of governance and service realignment, we see an increased policy drive to counter the entrenched interests within the public sector by encouraging organizations and professions to move away from silo or tribal type behaviour towards joined-up thinking and collaborating across boundaries. However, this requirement coexists with the need at the organizational level to meet short-term targets and efficiency savings demanded by government. As a consequence, combined with professional tribalism, aspirations for network forms of delivering public services are unlikely to be met (Currie and Suhomlinova, 2006).

Fourthly, we perceive a tension within the modernization agenda between centralization and decentralization. Policy encourages devolution and flexibility, so that organizations are innovative and entrepreneurial. At the same time, as outlined earlier, central government seeks to ensure standards and performance targets are delivered with a particular concern for short-term targets and efficiency savings. Measures of performance towards which auditing bodies orientate are based upon managerialist notions of effectiveness that privilege the economic and marginalize other notions of performance held by professionals. Managers within public service organizations became preoccupied with managing what gets measured or inspected and this has possible perverse effects, such as diverting resources from mainstream activity or squeezing out innovation within the organization (Newman, 2001). The auditing process seems designed to ensure that public sector organizations are working towards meeting their obligations to delivering government policy objectives.

Finally, public services organizations are required to imagine themselves as businesses. Linked to this, public services organizations have developed the apparatuses of contemporary business management (e.g., knowledge management; organizational learning; competence-based leadership development; total quality management; business process re-engineering; culture change programs; human resource management interventions, such as appraisal; strategic planning; mission statements). Marshalling the tools of managerialism, in particular, effective leadership is promoted by policy as the panacea for organizational ills within public services. Yet this, as with much of managerialism, appears inimical to professional practice with its emphasis on collegiality and team working. Following principles associated with human resource management, the labor process has been intensified, and in pursuit of flexibility, the labor force has been divided into core and periphery workers, both aided by the weakening of trade unions and decline of collective bargaining, replaced by individualized labor force/management relations. In short, managerialism both provides the appropriate forms of internal discipline and discretion and constitutes the conduits of implementation, control, and performance audit that are identified as the conditions of accountability to central government (Clarke and Newman, 1997).

BRINGING PUBLIC SERVICES POLICY AND MANAGEMENT TOGETHER CRITICALLY

While we have highlighted the policy tensions previously, we are keen to redress the balance in critical public services policy research that does not sufficiently privilege significant effects of policy at the local management level, which is likely to be acutely felt by much of our readership. Critical public services policy studies touch on issues of relevance to the management community but, for us, remain too focused at the policy level and less focused on everyday management practice. At the same time, while CMS has developed as a strong force within the business and management field, there is limited work that considers public services organizations. Where public services organizations are the site for CMS studies, analysis has taken little account of the policy context that frames management activity. Hence the needs of those academics and practitioners, both management and professional, appear poorly served. To serve these groups adequately, there is a need to take a more critical perspective upon changes from within the business and management literature, but within which critical policy analysis is embedded.

So this book aims to fuel the development of CMS perspectives specifically within public services management research. The work is not without precedent—a volume of critical essays has been recently published on health services management (see Learmonth and Harding, 2004). But we intend to build on this kind of work in order to develop further insights and perspectives. And we do not merely seek to influence academic debate—we believe that CMS can be relevant to people working in public services, not least to practicing managers themselves. We sense there are many within public services looking for a language of contestation to enable them to think through and challenge those management practices with which they are uncomfortable—but which seem to have no alternatives (Learmonth, 2007). We believe therefore that many people might feel more 'at home' with the theoretical ideas in CMS than in so-called 'mainstream' analyses. Furthermore, because many changes in public services have been highly contested, by people with a variety of interests (including different staff groups and representatives of the public) we believe that public services is a particularly fertile ground for a more critical appreciation of management practices (Clarke and Newman, 1997).

With a distinctive CMS flavor, we move away from what we consider to be orthodox critiques of public services policy (exemplified by Ferlie et al., 1996). Our volume couples our concern with CMS with what we regard as a more radical critical 'take' on the policy context that frames management activity within public services organizations, which is consistent with CMS concern for reflexivity and alternative ways of organizing, rather than remains within a functionalist paradigm for organization that privileges performance and top management's viewpoint. In particular, we highlight the interaction of critical public services policy studies and critical management studies (critical public services policy and management studies, henceforth referred to as CPSPMS) with some of the far-reaching managerial changes observable within the public sector. Our edited collection opens up some of the taken-for-granted assumptions about managerialism embedded in policy regarding the right to manage, that there is one best way to manage and the effects of and responses to managerialism.

In summary, we hope to appeal both to public services academics and practitioners new to CMS, but who intuitively connect with such analyses, as well as those more familiar with the area. Particularly perhaps, those people in public services who are also studying in postgraduate programs, and who want help to be critical, in academically legitimate ways, about the practices they observe and take part in within their working lives.

Our collection presents chapters from a broad range of public services domains (e.g., health, education, prisons, local and central government). The collection is cross-disciplinary with contributions from business and management; sociology; psychology; social policy; medicine; political science; philosophy. Reflecting the relevance of contributions, a range of contemporary issues facing managers in public services organizations are examined, including: regulation of professions; risk management; user involvement;

marketing; leadership. Finally, within the collection an international perspective is embedded within contributions from a CMS viewpoint.

Our volume is structured, firstly, to set out and reflect the background to the delivery of public services. Within this part there are four chapters: a historical reflection upon the ethos of self-help and mutual aid that characterized early public services delivery; contemporary rhetoric of government in the United States; the managerialist context in which education is delivered in the United States; the relationship between academics and the practice of management in public services. Recognizing CPSPMS as a broad "church," the second part encompasses critiques of mainstream managerial orthodoxy: regulation of professions; quality and risk management; user involvement; political marketing. Appealing to those concerned for a narrower or more "purist" version of CPSPMS, we move onto more radical critique of public services policy and management in the third part of the book: feminist approaches to leadership; psychoanalytic approaches to policy implementation; Foucauldian-influenced critique of prison services; the application of queer theory to interactions in healthcare delivery; the potential contribution of existentialism to critical analysis of public services organizations; the importance of relations of value that characterise the work of managers and professionals in public services.

In our final chapter, we argue contemporary public services policy and management doesn't have to be this managerialist way. Drawing together debate about what critical constitutes 'critical' with respect to CPSPMS, we propose a more reflexive, more inclusive, less instrumental agenda for practice, pedagogy, and research in public services policy and management. In sum, our collection represents a 'call to arms' regarding how we take CPSPMS forward to build alternative organizations that counter some of the problems raised by our contributing authors.

REFERENCES

Alvesson, M. and H. Willmott. 2003. *Studying management critically*. London: Sage.

Clarke, J. and J. Newman. 1993. *The managerial state: Power, politics and ideology in the re-making of social welfare*. London: Sage.

Clarke, J., S. Gerwitz, and E. McLaughlin. 2000.*New managerialism, new welfare*. Milton Keynes, UK: Open University.

Currie, G. and O. Suhomlinova. 2006. The impact of institutional forces upon knowledge sharing in the UK NHS: The triumph of professional power and the inconsistency of policy. *Public Administration* 84(1): 1–30.

Ferlie, E., L. Ashburner, L. Fitzgerald, and A. M. Pettigrew. 1996. *The new public management in action*. Oxford, UK: Oxford University Press.

Fournier, V. and C. Grey. 2000. At the critical moment. *Human Relations* 53(1): 7–32.

Hood, C. 1991. 'A Public Management for all Seasons' *Public Administration* 69 (Spring): 3–19.

Learmonth, M. 2007. Critical Management Education in Action: Personal Tales of Management Unlearning. *Academy of Management Learning and Education* 6(1):109–113.

Learmonth, M. and N. Harding. 2004. *Unmasking Health Management: A Critical Text*. New York: Nova Science.

McLaughlin, K. and S. P. Osborne. 2002. Current trends and future prospects of public management: A guide. In *New public management: Current trends and future prospects*, eds. K. McLaughlin, S. P. Osborne and E. Ferlie, 1–4. London: Routledge.

McLaughlin, K., S. P. Osborne, and E. Ferlie, eds. 2002. *New public management: Current trends and future prospects*. London: Routledge.

Newman, J. 2001. *Modernising governance: New Labour, policy and society*. London: Sage.

Newman, J. 2002. The New Public Management, modernization and institutional change: Disruptions, disjunctures and dilemmas. In *New public management: Current trends and future prospects*, eds. K. McLaughlin, S. P. Osborne and E. Ferlie, 77–92. London: Routledge.

Osborne, D. and T. Gaebler. 1992. *Reinventing government*. Reading, MA: Addison Wesley.

Pollitt, C. 2002. The New Public Management in international perspective: An analysis of impacts and effects. In *New public management: Current trends and future prospects*, eds. K. McLaughlin, S. P. Osborne and E. Ferlie, 274–292. London: Routledge.

Part I

Rethinking the Background

1   From Collective Struggle to Customer Service

The Story of How Self-Help and Mutual Aid Led to the Welfare State and Became Co-Opted in Market Managerialism

Patrick Reedy

> It can be liberating for people with an interest in changing any situation, to try to understand its place in *time* and in *struggle* (Yeo, 1979, 52).

The obliteration of the past by the present has been a striking feature of the provision of public services through the mechanism of constant reform, or even 'permanent revolution.' Current government policy towards the provision of public services can be characterized in this way. Indeed the very idea of New Labour was to create a discontinuity with 'Old' Labour and an alleged public perception of its electoral unacceptability as a party of tax and spend and statist bureaucracy. As a result the provision of additional resources for public spending has been made conditional on 'reform' and 'modernisation' and such reform is frequently couched in the language of managerialism (Yeo, 1979; Pollitt, 1993; Clark and Newman, 1997). Any reformist agenda tends to stress the newness and the change it is introducing and be based upon a rejection of the past and this is largely what has happened in official discourse concerning the delivery of public services and welfare. However, paradoxically, another trend in government policy towards voluntarism and the ostensible decentralization of public service delivery in the face of a perceived failure of statist solutions to meet welfare need is leading to a renewed interest in the prewelfare state history of alternative provision including self-help and mutualism (Levitas, 2000; Harris, 2004; Kelly, 2007).

However, an exploration of the history of self-help and mutual aid reveals a surprising degree of continuity between official discourse now and in the past. Speeches by contemporary politicians regarding the political dangers of a hostile alienated underclass or of how benefit payments encourage idleness and welfare dependency are couched in strikingly similar terms to those that were being made by the governing classes in the eighteenth century. The design of welfare systems to avoid providing an incentive not to work was as much a feature of government policy two hundred years ago as it is today. The one marked discontinuity is that, whilst politicians of the Right and Center are happy to revive the tradition of nineteenth century charity and voluntarism they are much less likely to refer to the equally significant tradition of working-class mutual self-help. Despite the rhetoric there is still an apparent preference for what Yeo has described as the "passive, individuated, alienated, centralized *consumption*" of welfare as opposed to the "active, associated, accessible, controlled *production* by and for the majority" (1979, 49).

This chapter, therefore, examines the history of working-class self-help and its relationship to the emerging state provision of welfare. I shall argue that the emergence of centralized state public welfare was not inevitable or necessarily wished for by those it was designed to aid and that far from being a purely humanitarian impulse on the part of progressive governments, the model of centralized welfare that emerged beginning with a series of Liberal administrations from 1906 was based on many of the same regulatory and disciplinary motives as the Poor Law that preceded it. In the process, an alternative model of decentralized and democratic provision was rejected despite its being championed both inside government and outside by the friendly societies and other working-class mutual organizations.

One of the ironies of this process that I shall describe later is that the idea that the state should centrally administer welfare, though now questioned from both the Left and the Right, was at least partially brought about by the collective struggle of the labour movement to ameliorate the harsh conditions of market capitalism that arose from the industrial revolution (Harrison, 1984; Thompson, 1991). Thus there were two strands to working-class attempts to improve their economic security, the first being self-help and mutual aid, the second, a struggle for political representation leading to effective demands for a welfare state. The reasons for the victory of the latter over the former are discussed in more detail later. Initially though, I shall discuss the emergence of collective self-help on the part of working people and the response of the authorities to it. I shall then go on to discuss the absorption of mutual aid into the centralized professional bureaucracy of state provision that developed in the twentieth century and its consequences. Finally I shall bring to bear this historical perspective on the official calls for a return to voluntarism and charity that have emerged as a central feature of contemporary public welfare reform, critically assessing this seeming return to community-based welfare against the earlier traditions of mutual aid.

Before moving on to the history of working-class self-help some comments about the complexity of the politics of public service and welfare reform are required, for it cannot be seen as simply an issue of Left (for the Welfare State) and Right (against). To begin, a typical narrative of the story of the welfare state goes something like this: The strength of the labour movement combined with the enlightened self-interest of Liberal progressives at the start of the twentieth century initiated the founding of a comprehensive state welfare system which replaced the patchy, inadequate, and uncoordinated provision of welfare by Poor Law Boards, charity, philanthropy, mutual-aid societies, the private insurance industry, neighbors, and family. After the end of World War II the Labour Government consolidated these foundations and the public sector began its rapid expansion, primarily implemented by the growing army of public sector professional groups such as teachers, doctors, nurses, and social workers. By the 1970s the pressures for reform were becoming evident. The poor performance of the UK economy, increasing public demand on the system combined with an increasingly unwieldy centralized bureaucracy indicated the need for greater financial efficiency and responsiveness to users (Fraser, 2003). The adequacy of the welfare state was attacked both from the Right and the Left, although often for different reasons. The Left criticized it for failing to help those most in need, and for its hierarchical professional structures which tended to patronize and often pathologize its supposed beneficiaries (Hadley and Hatch, 1981). From the late 1970s, the very notion of welfare and state provision was attacked by the New Right which had a major influence on government policy following the election of Margaret Thatcher in 1979 (see Marsland, 1995, for a typical expression of these ideas). Efficiency savings and restructuring marked the early stages of state welfare reform with an increasing role for the private sector. The return of the Labour Party to power in 1997 has not fundamentally seen a move away from the trends set in place by preceding conservative governments. It has, however, placed even more emphasis on managerialist solutions to the problems of efficiency and value for money as well as an ostensible decentralization of provision to a local level, often through the voluntary and charitable sectors (Clark and Newman, 1997). Such a narrative, of course, is only partially true and conceals a great many subtleties. Critics of state welfare on the Left and the Right might, for example, articulate similar concerns regarding the lack of responsiveness of public services to their users but will derive an entirely different set of conclusions about why this is and what should be done about it. When seemingly the very idea of the welfare state and the public services is under attack, via 'rolling back the state,' to be on the Left and to criticize the welfare state could be seen as a self-indulgent and destructive form of disloyalty. Likewise 'self-help' has been recommended by the rich and powerful to the poor as a way of repudiating any responsibilities for the social structures that lead to poverty (again see Marsland, 1995, for an example) as much as having been a resource which the working class has used to build its own organizations and forms of community support (Harrison, 1984). My own preferred course through these complexities has been that I do not wish to lend any support to the attacks on the public provision of welfare on the part of the political Right and that the achievements of the welfare state in providing security to the many have been considerable. That said I do not regard it as a sacred cow that may not be criticized especially because the particular form of the welfare state that has developed was even at its inception not particularly welcomed by those it was designed to serve (Pelling, 1968; Benson, 2003) and in many ways provided a continuation of the regulatory effects of the Poor Law. Whether arguing from the Left or the Right, the typical view of welfare tends to present it as either the benign actions of progressives in the governing classes or as a result of the political pressure of a strengthening labour movement. In both cases it is framed as something given to those it was designed to benefit, not something that its users could themselves take a predominant role in producing and organizing. In the next section I shall outline an alternative tradition in the development of social assistance based upon working-class self-help.

WORKING-CLASS SELF-HELP

From the sixteenth century to the establishment of the welfare state the only official assistance the laboring classes could rely on was provided by the Poor Law. The Elizabethan Poor Law was conceived in response to widespread fears that idle laborers roaming the land were a threat to the stability of society and needed to be set to work or punished (a medieval short sharp shock in the stocks). The Poor Law made a sharp distinction, one that has emerged once more in recent times, between the 'deserving poor,' who could receive relief (the category of which included the 'impotent poor' and the 'able poor') and the 'idle poor' (those who could work but who refused) who should be punished. Although the system was codified through national legislation it was implemented at the parish level under the supervision of Justices of the Peace, assisted by their appointees, the overseers of the poor. The Law required that parishes tax householders to help finance its benefits, thus the system reflected and reinforced the social hierarchy of the day. Support took the form of 'indoor relief' and 'outdoor relief.' Indoor relief consisted of taking the poor within an institution such as a workhouse or almshouse and was designed for the 'impotent poor' and the 'able poor,' (i.e. those who were either incapable of work because of age, sickness or disability or who could not find work but were willing to accept it). Outdoor relief was designed more for those who were temporarily unable to work and took the form of payments of money, clothes, or food. As the building of workhouses was expensive, outdoor relief tended to be the main means of providing Poor Law support to individuals. The system came under increasing strain beginning in the eighteenth century, with war with France inflating the price of corn and leading to large increases in the level of outdoor relief. Some parishes developed systems for using the Poor Law to top up low wages for agricultural laborers, often to head off labor unrest and riots. The resultant increasing burden of the Poor Law led to an expansion of the workhouse system, although these institutions were designed to be unpleasant enough to act as a deterrent to all but the most desperate. In addition, calls for the reform of the Poor Law grew increasingly loud.

In 1834, the 'new' Poor Law Act was passed which largely reflected the concerns of the newly enfranchised middle classes who bore much of the burden of Poor Law rates and who were also concerned to repress growing discontent on the part of the laboring classes. Outdoor relief was scaled back and the workhouse system expanded. This reformed system was to be the basis of government support for the destitute until the Liberal reforms of the twentieth century. The Poor Law was characterized by many of the same concerns that are apparent today (i.e. balancing the danger of unrest with the tax burden on the middle classes and the avoidance of 'welfare dependency'). The system was managed by the governing classes and imposed upon the laboring classes and was designed for deterrence and repression more than for the relief of suffering.

That institutionalization in the workhouse was seen by most working people as a calamitous disgrace is perhaps not surprising given the above and the frequency of accounts of tyrannical overseers or arbitrary decisions were additional incentives to avoid coming under the Poor Law unless every other possible option was exhausted. A particular shame was attached to having a pauper's funeral. A whole range of forms of mutual self-help were utilized to avoid coming into the clutches of the Poor Law system including reliance on family, neighbors, the negotiation of credit with retailers, and the pawnshop. More organized forms of self-help also developed particularly as industrialization and migration from agrarian communities to the towns and cities took place (Harris, 2004). The most important of these institutions were the friendly societies which can be taken as a typical example of working-class mutual aid and one that came to have a significant role in the provision of welfare and on the development of the welfare state. They are therefore the primary example of the principle of mutual aid to be explored in this chapter.

Although the names of the more famous societies such as "The Loyal Ancient Independent Order of Oddfellows" or even "The Antediluvians" reflected their claims to great antiquity (Gosden, 1973), the first mention of friendly societies occurs in the early seventeenth century. They arose initially as 'box clubs' where members would pay a subscription to the box, which would be kept by the local publican and out of which payments could be made for members in need, most commonly to pay for funerals of members. These societies became known as 'friendly' because conviviality was an essential part of their function, with funds from the box also being used to provide the costs of a monthly meeting at the pub and an annual 'feast' as well as paying for attendance at member's funerals. Thus they both "provided welfare and helped migrants to urban centres to recreate the ties and dependencies of the agrarian community" (Harris, 2004, 79).

Thus the origins of friendly societies were small and localized and entirely run by their own members, but from the 1830s individual societies began to become subsumed into larger regional or national organizations, the 'affiliated orders' (Gosden, 1973; Harris, 2004). On the whole, friendly societies were considered as relatively benign by the upper and middle classes, particularly as they relieved pressure on the Poor Law rates, though they sought to regulate and control them through state registration. Many societies preferred an illegal independence to this legislative control, even though the state offered some protection from embezzlement. Official attitudes though were also frequently ambivalent. There was always the suspicion, sometimes justified, that friendly societies (exempt from the Combination Acts which made associations of working people illegal) were providing a front for illegal trade unions which were organized on very similar lines and also provided similar forms of mutual aid. The large affiliated friendly societies shared with trade unions their oaths of secrecy, rituals, passwords, and effective forms of organization and remained illegal until the second half of the nineteenth century (Gosden, 1973). The use of funds for conviviality rather than welfare was also disapproved of though it was unlikely that the societies would have been anywhere near as popular without their social function. However, attempts to establish 'official' or 'county' societies run by the local gentry were largely a failure as working people preferred their own societies.

The societies grew to provide a large scale system of social welfare and the large affiliated orders aimed at a universal provision for working people. By 1803 it was estimated that there were "10,000 individual societies, with a combined membership of 704,350. The number of members rose to more than 800,000 in 1813 and 1814, and to 925,000 in 1815" (Harris, 2004, 81). Around 80 percent of male industrial workers were members of societies in 1892. By 1904 there were approximately 6 million friendly society members as compared with 1.3 million trade union members (Thane, 1996, 28). "In 1912, the last year before the introduction of the statutory system of national insurance, the Chief Registrar estimated that there were approximately 7.2 million members of 'ordinary' friendly societies . . . 730,000 members of other friendly societies . . . and around 7.75 million members of collecting societies, throughout the whole of the United Kingdom" (Harris, 2004, 83–84).

Despite their aspirations to provide a universal system of welfare, members tended to be from the more prosperous sections of the working class and male, although some female friendly societies were established. Apart from the need to be able to afford to save the subscription, Benson (2003) has pointed out that mutualism is sometimes undermined by the sheer struggle for individual survival where desperate people become pitted against each other for economic opportunities in casualized occupations. There were also considerable variations in benefits between different societies. A large affiliated order such as the Manchester Unity of Oddfellows paid members ten shillings a week in sickness benefit in the mid-nineteenth century as opposed to the collecting societies which might only make a single payment to cover the funeral expenses of a deceased member (Harris, 2004). The range of benefits provided by the best societies, however, covered sickness, unemployment, pension, and funeral expenses. Trade unions also provided a range of similar benefits to around 60 percent of their members by 1908 (Harris, 2004).

Societies were organized on democratic, participative, and egalitarian lines which contrasted strongly with the hierarchy of the factory system. "The most important feature of the organization of the local societies was their complete independence. Each society had its own funds and was governed by its own rules as decided by the members" (Gosden, 1973, 14). Even the large affiliated orders, where direct participation became more difficult, retained their democratic ideals which contrasted strongly with the private insurance industry. Members of individual societies tended to be drawn from a variety of occupations partly because single occupation societies were liable to be suppressed as trade unions, which were illegal under the Combination Acts. The officers of the societies were normally selected by a rotation of the members, as was usual in trade unions and other working-class organizations, their period of office usually lasting for around six months (Gosden, 1973). Yeo has argued that their mode of organization constituted "quintessentially working-class or mass democratic devices, as opposed to the vertically organized business, political and cultural machines which private capital favours" (1979, 51).

One of the problems of the early societies was having no reliable way of calculating the income required to cover their expenses and financial failure was common. They tried to protect themselves from this risk by requiring that new members were under forty years of age and in good health. Workers in dangerous occupations such as mining might also be excluded leading such occupations to rely on trade unions rather than friendly societies. The failure of local societies was a major reason for state intervention. Government sought to ensure that magistrates only registered those societies they believed were financially sound, though they would not have had the expertise to make realistic judgements in this regard. Although moralists and critics were inclined to ascribe failure to excessive spending on drink and social activities (and this did sometimes happen) it was more frequently due to the lack of a reliable method of calculating risk. In time the friendly societies developed actuarial tables that provided more reliable sliding scales of benefits and contributions from different members and these became the basis of the private insurance industry and national insurance.

To summarize, friendly societies were, as Yeo outlines:

> enormous, but not universal, mutual associations of working men, the theory of whose practice was collective self-help. In their most

developed forms they practised and believed in federal, associated self-government and in the connections between social goods like recreation, drink, helping others, hospital care, proper funerals, and the maintenance of an adequate life when sick, old or unemployed. They were autonomous working-class products in which the state and respectable opinion showed an obsessive and shaping interest through the nineteenth century. Their "failure" to become universal, and the "failure" of their most advanced forms to fulfil their highest ambitions must not be attributed to their intentions, and thus be moralized rather than explained. It has, rather, to be attached to the material constraints of majority working-class life—the absolute deprivation of spare time, money and cultural resources for all but a minority stratum of workers (1979, 50).

FROM MUTUAL AID TO STATE WELFARE

How did the combination of Poor Law relief, charity, philanthropy, mutual aid and self-help become the welfare state and what was lost and gained in the transition? Some have argued that the welfare state was a product of a powerful and well organized mass labour movement and it is certainly true that "during the 1890s and the early-1900s trade unionists and friendly society members played an increasingly active role in campaigns for state welfare provision" (Harris, 2004, 154), largely in order to universalize benefits across the population and particularly so that the poorest sections of society (whom the friendly societies had found difficult to reach) would be assisted.

Through these campaigns, the societies fostered a strong sense of collective and, eventually, class solidarity which contributed towards the newly emerging working-class political movements (Hobsbawm, 1995). From the eighteenth century, working people, and sometimes their middle class supporters, engaged in various political movements, the prime example being that of Chartism (Harrison, 1984), in order to gain a foothold in the institutions of the state, particularly the legislature, thus enabling them to influence both law and government policy in their favor. These movements eventually developed into a relatively unified labour movement having socialism as its dominant ideology (Hobsbawm, 1995). As Marxism became the dominant variety of socialism, older forms of anti-statist socialism including communitarian anarchism became less popular and a major objective of the labour movement became to increase the representation of the working class in Parliament. The influence of Fabianism on the Labour Party including the work of the Webbs also favored the state as the primary mechanism by which welfare could be effectively and efficiently managed (Pelling, 1968).

Benson has argued that statist solutions became more attractive to the labour movement from the end of the nineteenth century partly because of a decline in working-class participation in their own organizations as living standards improved for many working people. "Workers in the high-wage sectors of the economy came to regard themselves as consumers rather than as producers; in fact they came to regard the new consumerism, rather than job satisfaction, religious certainty, or educational achievement, as the most accessible avenue of individual (and family) advance" (Benson, 2003, 147). One of the results of this process was the weakening of working-class solidarity and to a commitment to a "class alternative—the conception of an alternative society, a goal toward which one moves through the struggle with an opponent" (Benson, 2003, 152). The rapid expansion in union membership of skilled industrial workers is attributed by Benson to largely instrumental attitudes on the part of members rather than a wish for direct political involvement: "the unions' importance in working-class life depended less on their involvement in industrial disputes than upon their participation in more pacific activities that impinged less intermittently on the well-being of their members" (Benson, 2003, 179). In such a climate it is not surprising if the unions preferred statist solutions to ones that relied on the direct participation of their members, such as mutual aid.

It must also be remembered that although the Liberal reforms from 1906 would not have occurred without pressure from a well organized labour movement they were far from being on their terms. They were not so much moves towards socialism as attempts to head off working-class militancy and thus prevent socialism. The first of the major pieces of legislation founding the welfare state was the Old Age Pensions Act of 1908, this was bitterly criticized by the labour movement as being "a pension for the very poor, the very respectable, and the very old" (Harris, 2004, 159). However, it also signalled that the future shape of the welfare state was to be based on central government, rather than on the localism of the Poor Law or the mutualism of working-class self-help. The influence of 'war socialism,' the postwar prestige of the USSR within the UK labour movement and the predominance of progressive Liberals and Fabian rather than Marxist socialism in the 1945 Labour Party all ensured that this centralized statist approach would become the model of public sector welfare provision in the twentieth century (Pelling, 1968; Hadley and Hatch, 1981).

There is a common assumption that the welfare state was unequivocally welcomed by the labour movement and working people but some have argued that this is far from the case and that alternative models of delivery were proposed that were much closer to the mutual aid ideals of the friendly societies. Pelling argues that "the extension of the power of the state at the beginning of this [twentieth] century . . . was by no means welcomed by members of the working class, was indeed undertaken over the critical hostility of many of them, perhaps most of them . . . this hostility derived from working-class attitudes of suspicion or dislike towards existing institutions which were the expression of national social policy" (1968, 2). In other words, working people saw the new institutions as a continuation of the Poor Law. Even within the governing establishment there was not consensus. Yeo describes the battle that W.J. Braithwaite had with Lloyd George over the organization of national insurance. Braithwaite was George's principal treasury assistant on insurance and championed the proposals of the friendly societies for a decentralized approach to national insurance. Braithwaite argued that national insurance should be run on "mutual, local, autonomous, self-governing lines in such a way that it 'could be run from a third floor office in the Strand'" (Yeo, 1979, 57). Likewise Beveridge himself, despite his statist predilections wished that "human society may become a friendly society" consisting of "an affiliated order of branches, some small, each with its own life in freedom, each linked to the rest by common purpose and by bonds to serve that purpose" (Beveridge [1948] cited in Yeo, 1979, 57).

Yeo concludes that far from constituting a "social settlement" (Clark and Newman, 1997, 2) between capital and labor, the formation of the welfare state constituted a battle over its underlying social relations that recalls the attempts to 'officialize' friendly societies in the eighteenth century. Much of the impetus for the solution that emerged can also be seen as a result of the growing power of the private insurance industry. The insurance industry lobbied government hard to water down many of the proposed elements of the original National Insurance Act, particularly any hint of democratic localized control. The friendly societies were thus to be entirely subordinated to the state even though the benefits available to an individual from the new state scheme were "not very much more that he would have obtained previously from a well-run Society" (Yeo, 1979, 62). Some contemporary commentators saw the imposition of a statist solution as an attempt to disarm the labour movement. The very term 'national insurance' stressed a one-nation nationalism rather than the interests of the common people as against other social classes. Hilaire Belloc wrote in 1912 that national insurance "had been designed to capture organized labor and cut its claws" (Yeo, 1979, 69).

It can be argued that the effects of this defeat of mutual aid and participative democratic social assistance have been serious and have given rise to many of the criticisms of a centralized, professional-bureaucratic welfare state which have become commonplace. "The welfare state has produced and been produced by national experts in 'social administration' . . . who then explain it to further professionals . . . who try to distribute its effects to consumers or clients" (Yeo, 1979, 53). It has been a common criticism of the management of public services that they exclude or alienate those they are meant to serve and this is ascribed by Yeo to the destruction of "the creative, public, associational voluntary life of so many English working people during the second half of the nineteenth century" (1979, 69) leading to a lack of identification with the new welfare state. One of the consequences of this has been that, despite the acquiescence of the friendly societies in the formation of the welfare state in the hope that those they had failed to reach could be provided for, those who are most deprived have still been least likely to benefit from it (Hadley and Hatch, 1981). In addition, the centralization of social assistance has contributed towards a "de-skilling of the working class in spheres other than the 'economic'" (Yeo, 1979, 55). If there is such a thing as welfare dependency it is possibly a product of this de-skilling rather than the result of over-generous welfare payments.

THE REVIVAL OF SELF-HELP

With the promises of reform and modernization from recent governments it would seem that self-help is an idea whose time has once more come around. New Labour appears to have accepted many of the criticisms of the statist welfare settlement of the twentieth century outlined above. Networks of diverse, community-based, small-scale voluntary bodies are proposed as being able to recover some of the legitimacy and participation of ordinary people that was previously lost, regenerating the spirit of mutual aid that sustained the friendly societies and other mutual aid organizations in the past (Kelly, 2007). However, a comparison with the history of friendly societies suggests that officially sanctioned and regulated forms of mutual aid are unlikely to be enthusiastically taken up by ordinary people any more than the 'patronized' friendly societies of the nineteenth century were. Despite the veneer of independence and autonomy, today's voluntary bodies tend to be incorporated into the government's reformed institutional structures of regulation and target-setting. In order to be acceptable bodies to government they must exhibit the same managerialism (arguably the latest manifestation of statist professional-bureaucratic technocracy) as within the rest of the public sector (Clark and Newman, 1997). The shift to the dispersal of public service delivery has as much to do with a belief in the superior efficiency of markets as anything else, including the primacy of 'choice' and 'personalisation.' Participatory democracy is unlikely to be the result of such market-led decentralization. In effect, the control of the state has simply shifted from bureaucratic control to a no-less onerous or regulative set of marketized relationships.

There is also the suspicion that the idea of self-help is being used once more as it was by the governing classes in the eighteenth and nineteenth centuries as a way of expecting groups of people who are poorly resourced to "pull themselves up by their collective bootstraps" (Levitas, 2000, 196). In other words the support of central government for self-help is, as it was 200 years ago, more about relieving the burden of supporting the poor from the shoulders of the middle classes than about supporting a democratic, participative form of mutual aid. If Benson is right then even if the government really did want to devolve the management of welfare back down to communities of its recipients the organizational tradition of ordinary people has been destroyed by the twin forces of commodifcation and bureaucratization. However, there are some examples that self-organization and mutual aid are not entirely dead but they are most unlikely to appeal to our current political leaders. Levitas cites one example provided by the 1983–1984 miners' strike: "The strike was maintained by a massive feat of local and national collective organization, involving soup kitchens, street collecting, and aid from trade unions and other groups" (2000, 195).

There is also a rich literature on the existence of alternative organizations and social movements that frequently involve major elements of participative democracy and mutual aid, demonstrating that spontaneous localized self-help is still a feature of everyday life for at least some (Kaufman, 1997; Katsiaficas, 1998; Albert and Hahmed, 1999; Abers, 2000; Ruggiero, 2000; Sen, Anand, Escobar and Waterman, 2003; Gold, 2004). However, once again these are unlikely to be amenable agents of governments wishing to devolve the provision of welfare. The paradox is that effective mutual aid arises in particular social conditions, often in ones where trust and confidence in government is very low. The history of friendly societies demonstrates that much of the glue the binds such groups together is opposition to authority as well as non-instrumental purposes such as conviviality or political objectives. Attempts by government to control, determine or regulate them are likely to be inimical to their survival and effectiveness. In addition the structures of consumerist market led individualism do not lend themselves to localized collective projects or forms of grass roots solidarity. Perhaps if governments really wish to see the revival of mutual aid they should devote their efforts to the production of the social and political conditions that stimulate their growth (Gorz, 1982). The democratization and liberalization of everyday life that this implies though would seem a most unlikely government objective for the foreseeable future.

REFERENCES

Abers, R. 2000. *Inventing local democracy*. Boulder, CO: Lynne Reiner.

Albert, M. and R. Hahmed. 1999. *Looking forward: Participatory economics for the 21st century*. Cambridge, MA: South End Press.

Benson, J. 2003. *Working class in Britain 1850–1939*. London: I.B. Tauris.

Clark, J. and J. Newman. 1997. *The managerial state*. London: Sage.

Fraser, D. 2003. *The evolution of the British welfare state*. Basingstoke, UK: Palgrave Macmillan.

Gold, L. 2004. *The sharing economy: Solidarity networks transforming globalisation*. Aldershot, UK: Ashgate.

Gorz, A. 1982. *Farewell to the working class*. London: Pluto Press.

Gosden, P. 1973. *Self-help; voluntary associations in the 19th century*. London: Batsford.

Hadley, R. and S. Hatch. 1981. *Social welfare and the failure of the state*. London: Allen & Unwin.

Harris, B. 2004. *The origins of the British welfare state: Social Welfare in England and Wales, 1800–1945*. Basingstoke, UK: Macmillan.

Harrison, J. 1984. *The common people: A history from the Norman Conquest to the present*. London: Flamingo.

Hobsbawm, E. 1995. *Age of extremes: The short twentieth century 1914–1991.* London: Abacus.

Katsiaficas, G. 1998. *The subversion of politics: European autonomous social movements and the decolonisation of everyday life.* Atlantic Highlands, New Jersey: Humanities Press.

Kaufman, M. 1997. *Community power and grassroots democracy: The transformation of social life.* London: Zed Books.

Kelly, J. 2007. Reforming public services in the UK: Bringing in the third sector. *Public Administration* 85(4): 1003–1022.

Levitas, R. 2000. Community, utopia and New Labour. *Local Economy* 15(3): 188–197.

Marsland, D. 1995. *Self reliance. Reforming welfare in advanced societies.* New Brunswick, NJ: Transaction Publishers.

Pelling, H. 1968. *Popular politics and society in late Victorian Britain.* London: Macmillan.

Pollitt, C. 1993. *Managerialism and the public services.* Oxford, UK: Blackwell.

Ruggiero, V. 2000. New social movements and the "Centri Sociali" in Milan. *The Sociological Review* 329(330): 167–185.

Sen, J., A. Anand, A. Escobar, and P. Waterman. 2003. *The world social forum: Challenging empires.* New Delhi, India: Viveka.

Thane, P. 1996. *Foundations of the welfare state.* Harlow, UK: Addison Wesley Longman.

Thompson, E. 1991. *The making of the English working class.* Harmondsworth, UK: Penguin.

Yeo, S. 1979. Working-class association, private capital, welfare and the state in the late nineteenth and twentieth centuries. In *Social work, welfare and the state*, eds. N. Parry, M. Rustin and C. Satyamurti, 48–71. London: Edward Arnold.

2 Toward Unprincipled Public Service

Critical Ideology, the Fetish of Capitalism, and Some Thoughts on the Future of Governance

Frank E. Scott

Not so long ago, Bill Clinton's apparently self-serving use of language drew widespread public expressions of outrage and ridicule. He had not actually had "sexual relations with that woman" according to his definition and, as he later solemnly swore in grand jury testimony, the issue of whether he had lied under oath actually hinged upon what "the meaning of the word 'is' is." It was largely on the basis of such language gaming that Clinton came to be described as America's first *postmodern* president; as a leader whose lack of principles permitted him to behave in virtually any way he wished. Yet Clinton was not the last American president to play such games or, at least arguably, to deserve such a description. Despite repeated appeals to principle, such as in his recent insistence that "you can't be the President unless you have a firm set of principles to guide you" George W. Bush (2007, ¶ 41) has sought to justify a number of highly controversial policies associated with his *War on Terror* precisely by shading the definition of such terms as "torture," "prisoner or war," and "terrorist" to suit his purposes.

This chapter adopts the perspectives provided especially by Thompson's (1984, 1990) *critical conception* of ideology and Lukács' (1971) Marxist-inspired concept of *reification* in examining how Bush and his administration have employed appeals principle in justifying a global project of domination, how the carrying through of that project has depended upon the concealment of the human relationships and human agency involved, and how the resulting state of affairs now demonstrates the failure of principles in providing a satisfactory basis for our lives together on the globe. It suggests that the cause of human freedom and dignity can best be pursued not through a retrenchment into principles, but through the articulation—much as neoconservatives have already done for their preferred beliefs—of a compelling justification for the relational morality that many already prefer. It further suggests that ideas currently arising from the lived experience of public service can play a crucial role in providing that justification, and in moving society beyond the depersonalized morality of principles toward more authentically human relational practices.

THE RESURGENCE OF IDEOLOGY ON
THE AMERICAN POLITICAL SCENE

An ironic consequence of today's increasingly relativist stance toward the nature of knowledge, according to White, is its conservative effect; its tendency to bolster the "idea that policy cannot be based on knowledge, but must be based ultimately on the judgment of men in positions of power" (Personal communication cited in Harmon 2007, 114). Thus in its post 9/11 ardor to spread American institutions across the Middle East, the Bush administration has been largely undaunted by its inability to support with facts a justification based upon the presumed threat of weapons of mass destruction, and has increasingly turned instead to an ideological justification that asserts the superiority of those institutions.

For the Bush administration, this approach dovetails neatly with Fukuyama's (1990) influential *end of history* thesis; the argument that the demise of European communism conclusively demonstrates American-style political and economic practices to be the ultimate forms of such practices and, thus, that the expansion of its Western institutions to all corners of the globe is now inevitable. Such end of history thinking has underpinned the Bush response to terrorism, one that anticipates the eradication of terrorism through the expansion of Western capitalism and democracy across the globe. In the words of Secretary of State Condoleezza Rice, "the absence of freedom in the Middle East, the freedom deficit, is what has produced the ideologies of hatred that led people to fly airplanes into a building on a fine September day" (Rice, 2005, ¶ 20). Guided by the parallel beliefs that a lack of freedom produces terrorism and that democracy produces freedom, and undeterred by the fact that the newly established democratic regimes in Iraq, Gaza, and Lebanon, have all been associated with eruptions of chaos and violence, the Bush administration continues to hold to its position that the spread of democracy—by violent force at its sole discretion—represents the only authentic path to peace around the world.

Perhaps owing in no small part to the pejorative view that ideology is a system of false and misleading beliefs, one that traces to the work of Marx, Bush and his administration initially took pains to label only the views of their enemies as such. In an April 2004 news conference, for instance, Bush (2004a) makes six references to the ideology of terrorists, variously characterizing it as an "ideology of murder," (¶ 20) an "ideology of terror" (¶ 24) and, as he does a great many times in his early speeches on the subject, as a "false ideology" (¶ 131). He also makes more than thirty references to *freedom*, variously characterizing it as "the deepest need of every human soul" (¶ 93), as "Almighty's gift to every man and woman in this world" (¶133), and as a "cause" (¶ 135), but never as an ideology. Yet by 2006 he had begun to refer to freedom itself as an ideology, as in "we will defeat the ideology of hatred with an ideology that's hopeful and light. And that's the ideology of freedom" (Bush, 2006a, ¶ 44), or "it's just going to take a long period of time . . . for [an] ideology that is hopeful, and that is an ideology of freedom, to overcome an ideology of hate" (Bush, 2006b, ¶ 14).

IDEOLOGY AND SOCIAL INTEGRATION

In their response to the horror of 9/11, Bush and American neoconservatives more generally appear to have forgot that the first to successfully destroy an American office building with massive loss of life were not swarthy foreign "evildoers" purportedly bent on destroying freedom, but white native-born "patriots" purportedly bent on preserving it. So it is that their current eagerness to assert the apotheosis of its institutions and forcefully spread them to the rest of the world would seem to beg the question of whether America's own sense of institutional legitimacy is solidly established, and there is much evidence that it is not. Such phenomena as low voter turnout, high levels of apathy and cynicism among citizens, antigovernment violence, and a nearly 50/50 polarization in the electorate would all seem to suggest that American support for its institutions of governance is far from unproblematic. Yet Bush's doctrinaire adherence to ideological purity regardless of its actual consequences is certainly consistent with the view, such as it is articulated by Gilman (2004), that the resurgence of the Republican Party in recent years is largely attributable to its transformation into America's first genuinely ideological party, and that the corresponding decline of the Democratic party over the same period is largely attributable to its continuation as a more traditional party, that is, as one responding to diverse interests and preferences not necessarily subsumable under a coherent ideological position.

The association of ideology with conservatism follows from the role it plays in sustaining social integration, argues Ricoeur (1991); in its ability to reinforce *existing* systems of authority and thereby fill what he terms a "credibility gap" between the claims of legitimacy and actual belief in the legitimacy of that authority (315). Thus although ideologies may preserve class power, perpetuate existing systems of authority or, more benignly, facilitate the "stable functioning of a community," the principal function of an ideology is to provide "pattern and continuity to the existing order" (318). Understood in this way, Thompson (1984) comments, an ideology serves as "a simplifying schema, an 'ism,' which persuades members of a group that they are right to think as they do" (187) and so it should come as no surprise that rising ideological fervor in response to a period of uncertain institutional legitimacy would manifest itself as a conservative turn.

Yet ideology is only one alternative response to the undermined legitimacy of an existing order, in the view of Mannheim (1968), who identified the alternative as *utopia*. Whereas ideologies serve to integrate, conserve, and consolidate the existing social order, he argues, utopias serve to "burst the bonds" of that order, to transcend it, to offer alternatives that are "not

realizable within the bounds" of that order (173). Yet if Republican thinking does in fact represent the ideological alternative in contemporary American political conversation, what then represents the utopian one? Is it that
of the Democrats? McIntyre (1984) is addressing this very question when
he observes that conservatives of today "are for the most part engaged in
conserving only older rather than later versions of liberal individualism"
(222). So to the extent that Democrats alternatively seek to conserve the
newer rather than the older version, that is, the more "welfare" rather than
the more "classic" liberal individualist stance, they appear to pursue a conservative ideological agenda themselves, albeit one more closely associated
with the now controversial New Deal era of the 1930s than with the eighteenth century Founding Period now held largely sacrosanct by Republican
ideologues.

In view of the role played by ideology in bolstering the legitimacy of
current institutional arrangements, however, perhaps the rise of ideological justification on the American political scene may be explained in terms
other than the apotheosis of its institutions. Rather than one of ultimate triumph for Western-style institutions, perhaps the current era may be more
accurately characterized as one of transition; as a period largely devoid
of utopia in the wake of the failure of communism, and during which the
United States in particular has turned to the integrating power of ideology to sustain the tenuous legitimacy of its institutions now under attack
from both within and without. Consider the similarity between the United
States' recent turn to ideologically-inspired violence in spreading its beliefs
and that of the various regimes of history that have relied on ideological fervor to bolster a failing legitimacy. Both the *Spanish Inquisition* of
the 1600s and Chinese *Cultural Revolution* of 1960s were, for example,
instances in which the eroding legitimacy of a dominant order, the Catholic
Church and the Communist Party, respectively, evoked an era of ideological intensity and an associated eruption of violence against the "heretics"
of the day. Today, the rise of Islamic fundamentalism—but not, at least
in the West, the corresponding rise of Christian fundamentalism—is not
uncommonly characterized as a dangerous ideological reaction to modernity's undermining of religious orthodoxy. Yet in an era when the number of
Americans who express either a "great deal" or "quite a lot" of confidence
in the institutions of *the presidency, the judicial system,* or *the congress* has
dropped to 33 percent, 25 percent, and 19 percent, respectively, in national
poll (PollingReport 2007), the United States now employs military force to
spread its institutions to far-off nations around the globe.

A CRITICAL APPROACH TO IDEOLOGY

For Ricoeur (1991), the functioning of ideology in social integration is
one "of which domination is a dimension but not the unique or essential

condition" (247). This normatively *neutral* view contrasts sharply with the more negative one that traces especially to the work of Marx, however; one in which an ideology is understood as an erroneous or illusory belief system, a *false consciousness* of the sort that has permitted, in the wake of the 9/11 events, ideology to be blamed for a blind fanaticism that engenders all manner of barbarism and inhumanity. Yet although drawing in significant degree upon Marx's ideas, Thompson (1984) seeks to avoid the "epistemological burden" traditionally imposed by the requirement that ideological analysis demonstrate the falsity and, therefore necessarily, the corresponding truth of alternative systems of belief, favoring instead what he proposes as a more "concrete" and useful basis of analysis. According to this *critical conception*, systems of meaning are ideological only insofar as "as they serve, in particular social-historical circumstances, to establish and sustain relations of domination" (56). Ideology is thus for Thompson, as it was for Marx, necessarily associated with forms of domination and marginalization, but although Thompson acknowledges that ideology may well serve to conceal or mask social relations, he differs from Marx in asserting that an ideology need not be demonstrably erroneous or illusory:

> What we are interested in here is not primarily and not initially the truth or falsity of symbolic forms, but rather the ways in which these forms serve, in particular circumstances, to establish and sustain relations of domination; and it is by no means the case that symbolic forms serve to establish and sustain relations of domination only by virtue of being erroneous, illusory, or false. (1984, 57)

By treating error, illusion, and falsity as contingent rather than necessary characteristics of ideology, Thompson turns the focus of his analysis to how meaning is "mobilized" through language in order to sustain an existing state of affairs. Although he recognizes that such mobilization of meaning is made possible by the "essentially open, shifting, indeterminate phenomenon" of signification, he does not accept the view that recasting ideological analysis from the pursuit of truth to the interpretation of symbolic forms renders it an entirely relativist undertaking.

> Although interpretations are contestable, it does not follow that they are arbitrary. There may be good reasons for offering a particular interpretation and adhering to it, reasons which may be quite convincing in the circumstances even if they are not altogether conclusive. An interpretation may be plausible, and considerably more plausible than other interpretations, without purporting to exclude all doubt; there is a great deal of room on the spectrum between uncontestable demonstration and arbitrary choice, and the interpretation of ideology, like all forms of interpretation, lies in the region in between. (1984, pp. 70–71)

Thompson's method thus avoids the modernist preoccupation with distinguishing the true from the false in favor of an interpreted and contestable "region in between," and, in so doing, skillfully wends its way between two potential pitfalls. One, as described by Rorty (1994), is the impossibility of discourse "about 'distorted communication' or 'distorting ideas' without believing in objects capable of being accurately or inaccurately, scientifically or merely fantastically, represented in these discourses" (230) and, thus, the necessity of a highly dubious claim to possess a genuinely undistorted perspective. The other, as is described by Hawkes (2003), is the inadvertent complicity of relativism, through its refusal to acknowledge the falsity of any consciousness, in sustaining the exploitive conditions of the current capitalist order. By permitting us to focus our attention on relations of domination and oppression themselves, without the necessity of an external historical-social vantage point, Thompson's approach to ideological analysis steps around both of these concerns.

In line with this focus on how beliefs operate in establishing and sustaining relations of domination, Thompson (1990, 61–65) identifies several specific modes of ideological operation. These include *dissimulation,* or the concealment of relations of domination by misrepresenting, concealing, denying, or obscuring their existence; *fragmentation,* or the construction of symbols either to differentiate individuals otherwise capable of effectively challenging the dominant group, or to orient forces of opposition "towards a target which is projected as evil, harmful, or threatening"; and *reification,* or the representation of a "transitory historical state . . . as if it were permanent, natural, outside of time," and thus foreclosing consideration of how things might be different (65).

Although employing the term in much the same way as does Thompson, Lukács (1971) draws upon the work of Marx in offering a broader conception of reification, linking it not merely with the pursuit of domination, but with the fostering of social consciousness. In the first chapter of *Capital*, Marx had described the process by which the social relationships involved in human productivity are cast into a "fantastic form of a relationship between things" analogous, he argues, to that of the "mist-enveloped regions of the religious world" (cited in Sayer, 1989, 55). He identifies this process with the *fetish* of the commodity. In the culturally and historically situated way of life that we call modern capitalism, he argues, the mode of production particular to it has been taken as universally applicable to every society and so, as Love (2006) suggests, "when Adam Smith refers to an 'invisible hand' that guides economic relations by the 'laws of supply and demand'" he has envisioned the operation of the market as a suprahuman reality governed by universal laws, and therefore one beyond human control. The "free market" thereby ceases to be a recognized as the form of human relationship it actually is; it becomes a fetish (90).

Lukács (1971) more fully draws out the implications of Marx's notion that the commodity structure recasts relationships between human beings as relationships between things, arguing that this structure has come to pervade Western consciousness far beyond our understanding of economics. In the wage-labor economy, he proposes, human productivity estranged from the human being and treated as an object of exchange itself becomes "subject to the nonhuman objectivity of the natural laws of society, and must [therefore] go its own way independently of man just like any other consumer article." The resulting reification of human action into suprahuman laws or principles increasingly comes to dominate not merely our economic relationships, but all aspects of the human life experience. Although they can appear to be "gradually discovered" and even used to advantage of human beings, these reifications come to be regarded as independent of and, therefore, inaccessible for modification by human action (87).

George W. Bush and the Ideology of Domination

The ideological analyses provided by Thompson and Lukács provide complementary and especially useful conceptual lenses for observing the ideological character of certain pronouncements by President Bush. Consider, for instance, his early 2003 turn to a fragmentation strategy in constructing an *axis of evil* of North Korea, Iran, and Iraq. Having in this way oriented an American population still traumatized by the events of 9/11 to an alternative threat of his choosing, he soon after began a verbal drum beat to war in Iraq with such statements as:

> If need be, if war is brought upon us like I said last night, I want to assure you, particularly those who wear the uniform and those who have a loved one in the military, we will commit the full force and might of the United States military. And for the name of peace, we will prevail. (Bush, 2003a, ¶ 11)

Although he does not hesitate here to use aggressive terms like "force" and "might," note how Bush forecloses alternatives to the use violence by casting a war as "brought upon us," that is, by a reification strategy that Thompson terms *passivization*. Note also how he redescribes the pursuit of war as the pursuit of peace, that is, his use of the dissimulation strategy Thompson terms *euphemization* (1990, 65). Bush's tone had changed by early 2005, however, or after it had become clear that no weapons of mass destruction were to be found in Iraq:

> The trend is clear: Freedom is on the march. Freedom is the birthright and deep desire of every human soul, and spreading freedom's blessings is the calling of our time. And when freedom and democracy take root in the Middle East, America and the world will be safer and more peaceful. (Bush, 2005, ¶ 13)

Here, Bush again employs several of the reification strategies described by Thompson (1990, 65): passivization in describing how freedom will "take root"; *nominalization* in converting violent human action to the noun form "spreading freedom's blessings"; and *naturalization* in describing a socially created event, the invasion of Iraq, as if it were the outcome of something as natural as the "birthright and deep desire of every human soul."

Yet perhaps most notable in this statement, as well as in the Rose Garden speech concerning freedom and democracy from which it is taken, is the disappearance of any reference to the human action involved in spreading his ideals. What now marches across the globe, according to this speech, is not an army under his command but a nonhuman thing he casts as *freedom* itself, and such references to freedom as a thing capable of independent action have by this time become increasingly common for Bush. In a statement honoring theoretical achievements of free market theorist Milton Friedman, for instance, he states:

> In contrast to the free market's invisible hand, which improves the lives of people, the government's invisible foot tramples on people's hopes and destroys their dreams . . . [A] free market system's main justification is its moral strength. Human freedom serves the cause of human dignity. Freedom rewards creativity and work, and you cannot reduce freedom in our economy without reducing freedom in our lives. (Bush 2002, ¶ 6–7)

Despite the rather odd metaphor of the "invisible foot," note here the distinction between the government, which is an identifiable set of actors who can be held responsible for their behavior, and freedom, which is an abstract thing that for all its presumed service to "the cause of human dignity" is beyond the realm of human responsibility or control. Consistent with Lukács analysis, the recasting of human relationships as relationships among things permits the violent spreading of American institutions across the globe to be attributed to the action of an abstract principle unfolding itself, that is, to an entity for which no human being can be held responsible.

THE URGE TO CARE, AND THE FUTURE OF GOVERNANCE

As long as we continue our quest for "consensus around what is real and good," suggests Gergen (1997), classes of the different, the undesirable, the *other*, will always be "under construction," and so it is that the major challenge we face in the twenty-first century is not what truths we can find to agree upon, but how we can manage "to *live together* on the globe" (149). Gergen thus not only parallels Thompson (1984) in redirecting our attention away from issues of error or illusion and toward issues of human relationship, but also highlights how the pursuit of ideological orthodoxy itself promotes the division of the *us* from the *them* that underpins relations of domination. A critical conception of ideology, or one principally concerned with the role that systems meaning play in promoting such relations, looks therefore upon the problem of ideology in much the same way as does Ricoeur (1991) when he argues that the failure of Marxism demonstrates not necessarily that that it is false, but that "the critical function of Marxism can be liberated and manifested only if the use of Marx's work is completely dissociated from the exercise of power and authority and from judgments of orthodoxy" (260). From this perspective, a system of meaning is problematic only to the extent it is *ideological* in Mannheim's (1968) sense, that is, only to the extent that it brings together power and appeals to orthodoxy in such a way as to prevent the emergence of *utopian* contestation and reevaluation of dominant beliefs. Yet note that the problematic of ideology thus identified does not inhere in its integrative function in persuading members of a group "that they are right to think as they do" (Thompson, 1984, 187). What members of other than dominant collectivities think about the current state of affairs may in fact be strikingly different from the dominant view, and may well lead them to search for alternative systems of meaning—of which Protestantism, liberalism, anarchism, socialism, and neoconservatism have all been examples—to justify their preference for an alternative order.

Consider in this regard two contemporary systems of meaning. The first follows from Fukuyama's (1990) highly influential assertion that his "end of history" represents an "end of the *evolution of thought* [italics added] about . . . first principles [of political and social organization]" that now comes "to rest in the liberal-democratic states descended from the French and American revolutions and based on the principles of liberty and equality" (75). Our very own preferred principles have received the ultimate vindication of history, he tells us, and so there is now no longer any need for us even to *think* about, much less contest, those principles. In short, Fukuyama provides American neoconservatives not only a persuasive argument that they are right to believe as they do, but also a self-sealing theory of orthodoxy under which no further examination of those beliefs will be necessary. As is frequently demonstrated in the pronouncements of George W. Bush, American neoconservatives now in power in the United States have relied on this theory in justifying the forcible spread of their preferred beliefs across the globe.

The second is less a cohesive system of meaning than a cluster of critiques, yet it follows from a shared inclination to abandon rational principles in favor of human relationship as the normative basis of our lives together. Having argued that the "project of providing a rational vindication" of morality has decisively failed, for instance, MacIntyre (1984, 50) proposes that we return to an Aristotelian-inspired notion of *virtue,* one understood as the pursuit of excellence in social practices. Rorty (1991) describes two principal ways through which thoughtful human beings seek to "give sense" to their lives. One, which he calls *objectivity*, involves some description of our relationship toward a "nonhuman reality." The other, which he calls *solidarity*, involves some notion of one's place in a particular community, and of the importance of making a contribution to that community (21). In his *Postmodern Ethics*, Bauman (1993) suggests that the moral failure of modernism springs directly from its attempts at objectification; from its emphasis on abstract universals and, ultimately, from its use of rules or laws that reduce morality to the performance of *duty*. He argues that this "depersonalization" (47) of morality in effect circumscribes and limits moral obligations, "absolves the conscience" and, ultimately, overcomes our deepest moral impulses (51). For Bauman, morality is not about the limits of our duty, but about our unlimited *responsibility* to care for one another. He therefore rejects rationalism, including such notions as universalized reciprocity, in arguing for the distinctly personal character of morality:

> I suggest . . . that morality is endemically and irredeemably *non-rational*—in the sense of not being calculable, hence not being presentable as following impersonal rules, hence not being describable as following rules that are in principle universalizable. The moral call is thoroughly personal; it appeals to my responsibility, and the urge to care thus elicited cannot be allayed or placated by the awareness that others do it for me, or that I have already done my share in following to the letter what others used to do. (60)

Because these critics of moral rationalism use reasoning to make sense of their preferred beliefs, just as do Fukuyama and American neoconservatives, their work is similarly ideological in the neutral sense described by Ricoeur (1991). Yet whereas neoconservatives ground their moral arguments in suprahuman principles, their critics regard the same appeal to abstract entities beyond the human realm as the chief culprit in contemporary moral failure. For this reason, the conclusion they draw, if not their exact means of getting to it, mirrors Lukács' (1971) assertion that in recasting human relationships as relationships between things, reified laws or principles increasingly come to dominate all aspects of the human life experience. And in proposing not for the retrenchment of the dominant normative system but instead for an alternative and now marginalized system of belief grounded in the morality of human relationship, these critics of moral principle also advocate a system of meaning not dependent upon associations with power, authority, and orthodoxy; one without the basis for relations of domination—and the attendant projects for ideological hegemony—so characteristic of their neoconservative counterparts.

ON THE FAILURE OF PRINCIPLES

Less than a year after Bush (2003b) publicly asserted that "freedom from torture is an inalienable human right" (¶ 2) and that the United States was leading the pursuit of its worldwide elimination "by example" (¶ 4), the unfolding events at Abu Ghraib had sent the world a very different message. Despite repeated assurances that its policy is not to "torture," the Bush Administration has reserved the right to interpret the meaning of that term in any way that suits its purposes. Repeated appeals to moral principle notwithstanding, the actions of the Bush administration have in fact been far more consistent with what MacIntyre (1984) terms *emotivism*, or the doctrine that "all moral judgments are *nothing but* expressions of preference, expression of attitude or feeling" (12). The resulting American leadership has been in the direction of undermining, if not entirely shattering, the international framework of principles intended to prevent such things as aggression by strong nations against weak ones and the torture of prisoners—a framework put in place following the horrors of World War II. Under the ideologically-driven aegis of the Bush administration's project of globalization, this framework has been put to the test, and it has failed.

Drawing upon the work of Lukács (1971), this paper has argued that by recasting human relationships into the suprahuman realm of abstraction, the assertion of universal principles actually serves to conceal from us the humanity inherent in our relationships with one another. Drawing upon the work of Thompson (1984, 1990), it has also argued that the problem of ideology lies not in the inherent truth of falsity of the consciousness it promotes, but in its function in establishing and sustaining relations of domination. These arguments have been drawn out here to suggest that the principal threat posed by the Bush administration against our lives together on the globe has followed less from its abandonment of universals in favor of merely justifying its preferred beliefs, than from its having promoted a preference for system of meaning in which relations of domination and oppression are concealed under the guise of the universals themselves. So the lesson to be learned for those of us who would counter that threat may not be that our efforts should now be redoubled in the quest for some or another more acceptable alternative principle—of *justice*, for instance— but rather, and much in the way that neoconservatives have already done, that we must now seek to develop a compelling system of meaning, an ideology by some definitions, for making sense of the relational morality that many already prefer.

Toward Unprincipled Public Service?

In suggesting that whereas the "power game" of politics represents youth, the "suffering and struggle" of administration represents maturity in the developmental cycle of society, White (1990, 236–237) emphasizes the danger of disconnecting the idealism of the former from the lived experience of the latter. It is a danger we have seen played out in recent years as ideologically-inspired dreams of conquest, power, and fame have been crushed and broken against such administrative realities of Iraqi "reconstruction" and Hurricane Katrina disaster relief. However slowly and grudgingly they may have been learned by those in need of them, powerful lessons have been presented both in how ideals disconnected from lived experience can run amok into catastrophe, and in the necessity of engaging the tensions between the abstractions of principle and authenticity of relationship that is required for mature and competent public service.

American public servants—soldiers, law enforcement personnel, CIA agents—have been the ones actually charged with carrying out the globalization project of the Bush administration abroad. Yet within the United States itself, that expectation has been largely reversed in the project that would subject American public service to the "invisible hand" of market forces. And it is perhaps in view of its experience as the target of that project that the alternatives to marketization now arising among a cluster of American public administration theorists may have particular relevance to the arguments made here.

Despite the diverse influence of postmodern, critical, phenomenological, feminist, communitarian, and related ideas, we find in a cluster of *alternative* public administration theorists a common advocacy of an essential role for public service in fostering more participative and relational practices in society. Among these are Harmon's notion of "moral community" (1995, 207), King and Stivers' advocacy of "active citizenship" (1998, 197), McSwite's belief that public administration should provide "the venue for our working out among ourselves how we want to live together,"(2002, 112) and Denhardt and Denhardt's argument that "participative and inclusive approaches are the only ones that build citizenship, responsibility, and trust" (2003, 166). Drawing upon the lived experience of a principal institutionalization of the urge to care, the public service, such ideas are directed at moving beyond the realm of abstraction that has come to pervade our social experience, and toward an opportunity to live out a preference for a more genuinely relational life.

REFERENCES

Bauman, Z. 1993. *Postmodern ethics*. Oxford, UK: Blackwell.
Bush, G.W. 2003a. Iraq: Denial and deception. Excerpts from Grand Rapids speech. http://www.whitehouse.gov/news/releases/2003/01/20030129–2.html (accessed December 5, 2005).
Bush, G.W. 2003b. Statement of the president: United Nations International Day in support of victims of torture. http://www.whitehouse.gov/news/releases/2003/06/20030626–3.html (accessed March 14, 2007).

Bush, G.W. 2004. President addresses the nation in prime time press conference. http://www.whitehouse.gov/news/releases/2004/04/20040413–20.html (accessed May 23, 2005).

Bush, G.W. 2005. President discusses freedom and democracy. http://www.whitehouse.gov/news/releases/2005/03/20050329.html (accessed 23 May 2005).

Bush, G.W. 2006a. Remarks by the president at Citizens for Judy Garr Topinka Lunch. http://www.whitehouse.gov/news/releases/2006/07/20060707–2.html (accessed July 1, 2007).

Bush, G.W. 2006b. President Bush meets with Prime Minister Howard of Australia. http://www.whitehouse.gov/ news/releases/2006/11/20061117–2.html (accessed May 23, 2005).

Bush, G.W. 2007. Press conference by the president. http://www.whitehouse.gov/news/releases/2007/12/20071220–1.html (accessed December 22, 2007).

Denhardt, J.V. and R.B. Denhardt. 2003. *The new public service: Serving, not steering.* Armonk, NY: M.E. Sharpe.

Fukuyama, F. 1990. Are we at the end of history? *Fortune* 121(2): 75–78.

Gergen, K.J. 1997. *An invitation to social construction.* London: Sage.

Gilman, N. 2004. What the rise of the Republicans as America's first ideological party means for Democrats. *The Forum 2(1).* http://www.bepress.com/forum (accessed June 24, 2006).

Harmon, M.M. 1995. *Responsibility as paradox: A critique of rational discourse on government.* Thousand Oaks, CA: Sage.

Harmon, M.M. 2007. *Public administration's final exam: A pragmatist restructuring of the profession and the discipline.* Tuscaloosa, AL: University of Alabama Press.

Hawkes, D. 2003. *Ideology,* 2nd ed. London: Routledge.

King, C.S. & C. Stivers. 1998. *Government is us: Public administration in an anti-government era.* Thousand Oaks, CA: Sage.

Love, N.S. 2006. *Understanding dogmas and dreams: A text,* 2nd ed. Washington, DC: CQ Press.

Lukács, G. 1971. *History and class consciousness: Studies in socialist dialectics.* Trans. R. Livingstone. Cambridge, MA: MIT Press.

MacIntyre, A. 1984. *After virtue: A study in moral theory,* 2nd ed. Notre Dame, IN: University of Notre Dame Press.

Mannheim, K. 1968. *Ideology and utopia: An introduction to the sociology of knowledge.* New York: Harcourt, Brace & World.

McSwite, O.C. 2002. *Invitation to public administration.* Armonk, NY: M.E. Sharpe.

PollingReport.Com (2007) Gallup Poll. June 1–4, 2006. http://www.pollingreport.com/ institut.htm (accessed June 29, 2007).

Rice, C. 2005. Rice urges Iraqis to pursue inclusive political process. http://usinfo.state.gov/dhr/Archive/2005/May/17–421926.html?chanlid=democracy (accessed May 22, 2005).

Ricoeur, P. 1991. *From text to action: Essays in hermeneutics II.* Trans K. Blamey and J.B. Thompson. Evanston, IL: Northwestern University Press.

Rorty, R. 1991. *Objectivity, relativism and truth: Philosophical papers, volume 1.* Cambridge, UK: Cambridge University Press.

Rorty, R. 1994. Feminism, ideology, and deconstruction: A pragmatist view. In *Mapping ideology,* ed. S. Žižek, 227–234. London: Verso.

Sayer, D., ed. 1989. *Readings from Karl Marx.* London: Routledge.

Thompson, J.B. 1984. *Studies in the theory of ideology.* Berkeley, CA: University of California Press.

Thompson, J.B. 1990. *Ideology and modern culture: Critical social theory in the era of mass communication.* Stanford, CA: Stanford University Press.

White, O.F. 1990. Reframing the authority/participation debate. In *Refounding public administration,* eds. G.L. Wamsley, R.N. Bacher, C.T. Goodsell, P.S. Kronenberg, J.A. Rohr, C.M. Stivers, O.F. White, & J.F. Wolf, 182–245. Newbury Park, CA: Sage.

3 Sheep in Wolf's Clothing
Schools, Managerialism, and Altering Ideologies

Patricia A.L. Ehrensal

In US schools there has been an increasing trend to both assimilate management models and practices of, and recruit educational leaders (principals and, more particularly, superintendents) from corporations and the military. This looking to and adulation of the private and military sectors is the foundation of the greatest archetypal shift in US education since the reform movements of the early twentieth century. This shift can be traced to four intersecting discourses: privatizing leadership, privatization of teacher preparation, privatization of educational purpose, and privatization of standards and accountability.

Privatizing leadership is at the center of this shift. Politicians who have influence over and control of public (state) education praise these noneducators for their *management* philosophies and practices. Further they advocate that values from business, industry, and the armed forces be adopted in the organization and management of schools. The subtext is that education is just another production function, and that anyone who can lead troops into battle, or a company into profitability, can lead schools and help children.

Privatization of teacher preparation by such groups as *Teach for America* and *Troops to Teachers* parallels the changes in leadership. These groups not only recruit individuals from outside schools and colleges of education (i.e., career changers from private sector and retiring military personnel) and train them as teachers, but also *manage* their placement in client school districts. The text of this discourse is that teaching is best taught *on the job* and that pedagogy is the purview of navel-gazing academics with little use in the *real world*.

The third discourse concerns the privatization of educational purpose. Most disturbing and underlying privatization as a movement is the firm belief that schooling is primarily a private, individual and corporate interest. Each student, and family, strives to promote their own achievement. Consequently, notions of the common good, the democratic ideal, and the shared responsibility are fading from various discourses concerning education.

The final discourse concerns the privatization of standards and accountability. The *No Child Left Behind* legislation, passed in 2001, requires the notification of the parents/guardians when a school does not meet "adequate yearly progress" and is *failing*, so that they may transfer to their children to other (nonfailing) schools. While this *choice* option has been touted empowering parents, the effect is imposing the responsibility of choice (often when there is little or no actual real choice) on families, rather than ensuring a free and appropriate education for all children. That is, parents who are able (both in terms of economic resources and cultural capital) can remove their children from the bad schools, leaving the children of less knowledgeable and economically impoverished parents in the *sink schools*. The subtext is "it's every child for her/himself." Education then, becomes a competitive good, subject to market forces (Ball, 2007; Boyles, 2005; Molnar, 2005; Saltman, 2000; Molnar, 1996). Consequently, education as a shared concern of a democratic society is lost.

While policy discourses around the privatization of educational purpose, standards and accountability have been fractured and uncoordinated in the past, the addition of the privatization of leadership and teacher preparation have allowed for a synergy of these discourses which has never been experienced in US history. Further, the confluence of these discourses reinforce one another in ways which have the potential of fundamentally altering ideologies and organizational arrangements of schools

This chapter will trace the business-model discourses in US schools. It will explore how this confluence of four areas of privatization in education results from the convergence of two discourses; the schools as producers of human capital and the anti-public sector discourses. Finally, the chapter explores how the convergence of these two discourses with the discourse of "managerialism" (Enteman, 1993) obfuscates the distinctions between schooling and education, which allows for the reinforcement of the corporate model for school organizations, as well as further marginalizing the *school as public good* discourse. This raises serious concerns about the ability of the next generation of citizens to participate in a self-governing democracy.

This tracing of the business-model discourse will be guided by Foucault's "history of the present" (1979, 30–31). Here then, the "primary goal is not to understand the past but to understand the present; . . . to use an understanding of the past to understand something that is intolerable in the present" (Gutting, 1994, 8). Further, the concern here is the "discourse itself as practice" (Foucault, 1972, 46). As such, it will examine the "archive," which Foucault defines as the "systems that establish statements as events (with their own conditions and domain of appearance) and things (with their own possibility and fields of use)" (1972, 128). Additionally, these archives are "strategies that continue to function, transformed through history and providing the possibility of appearing in other discourses" (Flynn, 1994, 29).

ILLUSIONS OF POLITICAL DISCOURSE IN DEMOCRATIC SOCIETIES

As Chomsky has pointed out in his writings on the "propaganda model" of the media (Chomsky and Herman, 1988; Chomsky, 1989), in "democratic" societies, public opinion must be carefully controlled. He argues "in a democratic political order, there is always the danger that independent thought might be translated into political action, so it is important to eliminate the threat at its root" (Chomsky, 1989, 48). This imposition of the "necessary illusions" is done through methods fundamental to the democratic process. Chomsky argues that "[d]ebate cannot be stilled, and indeed, in a properly functioning system of propaganda, it should not be, because it has a system-reinforcing character if constrained within the proper bounds. What is essential is to set the bounds firmly" (1989, 48). Further, "[c]ontroversy may range as long as it adheres to the presuppositions that define the consensus of elites, and it should furthermore be encouraged within these bounds, thus helping to establish these doctrines as the very condition of thinkable thought while reinforcing the belief that freedom reigns"(ibid., 48).

What is essential here is that power sets the agenda and determines the course and truths within the debate. Thus, from this perspective, both general political discourses and their discussions in the media can not be seen as independent from the operations of the interests of powerful elites.

Flyvbjerg (1998) explored the role of power in political/administrative decision-making and action. Flyvbjerg asserts that the relationship between power and knowledge is exercised through a strategy of *rationality*. "Power concerns itself with defining reality rather than with discovering what reality 'really' is" (Flyvbjerg, 1998, 227). Further, power-based political decisions are obfuscated by being presented as having been taken in a technical-rational and democratic fashion (Flyvbjerg, 1998). For Flyvbjerg, "power *defines* what counts as rationality and knowledge and thereby what counts as reality" (1998, 227). Thus, "power defines, and creates, concrete physical, economic, ecological, and social realities" (Flyvbjerg, 1998, 227). Additionally, "power seeks change, not knowledge. And power may very well see knowledge as an obstacle to the change power wants" (Flyvbjerg, 1998, 36). Consequently, power engages in strategies in which allows only that knowledge which suits its purposes.

This is not to imply that there is an active conspiracy, but rather those with power act in ways which serve their interests. To the degree that powerful elites have overlapping interests, they will champion those discourses and knowledge, which serve those interests while ignoring or suppressing those discourses or knowledge that they see as contradictory to their interests.

In its role as *regulator* (Bernstein, 1990), the government, in order to define, monitor, and limit the activities in school, had to interpret many documents and testimonies concerning them, this "process of interpretation is first and foremost a political process" (Mumby 1998, 160). Mumby (1998) states that interpretation is "an act which has direct implications for the way that discourse structures systems of domination in our society" (160). Further, from the political perspective of interpretation "certain dominant readings become incorporated into texts, such that a certain view of the world is maintained and reproduced" (ibid., 160).

Policy, then "is more than simply the policy text; it also involves processes prior to the articulation of the text and the process which continue after the text has been produced, both in modifications to it as a statement of values and desired actions and in actual practice" (Taylor, Rizvi, Lingard, and Henry, 1997, 28). That is, it is both a text and a process. The process is an ongoing and dynamic one in which *problems* are identified requiring a policy response (Taylor, Rizvi, Lingard, and Henry, 1997). Taylor et al. also argue that because policies "represent compromises over struggles" (28), they are value laden. Finally, they argue, policies are not written *tabula rasa*, rather they are based on existing laws, policies, and organizational arrangements. "Policy is thus an instrument through which change is mapped onto existing policies, programs or organizations, and onto the demands made by particular interest groups" (ibid., 5).

Consequently, in order to understand the current policies of privatization, adopting business organizational and management arrangements, as well as recruiting corporate managers and military officers to manage school buildings and districts, one needs to examine the history of school management/administration.

A (BRIEF) HISTORY OF BUSINESS-MODEL MANAGEMENT IN US SCHOOLS

Separating the Head from the Heart in School Organizations

The first introduction of school management/administration, separate from teaching, occurs during the Common School reform movement. In the 1830s, Horace Mann sought to mitigate the strife between the rich Protestants and poor Catholics of Boston through education reform. He established the Common School in which all (white) children would not only receive the same education, they would be educated in a common school house. The purpose of this model of schooling was to ensure that children learned to view themselves as *citizens* of the United States, rather than members of a particular social group (workers, Catholics, Protestants, etc.). Mann and other Common School reformers believed that educating (rich and poor) children in this way would teach them to accept and value their place in society, thus eliminating the root of social unrest of the time (Tharp, 1953; Cremin, 1957; Spring, 2001).

In order to implement the Common School reform, three steps needed to be taken. First, was the creation of a stable, inexpensive teaching force that would uphold the morals and ideals of the Common School Reform in the classroom. Second, there needed to be a standardization of the organization of schools to ensure common education. Finally, was the creation of a uniform (common) curriculum (Tharp, 1953; Cremin, 1957; Spring, 2001).

To establish a stable yet inexpensive teaching force, women would be recruited. Women were considered to be well suited for teaching because of their *natural* child rearing abilities (maternal instincts). Additionally it was argued that female minds are less distracted by worldly gain, simply because there was no other employment for them—which also made them cheap labor. Finally, women were considered to be *pure* and naturally moral (Tharp, 1953; Cremin, 1957; Spring, 2001).

In addition to a stable teaching force, schools had to be organized in a way which would ensure control over all activities. The characteristics of bureaucracies ensured not only stability, but also uniformity across an organization. Therefore, it was considered the ideal organizational model for the Common School system. Standard operating procedures were established for all activities, relationships, and processes to ensure uniformity across the school house. This included the standardization and routinization of lessons and teaching methods. In short, for every imaginable (and unimaginable) occurrence in the school organization there would be rules and procedures to define, regulate, and control them (Tharp, 1953; Cremin, 1957; Spring, 2001).

A hierarchical *chain of command*, based on the *natural* gender roles found in society (men ruled and women served; men are decision makers and women are nurtures; men are rational and women are emotional), was established. This division of labor, which draws from the "natural strengths" of men and women, ensured maximum efficiency of the work of the school organization. Additionally, with men in administrative roles—planning, organizing, controlling, and leading (the four functions of management)—women teachers would be kept under close control. That is they would be prevented from acting on their emotions, being taken advantage of by their students and/or the parents. Under male administration, school organizations would be logical, rational, and fair institutions (Spring, 2001).

The business/industrial organizational arrangements and management, with its particular discourses, then was first introduced as part of the Common School Reform movement. It was argued that this was the best means for maintaining uniformity across such a large enterprise. Additionally, this uniformity was necessary to ensure everyone was treated impartially. Finally, this form of organizational arrangement and management was the most efficient means of running a large school system, thus allowing the greatest number of children to be educated. Embedded in this *industrial model of school organization* discourse however, are constructs of patriarchy, hierarchy, as well as efficiency and impartiality being equated with equity and social justice. Consequently, schools facilitated social reproduction, with its asymmetrical power relationships. Additionally, these constructs become *normal* (Habermas's *life world*; 1987), and therefore unquestioned, in the discourse of school.

Scientific Management of Schools and the Production of Human Capital

At the turn of the twentieth century, in response to public indignation, fueled by liberal journalism (muckrakers), at the power of the new industrial regime, mass poverty, and municipal corruption, progressive reformers employed several strategies and policies to address these problems (Callahan, 1962; James, 1968; Spring, 1972; Tyack, 1974; Wallace, 1991; Berube, 1994). "At the heart of progressivism were efforts to expand democracy, sympathy for the immigrant poor, attempts to counterbalance the rise of unbridled wealth of with the new industrialism, and a drive against municipal corruption" (Berube, 1994, 1). Salient to this chapter are the criticisms of schools and the reforms instituted to address them.

While the Common School reform movement introduced business/industry organizational arrangements and management to schools, Callahan (1962) argues that during the progressive era it "was the rise of business and industry to a position of prestige and influence, and America's subsequent saturation with business-industrial values and practices [and] the reform movement . . . spearheaded by the muckraking journalists [coupled with] the vulnerability of the school administrator" (2) which allowed for the imposition of the business-industrial ideology on education. "Indeed, the acceptance of the business philosophy was so general that it has to be considered on e to the basic characteristics of American society in this period. Calvin Coolidge was not overstating the case when he said in 1925: 'The business of America is business'" (Callahan, 1962, 2).

This imposition of the business-industrial ideology on education had two major effects on school organizations. First, it altered the purpose of publicly funded education from the education of citizens for a self-governing democratic society to the production of human capital. Second, schools had to be organized and managed according to business-industrial standards of efficiency.

The social efficiency model of education reform (Spring, 1972, 2001) was based on the assumption that if a skilled workforce could be developed, then industry would operate more efficiently. This would lead to more employment and rising wages, which would in turn solve the problem of poverty. The task of teaching the appropriate skills fell on schools.

To accomplish this, several reform policies were enacted. There was the development of the comprehensive high school, as well as the junior high school. With the aid of a new technology—standardized/IQ tests—children were sorted/tracked into different courses of study based on *ability*. Children then were sorted by age and ability, which it was argued would make

teaching more efficient, thus better serving the students. Vocational education was also introduced. The purpose of this education was to produce
greater degrees of efficiency both in workers/students and the educational
process. Snedden and Prosser, the major proponents of this education,
argued that a utilitarian education was best suited for the working class.
They claimed that liberal studies such as Latin and Greek, not poverty, was
the primary reason why the children of the poor and working class did not
attend school (Spring, 2001). Finally, the *Smith-Hughes Act* (1917)—the
first time the federal government intervened in education—removed vocational education from departments of education and established the *Federal
Board for Vocational Education*, which included the Secretaries for Labor,
Commerce and Agriculture, as well as three civilian representatives form
those areas. The purpose of this act was to ensure that vocational education
was meeting the need of industry (Callahan, 1962; Spring, 2001).

Schools at this time still had a bureaucratic organizational arrangement.
However, administrators began to adopt the principles of scientific management, again from industry. Under these principles there was *one best way*
to approach teaching and learning (Callahan, 1962; Tyack, 1974). Consequently, curriculum and pedagogy became standardized and routinized.
Administrators (managers) were not only differentiated from the teaching
force by gender, but also by education. Universities and graduate school
training conferred *elite* and *expert* status on school administrators. Thus,
owing to their advanced education, administrators, not teachers, were best
suited to determine how policy was to be carried out in schools. Additionally, these administrators (managers) selected and trained teachers (workers) in the *one best pedagogy* for their school. Teaching then was reduced
to carrying out prescribed curriculum. Thus, as in industry, the brains of
education were located in administration/management, while the teachers/
workers provided the brawn (Spring 2001).

Education and National Security

The discourse of managerialism, then has been entrenched in the discourse
of school organization for nearly 175 years. Further, the *social efficiency*
model of progressive school reform also imposed the construct of education
for the production of human capital. In the latter part of the 1950s, the
construct of education for national defense was introduced.

With the end of World War II came the start of the Cold War, and with
it the arms race between the United States and the USSR. The launching
of Sputnik I by Russia in 1957 caused great consternation in the United
States. Eisenhower noted that in only forty short years the USSR went from
a feudal society to an industrial power (Spring, 2001). Public schools were
criticized for poor science and math curricula, thus hindering the development of the cadre of science and engineers needed to win the Cold War.
In response to this *problem*, the Congress passed the *National Defense*

Education Act (*NDEA*) in 1958. The purpose of the *NDEA* was "[t]o strengthen the national defense and to encourage and assist the expansion and improvement of educational programs to meet critical national needs" (*NDEA* reprinted in McCoy, 1961, 421).

The *NDEA* made recommendations for five specific areas. First, it called for a five-fold increase of educational activities by the *National Science Foundation* (*NSF*). Second, it called for a decrease in the waste of human talent. This was interpreted as increases testing and tracking, as well as additions of advanced math and science courses in high schools. Third, federal funds were made available for the training of math and science teachers. Fourth, graduate fellowships were instituted to prepare future professors and researchers in the fields of math and science. Finally, it recommended an increase in the study of foreign languages, particularly German and Russian.

The passage of the *NDEA* marks the second time that the Congress intervened in school practices. However, it was argued that education had become to important for national security, and therefore warranted the involvement of the federal level (Spring, 1972, 2001).

BACK TO THE FUTURE

Thus, embedded in the discourse of public education in the United States are *common sense* notions of business/industrial principles of managerialism and organizational arrangements. With these principles also comes the *common sense* view that business/industry models are the most efficient and are transferable to school organizations. The *social efficiency* model of the progressive school reform movement added the *common sense* position that the work of schools is to produce human capital for the industrial complex. Finally, the *NDEA* imposed the construct of education as vital for national defense to the discourse of schools. These constructs have shaped the discourse in such a way that the discourses of *markets, excellence, standards*, and *accountability* seem a natural part of the discourse of public schools.

The War Against the Civil Service

"Civil Service Will Remember Regan as an Anti-Government President." So stated the headline of Stephen Barr's Washington Post article commemorating the death of Reagan in June 2004. Indeed Reagan's *Inaugural Address* (1981) was tantamount to a declaration of war on the civil service when he stated "Government is not the solution to our problem; government is the problem." In that memorable speech, Regan (1981) went on to say:

> It is my intention to curb the size and influence of the Federal establishment and to demand recognition of the distinction between the powers

granted to the Federal Government and those reserved to the State or to the people. All of us need to be reminded that the Federal Government did not create the States; the States created the Federal Government.

He further stated that "[i]t is no coincidence that our present troubles parallel and are proportion to the intervention and intrusion in our lives that result from unnecessary and excessive growth of government" (Reagan, 1981). The message was clear, the economic crisis was not due to bad management decisions on the part of corporate CEOs, rather it was the life-sucking civil servants' parasitic existence at the root. Additionally, it was not the duty of the federal government to supply services to the citizens. Rather, this duty fell on the states only if the people deemed it necessary. Said another way, families were to take care of themselves and only turn to state government as an absolute last resort. Thus, embedded in Reagan's discourse were constructs of individualism and a preference of private over public. Like his British counterpart, Margaret Thatcher, Reagan's rhetoric claimed, "there was no society."

George H.W. Bush continued this anti-government discourse. He claimed that cadres of community volunteers could replace government services. In his *Thousand Points of Light* proposal he called on citizens to offer unpaid assistance to their neighbors and community:

> The old solution, the old way, was to think that public money alone could end these problems. But we have learned that this is not so . . . I am speaking of a new engagement in the lives of others, a new activism, hands-on and involved, that gets the job done . . . I have spoken of a thousand points of light, of all the community organizations that are spread like stars throughout the Nation, doing good. We will work hand in hand, encouraging, sometimes leading, sometimes being led, rewarding. We will work on this in the White House, in the Cabinet agencies. I will go to the people and the programs that are the brighter points of light, and I will ask every member of my government to become involved. The old ideas are new again because they are not old, they are timeless: duty, sacrifice, commitment, and a patriotism that finds its expression in taking part and pitching in. (Bush, G.H.W., Inaugural Address, 1989)

Again, it is the duty of individuals, not government, to render assistance and offer social services.

Clinton, a Democrat, continued this anti-government discourse when he proclaimed in his 1996 *State of the Union Address*: "The era of big government is over." In that speech he also stated that:

> We know big government does not have all the answers. We know there's not a program for every problem. We have worked to give the American

people a smaller, less bureaucratic government in Washington. And we have to give the American people one that lives within its means.

While he did state, "we cannot go back to the time when our citizens were left to fend for themselves," "self-reliance and teamwork" are to act in concert to address social need. In other words, government is the option of last resort.

Finally, George W. Bush also cautioned against the problems of too much government, especially in the social service arena.

> Government has a role, and an important role. Yet, too much government crowds out initiative and hard work, private charity and the private economy. Or new governing vision says Government should be active but limited, engaged but not overbearing. (Bush, G.W., *State of Union Address* 2001a).

Wasting no time, the next day Bush issued an executive order establishing the *Whitehouse Office of Faith-Based and Community Initiatives* to:

> establish policies, priorities, and objectives for the Federal Government's comprehensive effort to enlist , equip, enable, empower, and expand the work of faith-based and other community organizations to the exted permitted by law. (Bush, G.W., 2001b)

Through this office various church or faith based groups can receive federal funds to provide various social services in their communities.

> Faith-based and other community organizations are indispensable in meeting the needs of poor Americans and distressed neighborhoods. Government cannot be replaced by such organizations, but it can and should welcome them as partners. (Bush, G.W., 2001b).

While acknowledging that social services are the responsibility of government, it should be shared with private, including faith-based organizations. In short, the G.W. Bush administration has *outsourced* social services.

The political discourse since 1981 then has been one, which vilifies the civil servant. At best there are too many of them, and at worst they are leaches living off the taxpayers' gravy-train. In short we are better off without them. Individuals and families should be more self-reliant, and those who are not can either hope for a benevolent neighbor or pray for the assistance they require.

It's Still About the Production of Human Capital

In addition to the civil service, public education was also at the center of political discourse. In 1983, the report, *A Nation at Risk*, proclaimed, "the educational foundations of our society are presently being eroded by a rising tide of mediocrity that threatens our very future as a Nation and a people." This problem was so serious that "[i]f an unfriendly foreign power had attempted to impose on America the mediocre educational performance that exists today, we might well have viewed it as an act of war." Further, any gains made in the post-Sputnik era have been eroded. "We have, in effect, been committing an act of unthinking, unilateral educational disarmament" (*A Nation at Risk*, 1983). Consequently, once again national security is threatened because of bad public education.

This national security crisis, however is not a military one, rather it is an economic one. The United State's ability to compete in the global market place had decreased, and the blame for this was laid at the schoolhouse gate.

> It is also that these developments signify a redistribution of trained capability throughout the globe. Knowledge, learning, and skilled intelligence are the new raw materials of international commerce and we are today spreading it throughout the world . . . If only to keep and improve on the slim competitive edge we still retain in the world markets, we must dedicate ourselves to the reform of our educational system. (*A Nation at Risk*, 1983, 2)

Thus, while giving a nod to the preparation of citizens to participate in a self-governing society, the purpose of education according to *A Nation at Risk* is the development of human capital for the corporate/industrial/military complex.

The solution to this problem is *excellence in education*, where "[w]e should expect schools to have genuinely high standards rather than minimum ones, and parents to support and encourage their children to make the most of their talents and abilities" (*A Nation at Risk*, 1983, 5). Additionally, "[t]he search for solutions to our educational problems must also include a commitment to life-long learning" (ibid, 5). Hence, skills training needs not only be acquired in school *before* entering the workforce, it is the duty of every citizen to continually update these skills so that they meet the needs of the corporate/industrial/military complex.

Looking to Business Leaders for Guidance

In the early 1990s, an *Educational Summit* was held to come up with strategies to ensure *excellence in education*. The group who met at this summit included the *Business Round Table* (the CEOs of the *Fortune 500* companies) and the state governors, including then Governor Bill Clinton. Members of the education profession were not included. The purpose of this summit was to elicit advice from these corporate leaders on how to improve education. The Governors wanted to know what schools should be teaching to best prepare children to be successful in the global market place.

The result of this, and subsequent meetings, was *Goals 2000*, a list of 8 strategic goals designed to improve educational outcomes by the year 2000. In 1994, the Congress with the passage of the *Goals 2000: Educate America Act* formally accepted these goals. These goals sought to improve math and science scores, literacy rates, high school graduation rates, as well as discipline (Borman, Cookson, Jr., Sadovnik, and Spade, 1996).

In addition to *Goals 2000*, a plethora of other policies and strategies were adopted from the corporate world to improve school organizations and educational outcomes. These included: *Total Quality Management*, *Total Quality Improvement*, *Strategic Planning*, *Site-Based Management*, and *School-to-Work*, to name but a few. Programs such as *Principal for a Day* have been instituted for principals to obtain advice from corporate managers who spend one day a year in their school. Additionally, principals and superintendents were reading books by management gurus such as Tom Peters.

Market ideologies such as choice and competition have become the hallmarks of school reforms since *A Nation at Risk* (Molnar, 1996; Engel, 2000; Boyles, 2005; Molnar, 2005). That is, parents should be able to choose which school their children would attend and schools needed to compete for students. After all, business had to compete for customers, so it is only *natural* that schools should be subjected to the same market forces. It was argued by the market reformers, that as long as public schools maintained a monopolistic hold, there would never be true school reform (Molnar, 1996; Engel, 2000; Boyles, 2005; Molnar, 2005; Ball, 2007).

Indeed, William Ouchi (the author of *Theory* Z) has recently published a book outlining seven key steps for school improvement. One of these key steps is "every principal is an entrepreneur" (Ouchi, 2004, 51). Here he defines an entrepreneur as "a principal who has the freedom to organize her school in whatever way will work best for both students and staff. That is to say, and entrepreneur is a problem-solver rather than a rule-follower" (Ouchi, 2004, 58). He goes on to outline four steps to become an entrepreneur.

Step 1:   Analyze your customers
Step 2:   Design a staffing plan that fits your needs
Step 3:   Arrange the schedule to fit the plan
Step 4:   Choose teaching materials to fit the students (ibid., 58)

Not only is he advocating against the centrally controlled bureaucratic organizational arrangement of schools, he depicts good schools as ones that are customer oriented and have the flexible organizational arrangement so popular with corporate leaders today. For Ouchi, successful schools are those which adopt business/market practices and values, including competition resulting from the ultimate market value—choice. In short, the *revolutionary* concept that Ouchi is touting is schools would be more efficient/effective if they just behaved more like corporations.

Large School Organizations Need Real Managers

For over a decade, large urban school districts have been recruiting teachers from nontraditional sources such as programs like *Teach for America* and/ or developed their own *Teaching Fellows* programs. In these programs, recruits are either new college graduates who did not major in education, or they are "career-changers." Additionally, the Clinton administration initiated *Troops to Teachers*, which offers opportunities for soldiers to become teachers in public schools. In both programs the students are given accelerated (crash) courses in teaching methods and then put into a classroom while they work on obtaining state certification. These programs were instituted to alleviate the chronic teacher shortage that many urban districts face (Darling-Hammond, 1996; Shaul, 2001; Tell, 2001; Owing, Kaplan, Nunnery, Marzano, Myran, and Blacburn 2006).

In recent years this trend has extended to school administration. When the Pennsylvania State Department of Education classified the Philadelphia School District as *failing*, one of the strategies it imposed to improve the school was placing several of the *worse* schools under the *professional* management of the for-profit *Edison Schools*. In several large cities, "[d]rawing on theories of public administration, analogies to corporate practice, and what has been heralded as a proven success led by Chicago's Mayor Richard M. Daley, more and more school reformers are looking to mayors for leadership" (Henig and Rich, 2004, 4). The rationale for "mayor-centrism" suggested by Henig and Rich is that "today's generation of locally elected executives by training, orientation, and stronger links to the corporate sector may be better able to open up the education decision-making process so that it incorporates and responds to signals from the global economy" (ibid., 11). Thus mayors have seized control of the schools and hired corporate CEOs to oversee reform efforts. Programs such as *New Leadership for New Schools*, a not-for-profit organization, are competing with university-based degree programs for training and certifying principals. In New York City, Mayor Michael Bloomberg established the *Leadership Academy* to train principals for the city's schools. Here, students take *practical* courses in finance, school plant, management, and so on. In short these programs emphasize the *business* of schools with little consideration of the educational processes and practices in them.

SHEEP IN WOLF'S CLOTHING

The purpose of this chapter is not to examine the effects of market ideologies or corporatism on education. Indeed, many books have already been written on that topic (see, for example, Shapiro, 1989; Ball, 1990; Aronowitz and Giroux, 1993; Purpel and Shapiro, 1995; Jonathan, 1997; Goodman and Saltman, 2002). Rather, it was to explore the "history of the present" by examining the business/industrial model of schools "archives." That is, probing the business/industry organization and managerialist discourse practice of schools as a means of understanding the current policy of recruiting noneducationalists as principals and superintendents.

These discursive practices connect constructs, ideas, and events, as well as open possibilities for other discursive practices. In doing so they compose a *"historical a priori,"* which, "defines a field in which formal identities, thematic continuities, translations of concepts and polemical interchanges may be deployed" (Foucault, 1972, 127).

The archives outlined in this chapter have revealed a *historical a priori* of school organizations, which includes hierarchical organizational arrangements; division of labor; specialization; professionalism; standardization; efficiency; and production of human capital. These business-like discursive practices have opened the possibilities of furthering such practices, however it also opens vulnerabilities.

One of the major critiques of education in the United States since the early twentieth century has been that schools are controlled by education professionals (Campbell, Fleming, Newell, and Bennion, 1987). Then administrators responded by acquiring specialized school management education and credentialing. This however, did not eliminate the vulnerability and actually opened the possibility of a new one.

After the publication of *A Nation at Risk*, the critique that educational professionals' controlled of school was again raised. As noted previously, in the standards reform movement that followed, professional educators were not included in policy and strategy decision-making groups. Among the strategies deployed by the standards reform movement is a mixture of centralizing and decentralizing of processes. The real irony here, however, is that curriculum and assessment (for which educational professionals have specialized training and credentialing) have been centralized, while responsibility for managing test out-comes (league tables), student recruitment and budgets (for which educational professionals have little training or control over) had been decentralized.

Consequently, school administrators are left with autonomy in regards to maintaining a safe and functional school facility; competing with other schools in the recruiting of better students (raw material), and recruiting better teachers (workers); answering the demands of parents (customers), and meeting the demands of business/industry for good workers (human capital) for the global market place; and obtaining high scores on statewide assessments (producing deliverables). However, this must all be accomplished with maximum efficiencies (i.e., minimum cost).

Educational professionals consider themselves ill qualified to carry out these managerial duties, and most dislike them. Indeed, many retired or left the field rather than adopt this new role. This professionalism of school administrators' discursive practice ironically resulted in a short-age of administrators, opening opportunities for newly formed corporations such as Education Alternatives Inc. (EAI) and the Edison Project to take over the management of schools in several cities (Molnar, 1996).

Thus, the discourses of the global market place and privatization with the *historical a priori* of business-like practices in schools opened an important shift in the discursive practices of schools. No longer was it enough for school organizations to *act* like business, they had to *become* businesses. This schools-as-business discursive practice opens the possibilities of other discourses. As businesses that must be competitive and efficient, traditionally educated school administrators are ill qualified and/or do not want to "manage" them; the governing bodies responsible for these enterprises (school boards or mayors) need to seek out experienced applicants—corporate managers and military officers.

The irony here is that these corporate managers and military officers may find themselves even more vulnerable than the traditional school administrator. These new-styled school administrators, like their traditional counterparts, are charged with producing high scores on state-wide assessments (deliverables) efficiently (inexpensively). Thus, a routine organizational arrangement (Perrow, 1967) would seem appropriate. However, they are to carry out this task in a context, which includes state constitutional guarantees of free education for all children and compulsory education laws. While competing for "better" students (raw material) then, they must also accept any child who lives within the catchment area of their school. Consequently, it is difficult (if not impossible) to control for the "quality" of the students. Drawing from Perrow (1967) again, given the variations (exceptions) and believing that it is an analyzable problem, an engineering organizational arrangement would then be appropriate. (This would include traditional testing and ability tracking the children, as well as test-prep drills.) However, at the end of the day, what school administrators are dealing with are children, in all their developing and unpredictable glory. Hence, while fields such as child development and pedagogy make them more knowable, there will always be a great number of exceptions.

While the managerial discursive practice has tried to engineer education into a more routine technology, it is actually more akin to the craft industries as described by Perrow (1967), with its specialized knowledge. This knowledge includes curriculum, assessment and pedagogy. However, curriculum and assessment has been centralized, and these new-style school administrators have had little to no education in pedagogy. This lack of educational knowledge also impedes their ability to "engineer" the change they've been charged to make in schools. Ironically, then, these new-styled school administrators are most likely less effective as change agents. They may indeed be no more than sheep in wolves' clothing.

POST SCRIPT

On July 1, 2008, Terry Stecz, CEO of Edison Schools announced that the company was changing its name to **edison**learning, moving out of the business of school management, and intends to become a player in education software. After sixteen years, Edison Schools had not turned a profit and recently lost its contract with the Philadelphia School District because of lack of progress in the schools it managed. Perhaps the era of big business school management is ending—one can only hope.

REFERENCES

2008. The company formerly known as Edison Schools. The Quick and the ED.

Aronowitz, S. and Giroux, H.A. 1993. *Education still under siege*. Westport, CT: Bergin and Garvey.

Ball, S.J. 1989. *Politics and policy making in education: Explorations in policy sociology*. London: Routledge.

Ball, S.J. 2007. *Education plc: Understanding private sector participation in public sector education*. London: Routledge.

Barr, S. 2004. Civil service will remember Reagan as the anti-government president. *The Washington Post*. June 8th, P. B02.

Bernstein, B. 1990. *The structuring of pedagogic discourse: Class, codes and control*. London: Routledge.

Berube, M.R. 1994. *American school reform: Progressive, equity, and excellence movements, 1883–1993*. Westport, CT: Prager.

Borman, K.M., Cookson, P.W. Jr., Sadovink, A.R. and Spade, J.Z. 1996. *Implementing educational reform: Sociological perspectives on educational policy*. Norwood, NJ: Ablex.

Boyles, D. R., ed. 2005. *Schools or markets? Commercialism, privatization, and school-business partnerships*. Mahwah, NJ: Lawrence Erlbaum Associates.

Bush, G.H.W. 1989. Inaugural address. Washington D.C.

Bush, G.W. 2001a. State of the union address.

Bush, G.W. 2001b. Executive order: Establishment of the White House Office of Faith-Based and Community Initiatives.

Callahan, R.E. 1962. *Education and the cult of efficiency: A study of the social forces that have shaped the administration of the public schools*. Chicago, IL: Chicago University Press.

Campbell, R.F., T. Flemming, L.J. Newell, and J.W. Bennion. 1987. *A history of thought and practice in educational administration*. New York: Teachers College Press.

Chomsky, N. 1989. *Necessary illusions: Thought control in democratic societies*. Boston: South End Press.

Clinton, W.J. 1996. State of the union address.

Cremin, L.A., ed. 1957. *The republic and the school: Horace Mann on the education of free men*. New York: Bureau of Publications.

Engel, M. 2000. *The struggle of control of public education: Market ideology vs. democratic values*. Philadelphia, PA: Temple University Press.

Flynn, T. 1994. Foucault's mapping of history. In *The Cambridge companion to Foucault,* ed. G. Gutting, 28–46. Cambridge, UK: Cambridge University Press.

Flyvbjerg, B. 1998. *Rationality and power: Democracy in practice.* Chicago, IL: Univerity of Chicago Press.

Foucault, M. 1972. *The archaeology of knowledge: And the discourse on language.* New York: Pantheon Books.

Foucault, M. 1979. *Discipline and punish: The birth of the prison.* New York: Vintage Press.

Goodman, R.T., and K.J. Saltman. 2002. *Strange love: or how we learned to stop worrying and love the market.* Lanham, MD: Rowman and Littlefield.

Gutting, G. 1994. Introduction. In *The Cambridge Companion to Foucault,* ed. G. Gutting, 1–27. Cambridge, UK: Cambridge University Press.

Habermas, J. 1987. *The theory of communicative action: Lifeworld and system.* Boston: Beacon Press.

Henig, J.R., and W. Rich. 2004. Mayor-centrism in context. In *Mayors in the middle: Politics, race and mayoral control of urban schools,* eds. J.R. Henig and W.C. Rich, 3–24. Princeton, NJ: Princeton University Press.

James, H.T. 1969. *The new cult of efficiency and education.* Pittsburgh, PA: University of Pittsburgh Press.

Jonathan, R. 1997. *Illusory freedoms: Liberalism, education, and the market.* Oxford: Blackwell.

McCoy, R.F. 1961. *American school administration: Public and Catholic.* New York: McGraw-Hill.

Molnar, A. 1996. *Giving kids the business: The commercialization of America's schools.* Boulder, CO: Westview Press.

Molnar, A. 2005. *School commercialism: From democratic ideal to markey commodity.* New York: Routledge.

Mumby, D.K. 1988. *Communication and power in organizations: Discourse, ideology, and domination.* Norwood, NJ: Ablex Publishing.

National Commission on Excellence in Education. (1983) A Nation at Risk: The Imperative for Educational Reform. http://www.ed.gov/pubs/NatAtRisk/risk.html

Ouchi, W.G. 2003. *Making schools work: A revolutionary plan to get your children the education they need.* New York: Simon and Schuster.

Perrow, C. 1967. A framework for the comparative analysis of organizations. *American Sociological Review,* 32: 194–208.

Purpel, D.E., and H.S. Shapiro. 1995. *Beyond liberation and excellence: Reconstructing the public discourse on education.* Westport, CT: Bergin and Garvey.

Reagan, R. 1981. Inaugural address.

Saltman, K.J. 2000. *Collateral damage: Corporatizing public school—a threat to democracy.* Lanham, MD: Rowman and Littlefield Publishers, Inc.

Shapiro, S. 1990. *Between capitalism and democracy: Educational policy and the crisis of the welfare state.* Westport, CT: Bergin and Garvey.

Spring, J.H. 1972. *Education and the rise of the corporate state.* Boston: Beacon Press.

Spring, J.H. 2001. *The American school 1642–2000.* New York: McGraw-Hill.

Taylor, S., F. Rizvi, B. Lingard, and M. Henry. 1997. *Educational policy and the politics of change.* London: Routledge.

Tharp, L.H. 1953. *Until victory: Horace Mann and Mary Peabody,* Boston: Little Brown and Company.

Tyack, D.B. 1974. *The one best system: A history of American urban education.* Cambridge, MA: Harvard University Press.

Wallace, J.M. 1991. *Liberal journalism and American education, 1914–1941.* New Brunswick, NJ: Rutgers University Press.

4 Public Sector Management?
But We're Academics, We Don't Do That Sort of Thing!

Michael Humphreys and Mark Learmonth

As academics, attending international conferences is, for many of us, one of the best perks that we enjoy. Since getting jobs in a business school ourselves, we have seen much more of the world than we would have expected to have seen courtesy of our former (public sector) jobs; what is more, we have been paid to do so. Perk it may be, but at certain times of the year, our lives as academics can be dominated by conferences.[1] It's not only presenting papers (along with all that's involved in arranging and subjecting oneself to international travel) but it's also having to present *ourselves* at conferences—both in the formal and the (often rather more challenging) informal arenas.

Given their tendency to consume so much academic energy, it is perhaps unsurprising that conferences are relatively neglected as research sites themselves, in spite of offering potential, especially perhaps for ethnographic work (for exceptions see Burrell 1993; Humphreys, 2005; Grey and Sinclair, 2006; Ford and Harding, 2008). In this chapter, we use autobiographical vignettes (Humphreys, 2005) to provide parallel accounts of our attendance at two deeply contrasting academic conferences in the United States: the Academy of Management (AoM), held in New Orleans in August 2004, and the Congress of Qualatitive Inquiry (CQI), held in Urbana–Champaign in May 2005. We pay particular attention to the emotional and personal effects the two conferences had on us, and reflect on the ways in which they continue to inform the paradoxical nature of working on the 'critical' wing of a mainstream business school. Indeed, we suggest that events surrounding these two conferences, compressed into a few days of intense personal experiences, evoke important tensions within our more routine life and work in a business school. An account of conferences, then, make such tensions easier to see, and so, more readily available for reflection and critique.

Thus, the aims of this chapter are twofold. One is to provide a greater awareness of the identity work (Watson, 2008) that we critical academics do as part of *all* our formal and informal duties within business schools—not just at conferences. Second, we aim to exemplify the value of autoethnography—that is, first-person, reflexive accounts of excerpts from our lives, placed within a wider social theoretical context. The intent here is to show how autoethnography can represent a powerful way to focus on issues that are typically ignored in (if not hidden by) more traditional scholarship.

The first section of our chapter evokes some experiences of working in a business school, especially for us as critical scholars (broadly defined), and suggests how autoethnography might inform academic identity. We then provide two brief parallel accounts of impressions from each conference—impressions that focus on our own emotional reactions to the contrasting experiences. Finally, we construct a critical discussion of life as a scholar outside the mainstream within a university business school—as well as suggesting ways in which we might hang on to our own values and beliefs (along with our jobs).

TALES OF THE FIELD: AN "I-WITNESS" ACCOUNT[2] OF THE BUSINESS SCHOOL

As many readers will doubtless appreciate, in both the United Kingdom and United States there is substantial heterogeneity among those university departments typically called 'business schools,' 'departments of management studies,' etc. Some schools focus on executive education and emphasize so-called 'cutting edge' management practice; at the other end of the spectrum, there are those that try to emulate traditions within social science and try to keep a critical distance between themselves and (at least managers' versions) of relevant knowledge (Grey, 2001). However, most, like ours, are 'mixed' schools. These have differing proportions of undergraduate and postgraduate teaching, some MBA provision, a PhD program, and a variety of approaches both to maintaining their intellectual credibility and ensuring their financial survival (Starkey, Hatchuel, and Tempest, 2004).

In mixed schools generally, and certainly in ours, the dominant research tradition strongly tends towards privileging quantitative methods. These methods, furthermore, whatever their intellectual lineage, *politically* are typically orientated towards meeting the educational and research needs of managers—as defined by managers.[3] So, our interests in critical ethnography and critical management education, for example, mean we are faced on a daily basis with an identity confusion that is caused by the conflict between our preferred roles as teachers and researchers and those that are institutionally approved. Indeed, some of our senior colleagues can, at least in private conversations with us, be overtly deprecating about the value of critical (or even any variety of qualitative) work.

If writing about the self within a business school context is uncommon[4] there has been a new flowering of autobiographical work in the academic literature, which has attracted the classification 'autoethnography.' Reed-Danahay defines autoethnography as "a form of self-narrative that places the self within a social context. It is both a method and a text" (1997, 9).

Indeed, there are now many autoethnographic publications in which, as Coffey has put it, "the self and the field become one" (2002, 320).[5] Auto-ethnographic subject matter includes, for example, prison life (Svensson, 1997); Corsican identity (Jaffe, 1997); Jewish identity in the workplace (Berg, 2002); aesthetics (Pickart, 2002); teaching (Pelias, 2003); art as research (Bochner and Ellis, 2003)—even managerial identity (Mischenko, 2005). The strength of such writing lies for us in the potential to evoke and illustrate the contradictions we experience (Ellis and Bochner, 2000, 738) in our lives as business school academics; as Jenks puts it, "[r]eal life is messy" (2002, 183).

In using autoethnographic first-person vignettes (Figure 1) to record our impressions of, and our reflections on, two conferences, we are not only setting out to dispel any notion of the author as an independent, objective observer (Stacey, 1996) or narrator (Hatch, 1996; Learmonth, 2006)—we also want to say something about our own ambivalences concerning our identities as academics. We are both late-starters in the world of business school academia and carry the baggage of previous careers and of being mature students in both our master's and PhD degrees. This places us in a different position to many of our colleagues. We have some things in common both with younger colleagues (relatively few publications) and older colleagues (life experience, established family connections), but we remain different because our disciplinary allegiances are tenuous, and we have hardly established any reputation. In other words, we are only at the beginning of the academic identity construction process—we remain fairly marginal and outside the established academic groupings—critical, main-stream, indeed outside of any classification of this sort.

This is an interesting place to be. We don't have to worry much about the loss of academic reputation that personal self-revelation—'opening our kimonos'[6]—might imply. Perhaps we worry less about the accusations of self-indulgence, narcissism and even of "academic wank" (Sparkes, 2002, 212) that are often made against autoethnography—and which might threaten our positions had we more established reputations. So, in address-ing for ourselves and for our readers the question of what it means to be an academic in a business school we aim to examine reflexively what Rosen refered to as the "enlightening and disequilibriating implications of view-ing a world which is our own" (1991, 15).

What, then, is academic life? Conventionally, being a university aca-demic involves activities like teaching, research, conference attendance, and the preparation and presentation of academic work (eg. Frost and Tay-lor, 1996). Each of these, however, can mean something different to differ-ent people. On the face of it, the relatively autonomous academic should be able to define what he or she does—and to construct what he or she 'is.' In practice though, the hegemonic influence of the typical business school— for example, the pressure to publish in the "right" journals and the edito-rial policies typically enacted by these journals—distorts any individual's attempt to construct a working life which extends beyond established norms (Boje, 1996). In our particular world, the AoM has an especially powerful influence, which one of the following vignettes is intended to illustrate directly; the other, perhaps a little more tangentially.

TWO TRAVELLERS' TALES

As fairly naïve newcomers to the academic game we (independently) submitted qualitative research papers to both the AoM and CQI conferences. We did this without considering the possibility of any radical differences between the two. Both conferences, in some respects, left us feeling marginalized and identity-confused in different ways. At AoM we felt we felt we were part of the quirky end of the continuum; at CQI we felt unadventurous—even boring. Before the AoM trip we had met only a couple of times at seminars and interviews. Our meeting at Manchester Airport for the flight to New Orleans was the beginning of a friendship and working relationship as colleagues. In both cases we travelled together and attended many common sessions and social events but the two accounts presented in Figure 1 were written without collaboration. They are meant to be a way to connect ourselves both as

Table 4.1   Two Travellers' Tales

Mike in New Orleans	Mark in Urbana–Champaign
I had been looking forward to this meeting of the AoM for a long time. The attraction was New Orleans itself and the prospect of lots of music in the birthplace of jazz. Although I had a large group of colleagues travelling with me there were only two or three who shared my musical interests so the conversations in airports and on the plane leaned towards issues of academic life, papers, reviews, and career moves. The overly-academic tone of the conversation was apparent in the stretch limousine which took us from the airport to our hotel. As we set off, the driver, a black man in his 50s, asked in his languid southern drawl "You guys all been to New Orleans before?" and one of my academic colleagues sitting nearest to him replied "No, we're neophytes." The driver didn't say another word.	London, Detroit, Urbana–Champaign: the last leg flown on a small prop-engine plane; we arrived at about 8 p.m. local time (1 a.m. UK time and we'd been travelling since 5 a.m.). So I just wanted to get into a taxi, head straight to the hotel and sleep off the jet-lag! But as we emerged out of the small airport concourse we saw there were no taxis—not even anyone to ask about getting one. And how far away, exactly, was Urbana–Champaign? There was little sign of major settlements as we landed—only endless fields. Welcome to the mid-West!
Installed in our hotel I felt compelled to get out and savor the atmosphere of	Having finally got a taxi to the hotel (which was only a short drive as it turned out), the next day we were free to explore the town in the warm spring weather. There was an out-of-town shopping complex, a memorably eclectic music shop, a few restaurants, the university campus, and, well, actually that was about it. Even bars *(continued)*

Mike in New Orleans (continued)	Mark in Urbana–Champaign (continued)

the place. The August humid heat was oppressive but we were soon wandering the French Quarter, sipping cold beer in bars with incredibly eclectic juke boxes. There were buskers on the street that would have been gigging session musicians at home. There were record stores where you could lose days just browsing the shelves. We found the brilliant PBS radio station WWOZ 90.7 with its output of jazz, blues, Cajun, Zydeco, and gospel music. We rode the street cars and took cab rides where the drivers offered us exotic experiences with "New Orleans Ladies." We opted for the live music which was everywhere. We took part in the Satchmo Summerfest and saw Aaron Neville, Ellis Marsalis, Irving Mayfield, and the New Orleans Jazz Orchestra all in one evening at the Mahalia Jackson Theatre. Eating gumbo and jambalaya, we marvelled at Jason Marsalis and Kermit Ruffins on percussion and bass at the Café Brasil and were mesmerized when an Italian trumpeter in the audience sat in and "blew up a storm." We ate red beans and rice watching second-line bands competing with each other outside the Louisiana State Museum's Old US Mint. Within a couple of days my suitcase was bulging with CDs and I was beginning to worry about airline baggage regulations.

Oh, yes, there was also a conference to attend. Six thousand delegates attending sessions in vast corporate hotels. There were suits and ties everywhere in the icy, air-conditioned rooms as young scholars vied with each other for the best faculty posts. We attended our own sessions to find that we had been given a twenty-minute slot alongside a strange mix of disparate papers. Mine was located in a session along with quantitative statistical pieces like "Measuring and Building Linear/Nonlinear Thinking Style Balance For Enhanced Performance."

proved hard to find—we slowly realized we'd arrived in the Bible belt. So while it was interesting for a Brit to see "small town America," the limited distractions in the town itself meant I was particularly pleased the conference turned out to be a good one!

The first afternoon of the conference consisted of special workshops—I went to one on performance ethnography. During the session we were split into groups and asked to prepare a performance on our first experiences of racism. We decided to start by telling one another our own particular story—a fascinating experience—especially as the group was made up of people from all over the world. For instance, someone had grown up in a black township in 1960s South Africa: what, he wondered, was his *first* experience of racism? Another group member had spent her childhood in a privileged family in the southern states of America, waited on by black servants: she wondered about her first experience of racism too. As for me, I contributed what I had to excavate from my subconscious—an almost forgotten memory of a racist incident I was part of at school when I was about fourteen years old.

Needless to say, the session was more than merely interesting—it was also challenging and personally involving. And it set the tone for the rest of the conference. Many subsequent presentations, like this first session, explored the political through the personal. The focus was very much on autoethnography and performance ethnography, though with room for more conventional papers (like mine). And my most enduring memories are of the effective performances. I particularly remember the almost unbearable accounts of child prostitutes in South America; reliving a father's funeral brought me close to tears; and hearing about someone else's adolescent angst helped me to understand

(continued)

Mike in New Orleans (continued)	Mark in Urbana–Champaign (continued)

I attended a few other sessions, but experienced a growing sense of alienation from the presentations and the presenters. I kept rushing back to the music, wherever and whenever I could. The *Journal of Management Studies* reception was the best AoM event for me. It was held on the first floor of a restaurant with a balcony overlooking Bourbon Street. There was wonderful Cajun food, lots of cocktails and of course a great four-piece jazz band playing high quality mainstream jazz.

In sum New Orleans was a fabulous experience. I loved the place, learned a lot about music and had a great time. But all the good parts of the experience were about the place. New Orleans welcomed me, I felt comfortable, involved, and immersed in things that really interested me (e.g., music, people, culture, food and drink). The AoM conference, on the other hand, I found dull, culturally alienating, and for the most part irrelevant to me as a person. Sessions were often unnecessarily adversarial and competitive. There was just too much sucking up to big names and obvious career-networking for my taste. I often felt completely out of place and disoriented in paper sessions yet completely at home in bars, cafes, record stores. The richness of my experience was entirely down to New Orleans as a town.

a surprising amount about my own current relationships as an adult.

There were very few papers on my putative interest—organization and management—but then that hardly mattered because of the rich experiences many of the other presentations provided. In fact, it wasn't just the content, but the atmosphere and overall feel of the conference that was refreshingly different from any management conference I'd been to. The apparent absence of people "networking" was particularly striking (a commodification of relationships that seems endemic to management conferences) as was the absence of publishers' drinks parties and people trying to sell you things.

Once, at a big management conference, a senior colleague suggested I go with him to a publishers' drinks party so that he could introduce me to some of the people there. I'm sure he intended this offer as a favor, but I told him that I didn't feel like it. "If you don't go," he warned, "it could be career limiting." I knew at the time that he was probably right, but in any case I turned down his offer. Here at CQI though, I felt I could appreciate the people I met for who they were, in themselves—without an eye on the position they held or what they'd written. And without seeing any interaction as significant in career terms.

writers and subjects with our readers and to encourage others to engage in similar ways with events in their own lives. After all, as Fletcher and Watson assert: "[a]lthough there are various shapes that ethnographic accounts take, they inevitably involve story-telling" (2007, 159).

BACK HOME: THE HOLIDAY SNAPS

In summary then, we had a great time at both events—but for different reasons. In New Orleans, it was all to do with the city and its people; in

Urbana–Champaign, the town had little to do with our enjoyment—which was down to the conference and the people there. Of course, both conferences are just memories now—our stories, like holiday photographs,[7] the only concrete thing we have left of the experiences. Yet we think that the juxtaposition has much to say about the nature of academic life back home in our day-to-day jobs. Indeed, CQI brought home to us how little natural affinity we have with many of the things involved in business school life: which is to say that working in our business school is rather more like being at AoM than at CQI.

Indeed, one of the effects of the juxtaposition has been to encourage us to reflect more deeply about what it means to be academics within a mixed business school like ours. The CQI conference lives on in our imaginations as a vivid reminder of something that seems to be akin to the life we were seeking when we first entered academia in mid-career. The AoM conference, on the other hand, has come to encapsulate many of our discomforts with the sort of academic role that is institutionally approved in most business schools, including our own. And, unfortunately, the AoM reminds us, not only of how we can resist seeking this kind of institutional approval, but also of how we might be rather too easily seduced by some of its charms.

But though there may be few institutional rewards for doing so, we like ourselves much better when we act in the sort of ways encouraged at CQI. We think this might be, in part, because both of us spent considerable time outside the academy—in the public sector—prior to obtaining university posts. And we both sought career changes, because, while studying for master's degrees, we were attracted by the contrasts with our current jobs that an academic career appeared to offer. As mature students peering in on the world and work of academics, it appeared that, on a daily basis, they dealt with the world of ideas; not only this, they did so within an organizational climate completely different (apparently) from the ones we faced.

These experiences as students gave us a reading of academic life that started to change the way we felt about our jobs—and our own selves. Hochschild's words about senior managers, for example, became increasingly resonant: "Years of training and experience, mixed with a daily carrot-and-stick discipline, conspire to push corporate feeling rules further and further away from self-awareness. Eventually these rules about how to see things and how to feel about them come to seem 'natural,' a part of one's own personality" (1983, 155).

Our insights into other ways to be—that is to say, insights into being academics (however partial these insights may have then been)—seemed to have started to reverse the process to which Hochschild points. They began to denaturalize the 'corporate feeling rules' and push them nearer to self-awareness. As a result, one of the attractions of teaching and researching in a university setting came to be that it held out the possibility of escape from corporate dystopias. We realized we were struggling against compliance to corporate feeling rules, many of which we now resented—and which we hoped to escape altogether via jobs in academia. These jobs would, we believed, allow us to do some of the things in which we had a real interest, within a setting where we could feel at home.

But now, after several years of working in business schools, and especially after CQI, we wonder just how complete that escape has been. Perhaps the CQI conference is a reminder to us of the utopian ideals which inspired our moves into academic careers in the first place. AoM, on the other hand, stands as a reminder of how easily these ideals can be compromised. CQI, juxtaposed against AoM, has also reminded us that a life and identity as a business school academic has, to use Hochschild's term, "feeling rules" too—rules that can equally well be pushed further and further away from self-awareness. So, just as being students allowed us to become more reflexive about the feeling rules of our previous jobs, so going to AoM and then to CQI has encouraged us to see more clearly something of the feeling rules that apply to business school academics: rules that seem to us uncomfortably close to those governing the sort of life we (thought we) had left.

So we want to suggest that it is possible to read many aspects of AoM as a caricature of the feeling rules in today's business schools. As Burrell (1993) was aware, the AoM conference "drips power, bureaucratic hierarchy and patriarchy. It reflects the institutions from which it is membership is drawn . . . it is the modern fair in which we and our relationships are all commodified. It is a three day market in which we are all likely to be bought and sold—unless we are very, very careful" (1993, 76).

Like most business schools, AoM is a virtual monopoly of white, middle-class, heterosexual, men: a monopoly that has certain consequences. One characteristic associated with masculinity is competitiveness—at AoM the intellectual cock fight is barely suppressed in the typical manner in which papers are presented, or in the pride expressed by having a 'hit' in a prestigious journal, or in the 'big names' being treated like celebrities—even to the extent of their being harried, on occasion, by young admirers. Indeed, the ability of prestigious men (mostly) to dominate those with less prestige (often women) is institutionalized most obviously perhaps, by AoM's role as a "market for intellectual meat"—Burrell's term for the widespread practice of conducting formal job interviews at the conference (1993, 75). And AoM is not just a market for meat—the sexual possibilities for such domination are, it seems, far from lost, even on the conference organizers, who provide the following advice concerning the conduct of job interviews in the official AoM Program (2004):

> Hotel guest rooms are usually inappropriate settings for conducting recruiting interviews. If interviews must be conducted in hotel guest rooms, we offer the following suggestions: have multiple recruiters meet with each candidate; leave the guest room door ajar; ensure that the room is properly prepared to conduct interviews (i.e., beds are

made, personal belongings are put away, etc.); maintain and encourage a professional demeanor by having all parties sit on chairs or sofas, wear shoes, and ask only appropriate questions; and above all, be sensitive to concerns of the other party by avoiding actions or comments that may make others uncomfortable (2004, 34).

Of course, *our* discomforts about aspects of AoM such as these were already apparent at the time—our self-conscious refusals to mimic the suits and ties, our sense of being out of place, our regular escapes by skipping sessions, etc.—might all be seen as symptomatic of such discomforts. But the oppressive atmosphere that AoM produces for us[8] was brought into clearer focus by just how refreshing it was at CQI to experience a much greater diversity in terms of race, class, sexual identity and preference—as well as to experience the virtual absence of all of AoM's masculinist paraphernalia, the commodification of relationships and the commercialization that takes place there.[9] The difference was perhaps most obviously evident at CQI because of the university classrooms (not hotels) in which the sessions were conducted, the far greater range of lifestyle choices evident among the participants, and people's interest in the substantive nature of what we write about—rather than just *where* it had been published. Indeed, the political, ethical, and emotional stances are vividly illustrated, we think, by the juxtaposition of excerpts from the welcome statements at the start of the respective conference programs (see Figure 2).

Table 4.2 Welcome Statement to Two Conferences

AoM	CQI
"This year's theme of "Creating Actionable Knowledge" encourages us to explore the influence and meaning of our research on management and organizations. The AoM has long been dedicated to creating and disseminating knowledge about management and organizations, and a key part of its mission requires that our science-based knowledge be relevant, responsible, and make a valuable contribution to society and its institutions. To accomplish this our knowledge must transcend purely scientific concerns and enable organizational members to make informed choices about important practical problems and to implement solutions to them effectively" (AoM Official Program, 2004, 2).	"The theme of the First International Conference focuses on qualitative inquiry and the pursuit of social justice in a time of global uncertainty. The congress is a call to the international community of qualitative researchers to address the implications of the attempts by federal funding agencies to regulate scientific inquiry by defining what is good science. Around the globe governments are enforcing evidence-based, bio-medical models of inquiry. These regulatory activities raise fundamental philosophical, epistemological, political and pedagogical issues for scholarship and freedom of speech in the academy" (Denzin, 2005, iv).

ETHNO-DRAMA WITH NO CATHARSIS:[10]
SELF-INDULGENCE OR SOMETHING MORE?[11]

While we could skip sessions with impunity at AoM, escaping from our day jobs is, of course, a little more complicated—particularly if the escape we plan is to be into a world like CQI. Several of our senior colleagues were highly skeptical of our attendance at CQI and explicit in their view that being interdisciplinary and unrecognized as a "business" conference it was a waste of the conference budget.[12] As Blaxter et. al. have noted, our sort of unconventionality can lead to us wandering "under the guise of inter-disciplinarity fac[ing] certain dangers of becoming lost souls on the way" (1997, 507).

The annual AoM conference, on the other hand, along with the AoM's journals, are considered prestigious by people whose opinions count in business schools. It is one of *the* places to present work in our field. And of course there are considerable career advantages in joining the mainstream—attending the major conferences, publishing in 'recognized' management journals, etc. As one of us has commented about life within universities:

> there seems to be an implicit notion of the 'ideal' or 'standard' career in which rising stars achieve their chairs as early as possible, often in their late twenties or early thirties. Their extraordinarily dense CVs burgeon with publications as they become increasingly valuable commodities in the university transfer market, and their talents are exhibited at a range of conferences on the global stage (Humphreys, 2005, 843).

But, as late starters, our *ideal* is to do what interests us rather than what will get us promoted. While we continue to go to AoM conferences (they are usually held in interesting places) and have even published papers in Academy journals, we hope our identity is not shaped too strongly by these things. We want to teach students who are interested in ideas—that surely is what we are here to offer them. The only trouble is that business schools promote themselves primarily on a competitive notion that makes learning a commodity—valued by the job market. And like the plush hotels of AoM, the institutional incentive is for our research to attract big external grants—even though the demands of corporate or government funders often constrain the free flow of ideas (Learmonth and Harding, 2006). As Sparkes (2007) observed, the academic currency of the day is one "where the slogan 'papers in and grants out' shaped the collective and individual consciousness" (2007, 532).

Then again, who are we kidding? After all, both of us have recently been promoted at the same time as drafting the manuscript of this chapter. And publishing in favored journals clearly assists in such things. Although we don't find it a particularly attractive aspect of ourselves, we are aware of the momentary frisson of pleasure when our names appear on the monthly email to all staff listing those with publications successes (and perhaps, even worse, we are aware of the frisson we get when certain others are *not* listed when we are). Perhaps in this chapter, then, we are furthering our career—by writing about not wanting a career.

NOTES

1. But let's not complain too much!
2. "[T]o be a convincing "I-witness," one must, so it seems, first become a convincing "I""(Geertz, 1988, 79).
3. Though the extent to which they succeed in meeting managers' self-defined needs may be a moot point.
4. For exceptions, see Frost and Taylor (1996); Reedy (2003); Parker (2004); Humphreys (2005); Grey and Sinclair (2006); and Learmonth (2007).
5. See, for example, Ellis (1993, 1994); Fine (1998); Spry (2001); Ellis and Bochner (2002); Saldana (2003); and Pelias (2003).
6. When one of us presented an autoethnographic paper at the 2003 AoM, the session chair likened the presentation to "opening your kimono."
7. Actually, we did take a lot of photos in both places.
8. Even for us—both of whom are white, middle-class, heterosexual, and male.
9. For example, advertisements and sponsorship dominate the AOM 2004 program, whereas the CQI 2005 program has none.
10. Pelias (2002).
11. Sparkes (2002).
12. No doubt these people (should they read this chapter) would be confirmed in their view; though, fortunately, we think they are unlikely to read it.

REFERENCES

Academy of Management. 2004. *Creating Actionable Knowledge.* Conference Program.

Berg, D.N. 2002. Bringing one's self to work: A Jew reflects. *Journal of Applied Behavioural Science* 38(4): 397–415.

Bochner, A.P. and Ellis, C. 2003. An introduction to the arts and narrative research: Art as inquiry. *Qualitative Inquiry* 9(4): 506–514.

Blaxter, L., C. Hughes, T. Lovell, and K. Scanlon. 1997. On the edge: Making meaning of flexible careers. *Gender and Education* 9(4): 505–510.

Boje, D 1996. Storytelling at Administrative Science Quarterly: Warding off the postmodern barbarians. In *Postmodern management and organization theory,* ed. D. Boje, 60–92. Thousand Oaks, CA: Sage.

Burrell, G. 1993. Eco and the bunnymen. In *Postmodernism and organizations,* eds. J. Hassard and M. Parker, 71–82. London: Sage.

Calás, M., G. Morgan, and L. Smircich. 2006. Editorial. *Organization* 13(1): 5–7.

Coffey, A. 2002. Ethnography and Self: Reflections and representations. In *Qualitative research in action,* ed. T. May, 313–31. London: Sage.

Denzin, N.K. 2005. Welcome from the Director. *First International Congress of Qualitative Inquiry: Offical programme.*

Ellis, C. 1993. "There are survivors": Telling a story of sudden death. *Sociological Quarterly* 34: 711–730.

Ellis, C. 2004. *The Ethnographic I: A methodological novel about autoethnography*. Walnut Creek, CA: Altamira Press.

Ellis, C. and Bochner, A.P. 2000. Autoethnography, personal narrative, reflexivity: Researcher as subject. In *Handbook of qualitative research, 2nd ed.*, eds. N.K. Denzin and Y.S. Lincoln, 733–768. Thousand Oaks, CA: Sage.

Fine, M. 1998. Working the hyphens: Reinventing self and other in qualitative research. In *The landscape of qualitative research: The theories and issues*, eds. N.K. Denzin and Y.S. Lincoln, 130–155. Thousand Oaks, CA: Sage.

Fletcher, D. and T.J. Watson. 2007. Voice, silence and the business of construction: Loud and quiet voices in the construction of personal, organizational and social realities. *Organization* 14(2): 155–174.

Ford, J. and Harding N. 2008. Fear and loathing in Harrogate, or a study of a conference. *Organization* 15(2): 233–250.

Frost, P.J. and S.M. Taylor, eds. 1996. *Rhythms of academic life: Personal accounts of careers in academia*. London: Sage.

Geertz, C. 1988. *Works and lives—The anthropologist as author*. Cambridge, UK: Polity Press.

Gray, R.E. 2003. Performing on and off stage: The place(s) of performance in arts-based approaches to qualitative inquiry. *Qualitative Inquiry* 9(2): 254–267.

Grey, C. 2001. Re-imagining relevance: A response to Starkey and Maddan. *British Journal of Management* 12: s27–s32.

Grey, C. and A. Sinclair. 2006. Writing differently. *Organization*, 13(3): 443–53.

Hatch, M.J. 1996. The role of the researcher: An analysis of narrative position in organization theory. *Journal of Management Inquiry* 5(4): 359–374.

Hochschild, A.R. 1983. *The managed heart: Commercialization of human feeling*. Berkeley, CA: University of California Press.

Humphreys, M. 2005. Getting personal: Reflexivity and autoethnographic vignettes. *Qualitative Inquiry* 11(6): 840–860.

Jaffe, A. 1997. Narrating the "I" versus narrating the "Isle": Life histories and the problem of representation on Corsica. In *Auto/Ethnography: Rewriting the self and the social*, ed. D.E. Reed-Danahay, 145–168. Oxford, UK: Berg.

Jenks, E.B. 2002. Searching for autoethnographic credibility, reflections from a mom with a notepad. In *Ethnographically Speaking: Autoethnography, literature and aesthetic*, eds. A.P. Bochner and C. Ellis, 44–56. Walnut Creek, CA: Altamira Press.

Kideckel, D.A. 1997. Autoethnography as political resistance: A case from socialist Romania. In *Auto/Ethnography: Rewriting the self and the social*, ed. D.E. Reed-Danahay, 47–70. Oxford, UK: Berg.

Learmonth, M. 2006. Doing critical management research interviews after reading Derrida. *Qualitative Research in Organization and Management* 1(2): 83–97.

Learmonth, M. 2007. Critical management education in action: Personal tales of management unlearning. *Academy of Management Learning & Education* 6(1): 109–113.

Learmonth, M. and N. Harding. 2006. Evidence-based Management: The very idea. *Public Administration* 84(2): 245–66.

Lerum, K. 2001. Subjects of desire: Academic armor, intimate ethnography, and the production of critical knowledge. *Qualitative Inquiry* 7(4): 466–483.

Mischenko, J. 2005. Exhausting management work: Conflicting identities. *Journal Of Health Organization And Management* 19(3): 204–218.

Parker, M. 2004. Becoming manager: Or, the werewolf looks anxiously in the mirror, checking for unusual facial hair. *Management Learning* 35(1): 45–59.

Pelias, R.D. 2002. For father and son: An ethnodrama with no catharsis. In *Ethnographically speaking: Autoethnography, literature and aesthetics*, eds. A.P. Bochner and C. Ellis, 35–43. Walnut Creek, CA: Altamira Press.

Pelias, R.D. 2003. The academic tourist: A critical ethnography. *Qualitative Inquiry* 9(3): 369–373.

Rawlins, W.K. 1998. From ethnographic occupations to ethnographic stances. In *Communication: Views from the helm for the 21ˢᵗ century*, ed. J. S. Trent, 359–362. Boston: Allyn and Bacon,

Reed-Danahay, D. E., ed. 1997. *Auto/Ethnography: Rewriting the self and the social*. Oxford, UK: Berg.

Rosen, M. 1991. Coming to terms with the field: Understanding and doing organisational ethnography. *Journal of Management Studies* 28(1): 1–24.

Saldana, J. 2003. Dramatizing data: A primer. *Qualitative Inquiry* 9(2): 218–236.

Sparkes, A. C. 2002. Autoethnography: Self-indulgence or something more? In *Ethnographically speaking: Autoethnography, literature and aesthetic*, eds. A.P. Bochner and C. Ellis, 209–232. Walnut Creek, CA: Altamira Press.

Sparkes, A.C. 2007. Embodiment, academics, and the audit culture: A story seeking consideration. *Qualitative Research* 7(4): 521–550.

Spry, T. 2001. Performing autoethnography: An embodied methodological praxis. *Qualitative Inquiry* 7(6): 706–732.

Stacey, R.D. 1996. *Complexity and creativity in organisations*. San Francisco, CA: Berret Koehler Publishers.

Starkey, K., A. Hatchuel, and S. Tempest. 2004. Rethinking the business school. *Journal of Management Studies* 41(8): 1521–1531

Svensson, B. 1997. The power of biography: criminal policy, prison life, and the formation of criminal identities in the Swedish welfare state. In *Auto/ethnography: Rewriting the self and the social*, ed. D.E. Reed-Danahay, 71–106. Oxford, UK: Berg.

Vickers, M.H. 2002. Researchers as storytellers: writing on the edge—and without a safety net. *Qualitative Inquiry* 8(5): 608–621.

Watson, T.J. 2008. Managing identity: Identity work, personal predicaments and structural circumstances. *Organization* 15(1): 121–143.

Part II

Critique of Mainstream Orthodoxy

5   The Inevitability of Professions?

Robert Dingwall

For more than half a century, successive generations of students have been taught that professional dominance is a problem. Professions are said, in the words of the Irish playwright, George Bernard Shaw, to be "conspiracies against the laity,"[1] cartels that exploit a market advantage, shield their incompetent members and use class, gender, and race privilege to exclude and oppress minorities in the interests of capital. This image has driven public policy in both the United States and the United Kingdom to create an environment where virtually all of these assertions are now empirically highly questionable, if not demonstrably untrue. Ironically, the result of these interventions has been to stimulate more sophisticated analyses of what professions do and why they may be socially desirable, to the point where it is clear that current policies are throwing out a nursery full of babies with the bathwater.

This chapter begins by reviewing the history of social scientific writing on the professions, particularly since World War II, when they first became a major object of scholarly attention. It will examine the debate between those analysts who stressed the 'demand' for professional licensing as a response to pressure from well-organized occupational groups and those that saw the 'supply' of licensing for the pursuit of state interests as more significant. This framework will then be used to examine recent policy developments, particularly in the United Kingdom; in effect, these developments close the debate by showing that professional licensing depends almost entirely on the coincidence between state and professional goals and that, where these come into conflict, state power is the lead that brings professions to heel. Finally, the chapter will seek to assess the costs of the attack on professional autonomy. Do we lose something significant when professions become subservient to post-liberal states? Should we care about this?

WHAT IS A PROFESSION?

Eliot Freidson (1983) noted the confusion that had arisen within the sociology of the professions as a result of the tendency of different authors to choose different referents for the term 'profession.' For some, this had a historical sense, denoting the traditional learned professions of medicine and law, to which would usually be added the clergy, and their offshoots in university teaching and some of the creative arts, and the military. Others were less concerned with tradition and more concerned with the legal forms that were developed in Anglo-American societies during the nineteenth century for the licensing of expert labor; lawyers and doctors still qualified but their companions would be groups like engineers and accountants. Yet others would concentrate more on professionalism as a cultural form, market labor that was not wholly subject to market values. As Evetts (2006) notes, this last definition has become more influential in recent years, partly because it better fits the circumstances of countries whose historical experience had differed from that of the United States, the United Kingdom, and the former UK Dominions, and partly because it allows analysts to address the post-WWII growth of wannabe professions, who have adopted the cultural forms in the hope of improving their market position and social status, and the recent response to this by employers who have sought to facilitate such gentrification as an alternative to economic reward in motivating workers. As a result, the field is now often described as 'the sociology of professional groups,' a somewhat looser category of occupations that is united by culture rather than by structure.

In the process, however, something of the original interest in the legal framework for the articulation of expert knowledge has been lost; much of the current discussion about the social control of expertise is now going on within the sociology of science without reference to the occupational basis of expertise (see Evans [2008] for a review of this material). This chapter will ultimately be concerned to explore the consequences of a change in legal forms that has been substantially obscured by changes in institutional rhetoric. Before doing so, however, it is important to outline the origins of the legally-closed occupational group, the licensed profession, and its relationship to expertise.

THE PROFESSIONAL DOMINANCE THESIS

Social scientists have long been fascinated by the professions as a distinctive element in the rise of the modern capitalist economy and society. There are, however, basically only two stories to be told to explain this (Dingwall and Fenn, 1987).

One is that professions are a solution to market failure in circumstances where clients present highly-variable and contingent problems demanding esoteric knowledge for their solution, and are ill-equipped to evaluate the quality of the service that they are offered. The client may receive an appropriate service but still fail to get an acceptable result because of the intrinsic nature of the problem. Lawyers cannot win all their cases and doctors cannot cure all their patients. If the client's evaluation is based on their assessment of qualities that anyone can judge, like courtesy, deference and civility, they may favour the genial incompetent over the spiky expert. Harold Shipman was a popular general practitioner with his patients.[2]

Many clients are one-shotters, dealing with professionals in isolated transactions, so that they cannot build up assessment skills or influence practice standards by taking their business elsewhere (Galanter, 1974). Historically, states have similar problems when they contract with professionals to supply particular services to poor people or to protect citizens more generally from adverse collective outcomes. When nineteenth century states began to develop public health systems, for example, how could they judge who was a fit and proper recipient of a fee or salary from the public purse? The legally-defined profession was a possible solution to these informational problems. The people who were best equipped to assess the competence of providers of a service that was critically important to states or users were other providers. The grant of a licence that closed the market to everyone except members of this cartel allowed them to define relevant expertise, set standards for acquiring and demonstrating it, and sanction or exclude those of their peers who failed to deliver service to an acceptable standard.

This analysis originates, perhaps surprisingly, with the work of Adam Smith (1976), where he specifically exempts the professions from his critique of guild monopolies. The quality of their workmanship cannot be guaranteed by devices like hallmarking, which he sees as an alternative to the restrictive practices of traditional crafts. Professional work, by which he largely means the practice of law and medicine, rested on a high degree of trust by consumers in the application of expert knowledge to their problems in uncertain circumstances. As such, it depended upon institutions that would promote and preserve that trust. Professional corporations were one such institution. This generally positive view of the professions was shared by most other writers until the 1960s (e.g., Spencer, 1886; Marshall, 1939; Parsons, 1939; Hughes, 1971; Durkheim, 1992). Professions were seen as an important feature of liberal societies, means of supplying trust and order to markets without concentrating power in states. There was a growing interest in the cultural model that they offered, particularly in articulating the moral infrastructure on which markets rested, but which markets could not themselves generate. Indeed, particularly for Parsons and Marshall, the degree to which professional values might restrain market opportunism was seen as a potential model for business management, as a reminder of the extent to which the legitimacy of enterprises, and, indirectly, of capitalism itself, might rest on normative judgements by entrepreneurs that traded off profit-maximization against its social impacts (see also Khurana [2007]). Could the businessman learn to be a professional, taking pride in the craft of management rather than in the naked exploitation of human or material resources?

This story, then, concentrates on the *supply* of regulation to create cartels that allow certain markets to operate where they would otherwise be vulnerable to failure, but where their successful functioning is seen to be critical for other valued social goals.

Since World War II, however, the dominant social scientific voices have become more critical, echoing Shaw's comment. The second story portrays professions primarily as monopolies, exploitative or oppressive institutions that should be tightly regulated, if not actually abolished (Friedman and Kuznets 1945). Smith's sympathy for the professions has come to be an embarrassment to economists, who generally regard the old boy as having had an off-day when he wrote it. Lees' verdict is more typical of contemporary sentiments:

> Getting rid of the medieval guild system and the producer privileges of mercantilism were essential pre-conditions of more rapid economic advance and greater equality of opportunity. The modern professions embody those same notions of conservatism, status and privilege which it was the abiding achievement of 18th century thought and 19th century capitalism to destroy (1966, 28).

Few go as far as Friedman (1962) in proposing the outright repeal of licensure laws and the exposure of the professions to the full rigors of antimonopoly legislation. Nevertheless, it is widely asserted that client interests would be better served by weakening professional monopolies.

A similar conclusion was reached within sociology during the 1960s as part of that decade's wider critique of all forms of inequality and social privilege; the users of professional services like law and medicine were oppressed in the same way as all other subordinate groups—indeed, if they were women or from minority backgrounds, they were potentially multiply oppressed. This analysis drew eclectically on Marxist and feminist traditions in social thought and is represented in the work of writers like Johnson (1972), Larson (1977), Witz (1992), Krause (1996) and Macdonald (1995). Larson, for instance, analyzes professionalization as a strategy to obstruct the free movement of labour and induce or accentuate social inequality.

> I see professionalization as the process by which producers of special services sought to constitute *and control* a market for their expertise. Because marketable expertise is a crucial element in the structure of modern inequality, professionalization appears *also* as a collective process of upward social mobility. . . [the] constitution of professional markets inaugurated a new form of structured inequality (1977, xvi–xvii).

The development of modern professions, since the mid-nineteenth century, may be seen as a service-sector equivalent of the attempt by corporate capital to enlist the state in regulating markets to restrain competition, and enhance the returns to established players. Cartelization is facilitated by enlisting the state's coercive power, to support it through a licensing regime. It is an analysis that emphasises the *demand* for regulation from well-organized occupational groups and gives priority to their lobbying for protection from competition. There are two common explanations for the success of groups in achieving this objective. One attributes it to imperfections in the market for votes (Buchanan, 1975; Peltzman, 1976; Tullock, 1982). Licensure is possible because democratic systems are vulnerable to the actions of organized groups who are seeking anticompetitive protections (Posner 1974). Larson (1977), for example, contrasts the relative success of medicine, dealing with dispersed and individualized consumers, who are difficult to organize in opposition, and the failure of engineering, facing organized and cohesive corporate interests. The other explanation views licensure as a way for capitalist states to offer privileges that co-opt certain groups to the tasks of repression (Waitzkin, 1991) or ideological legitimization (Cain, 1976).

The dominance of the demand story has come under increasing empirical challenge since the 1980s. There are three major problems with this thesis. First, it does not really explain the differential success and failure of occupational groups that are seeking licensing and the consequences of the grant or the different forms that it takes in different countries. In the United States, licensing is primarily a state matter. There is a great diversity in the range of occupations that are licensed and the terms on which this has been achieved. In the United Kingdom, relatively few occupations are licensed, despite some very long-term campaigns, like that by estate agents (realtors). Some of the occupations that are licensed, like plumbers who fit gas appliances and electricians who certify the fitness of installations, have effective, legally-backed, monopolies without any of the symbolic reward that goes with professional work. In mainland Europe, there is considerable discussion about whether "profession" in its Anglo-American sense is a meaningful term at all (Dubar, 1995; Evetts, 2006). Although Durkheim used it in a way that is broadly consistent with Anglophone contemporaries like Spencer, its referents have become more cultural. This has led to a focus on occupational identity and to seeing professions as intermediary associations, in a Durkheimian sense, rather than as a distinctive, legally-structured, form of work organization (Dubar, 2000; Sciulli, 2007a, 2007b).

Second, in the long run, gains from monopoly are always vulnerable to competition and innovation. Profits can be made from eliminating market imperfections; a persistent failure to do so implies that efficiency gains are actually being made (Thurow, 1975). What might these be? Economists have returned to the problem of informational asymmetry, and recognized its potential role in causing market failure (Akerlof, 1970; Leland, 1979). Smith's comments on the importance of trust between professionals and clients, because of the latters' limited capacity to evaluate the skills of the former, are less easily dismissed than seemed to be the case in the 1960s. There is greater acceptance of the idea that professions may not be a symptom of market failure but a solution. With the rise of national and global markets, for example, it is hard to assure the quality of services through the local knowledge that would have been available in small-scale societies. Local healers lose out because they are local rather than because they are systematically oppressed. Large-scale engineering projects require the skills of recognizable experts to secure the trust and confidence of potential investors in international capital markets. States also have their interests: UK solicitors acquired their monopoly from their role as tax collectors in property transactions and pharmacists from a moral panic about the free availability of organic poisons (see Dingwall, 1999).

Third, professions have also come to be seen as potential solutions to wider problems of governance, as mooted by the late nineteenth century English sociologist, Herbert Spencer (1886). Halliday (1987), for example, saw that professions could be an answer to "state overload," the challenge of sustaining order in markets in an era when direct state intervention had lost a degree of legitimacy. By contracting out functions to arms-length bodies, states might secure order while avoiding the need to raise taxation to resource supposedly inefficient or ineffective public bureaucracies or to intervene directly in "free" markets. These observations were extended by Dingwall and King (1995), Dingwall (1999) and Evetts and Dingwall (2002), to explore how professions could contribute to 'government at a distance,' a more flexible and resilient model of societal organization that avoided concentrations of state power while maintaining economic and social orderliness (see also Johnson, 1995; Light, 1995; Freidson, 2001).

The rebalancing of the social scientific thinking on professions is best exemplified in the intellectual journey of Eliot Freidson (Dingwall, 2006; Brint, 2006). Freidson's (1970a, 1970b) classic work of the early 1970s had been the most influential mainstream statement of the demand thesis, in its analysis and critique of the dominance of medicine in the US health system and its exploration of the need for a new kind of practice that was accountable to patients rather than designed to control them. He subsequently contributed a glowing cover endorsement to Larson's (1977) more overtly Marxist analysis. However, his picture of a free-flowing and competitive labor market where physicians had established their dominance and control through a victory in a succession of jurisdictional conflicts and the creation of subordinate jurisdictions (Abbott, 1988) was already being criticized by the 1980s for its lack of attention to the role of states (e.g., Rueschemeyer, 1983). His later work (Freidson, 1986, 2001) addressed this challenge and concluded that:

> In sum, [the state] is the key force required for the creation, maintenance, and enforcement of ideal typical professionalism. Whether or not it does so depends upon its own organization and agenda, which varies in time and space (Freidson, 2001, 128–129).

The crisis of the welfare state had displaced professions from their role as partners in a kindly but paternalist system of governance. Now they were increasingly subordinated to the interests of states in disciplining citizens to act as neo-liberal consumers. Autonomy and self-regulation were being replaced by state direction and executive control. The consequences were, in Freidson's view, increasingly inhumane:

> Where service is provided to individual humans in need, standardization runs the risk of degrading the service to some and failing to serve appropriately those who fall outside the norm . . . the institutions that support the professions [have become] more vulnerable to market and bureaucratic forces and less able to resist their pressure towards the

maximization of profit and the minimization of discretion . . . the professional ideology [is attached] to a transcendent value that gives it meaning and justifies its independence. By virtue of that independence members of the profession claim the right to judge the demands of employers or patrons and the laws of the state, and to criticize or refuse to obey them. That refusal is not based on personal grounds of individual conscience or desire but on the *professional* grounds that the basic value or purpose of a discipline is being perverted (Freidson, 2001, 218–221).

The licensed autonomy of the professions, coupled with material and symbolic rewards sufficient to establish genuine independence of judgement, were the individual's last protections against Fordist managerialism in the provision of personal services.

The competition between demand and supply theories of professionalization is one that is clearly subject to empirical test. The UK experience under New Labour provides a remarkable case study. In effect, the government's moves to deregulate markets and to bring professions under state control are a crucial endorsement of the supply model—when professions cease to serve a state interest, their licenses will be unilaterally torn up. The next section will examine this experience, before returning to consider whether Freidson's view of the consequences may be correct.

TUGGING THE LEAD

The United Kingdom has seen a remarkable process of reform in the structures and processes of professional governance over the last twenty years, which will be completed by the end of the present decade. In effect, it will have transformed all the licensing boards for traditional professions into agents of the state, rather than of the professionals, and brought a number of previously unregulated occupations into the same framework. The significance of these developments has often been missed by the narrow focus of UK commentators on particular sectors or their inattention to experience outside the United Kingdom. The substitution of the state-controlled licensing board for the arms-length self-regulation of a professional body has been well-established in the United States for many years, although the implications are rather different in an environment where the state has only limited responsibilities for the provision of the regulated services. More importantly, the tendency of writers on the UK legal and medical professions not to attend to each other's work means that each has tended to examine the developments in their own field as unique to that field rather than seeing them as evidence of a state project. By 'state project,' it is important to stress that the model is not one of a conspiracy of particular and named individuals so much as of the rise of a collective sentiment in government, and associated policy and administration communities, that state power should be directed in particular ways to achieve particular ends.

In the UK context, for example, there has been little comment on the parallels between the Clementi (2004) report on the regulation of legal services and the developments in the health sector. Clementi notes the desire of the government to introduce a new regulatory framework that will permit the introduction of new forms of business structures and promote the commercialization of legal work. The report dismisses the concerns of some lawyers about the implications of promoting business values at the expense of those of professionalism, and about the loss of independence from the state. It concludes by recommending the introduction of a radically reconstructed regulatory regime, supervised by a Legal Services Board (LSB). The individual professions would be required to split the representative and the regulatory functions of their associations, with the latter exercised only under delegated powers from the LSB. The majority of LSB members would be non-lawyers, with the chair and chief executive appointed by the relevant government minister. The eventual legislation extended the minister's role to the appointment of all board members, rather than leaving this with the board itself, and excluded government-employed lawyers from the scope of regulation (DCA, 2006; Legal Services Act, 2007).

In the health sector, the various licensing bodies have, since 2003, been subordinated to the Council for Healthcare Regulatory Excellence (CHRE, formerly Council for the Regulation of Healthcare Professionals). CHRE functions as a super-regulator, with the power to call in and override the decisions of any of the individual regulators in particular cases, in which respect it goes further than the LSB. Unlike the LSB, about half the membership is nominated by the licensing bodies, but the remainder are appointed indirectly by the government through the NHS Appointments Commission. CHRE was established on the back of the inquiry into deaths associated with paediatric cardiac surgery at the Bristol Royal Infirmary (BRI), chaired by Sir Ian Kennedy, which reported in 2001, under the NHS Reform and Health Care Professions Act 2002. The implementation of this act was barely complete, however, before further change was demanded, following the report of the Shipman Inquiry (see note 2), chaired by Dame Janet Smith, in 2004. This was followed by the Donaldson (2006) and Foster (2006) reports and a White Paper, *Trust, Assurance and Safety* in 2007. Large elements of these do not require primary legislation but are being implemented by 'Section 60 Orders' under the Health Act 1999. As with the legal services reforms, those bodies that combined representation and regulation, like the Royal Pharmaceutical Society, are being forced to demerge on a very tight timescale—the new licensing board for pharmacy is due to come into operation on January 1, 2010, with less than two years' preparation. All licensing boards are to have at least parity between lay and professional representation with a strong steer towards lay majorities. Their professional membership will no longer depend mainly on election by the profession but will be made up, wholly or in part, by government nominees, who will probably be excluded from holding office in any representative body for the profession. The CHRE will be reduced in size by reducing the number of professional members and selecting them by a process of government appointment rather than by nomination from the licensing boards.

These various changes are justified by reference to the BRI and Shipman Inquiries as if their findings are self-evident cases for reform. However, it is important to recognize that both of these are documents have their own history, which provides an important context for the subsequent recommendations. Kennedy, in particular, was a critic of the medical profession well before he was ever appointed to chair the BRI Inquiry. His 1980 Reith Lectures, published as *Unmasking Medicine* (1981), presented an academic lawyer's case against the medical profession's regulatory structures. Their arguments continued to attract considerable attention, as an expression of the monopoly case against professions. It is, however, worth recalling Freidson's verdict:

> To put it bluntly, the intellectual qualities of the book are stereotyped and thin . . . its overall tone is one of doctor-bashing, science-baiting and machine-smashing . . . the book does not go much beyond sloganeering . . . (1982, 96–97)

It is not clear to what extent Freidson's own shift of perspective was prompted by Kennedy's use of ideas that he had helped to develop, although the conclusion of the review hints at this, but it is also clear that, in appointing Kennedy in 1998 to chair the inquiry, ministers and civil servants would have known exactly what they were likely to get by way of an outcome.

The previous positions of Dame Janet Smith, the judge who chaired the Shipman Inquiry, are less clearly documented. However, the general problems of asking judges to review complex organizational failures are well-recognized (Dingwall, 1986). The life and career experience of judges, and the individualistic nature of legal reasoning and its application to cases, do not equip them to think in the systemic terms more characteristic of the social sciences, and arguably more relevant to the challenge of redesigning institutions. As a result, both reports place a great deal of emphasis on legal or regulatory change to require alterations in actors' behavior rather than seeking to understand how this behavior was institutionally possible and seeing law merely as one part of a portfolio of possible interventions to change this. This view of law as a form of command, which goes back to Bentham and Austin, early nineteenth century legal philosophers, models organizations as systems of command and control: law commands organizations, organizations command their members, their members act in accordance with these commands, end of story.

Although law is an important dimension of organizational environments (see Edelman and Suchman, 1997), contemporary analysts would find it hard to recognize this as a model of organizational behavior; laws are not self-interpreting and self-enacting so organizations must constantly decide what they mean, resolve conflicts between their commands and manage their interactions with other external signals. However, politicians have little difficulty in endorsing this version of their relationship with an institutional system. Austin (1998) saw law primarily as the embodiment of the commands of the sovereign power.[3] Historically, this might have been the monarch, but in the democracies that were emerging by the early nineteenth century, the source of authority was a constitution or a popularly elected legislature. The modern politician is the heir to this power to issue commands through law. Inquiries of this kind supply legitimacy to uses of this power, translating it into authority in the Weberian sense, but do not necessarily drive those usages. This is an important element of the case for taking a wider review of the reform of professional licensing in the United Kingdom—by looking across individual reforms in individual sectors, purportedly providing responses to sector-specific problems, we may identify patterns that are invisible in each sector taken alone.

The reconstruction of professional licensing, then, does not only apply to those occupations where there have been historic concerns about professional misbehaviour (medicine, nursing) or consumer protection (law), but also to occupations where there is no significant history of malpractice (pharmacy) and, indeed, to competing occupations where the jurisdiction has never been clear enough to define what would count as malpractice or drive a need for consumer protection (complementary medicine). The feature of all of these is the installation of lay-dominated regulatory bodies, with most members being nominated by relevant government interests, or recruited through the Public Appointments Commission and approved by ministers.[4] Government departments represent these changes as giving a clear priority to regulatory functions. The previous systems, which had evolved from professionally-dominated bodies to professional/lay partnerships, had often played a representative role for the professions, sometimes alongside other bodies and sometimes as a combined regulatory/representative body, like the Law Society or the Royal Pharmaceutical Society. Ostensibly, these functions are to be clearly separated, with professional bodies speaking for the professions and regulatory bodies speaking for their clients.

In practice, this is not quite so simple. The sponsoring government departments clearly envision that they will continue to control the representative bodies, which are expected to operate in the public interest, although they will actually be paid for by their members. Guidance to the Clarke Inquiry (2008), on the future of the Royal Pharmaceutical Society following the demerger of its regulatory elements and the end of compulsory membership, indicated that the Department of Health expected the professional body to support its own agenda for the reform of pharmacy education and services, rather than being member-driven, at least in policy terms. The sponsoring departments will certainly control the licensing boards; the planning for pharmacy was being led by a career NHS manager and a former Deputy Chief Pharmacist in the Department of Health, for example. As Martin (2008) has pointed out, lay involvement, at least in the health sector, does not rest on any representative principle so much as on an adherence to the policies and goals of the department. His argument is based on a discourse analysis of recruitment documents for lay members of NHS bodies, but these do not differ in any essential detail from those used for recruitment in other sectors, such as legal services. Lay representation supplies legitimacy to departmental goals and policies through the selection of "experts in laity" rather than through the traditional systems of representative democracy. These experts have knowledge by virtue of their disposition and social location that can provide insights to government in the reconstruction of its relations with citizens. Martin quotes Rose and Miller's comment that:

> . . . by means of expertise, self regulatory techniques can be installed in citizens that will align their personal choice with the ends of government. The freedom and subjectivity of citizens can in such ways become an ally, and not a threat, to the orderly government of a polity and a society (1992, 1188–1189).

Following Rose and, ultimately, Foucault, Martin tends to sideline the role of top-down regulation in this process, in favour of regulation through structured autonomy, where the choices made by citizens contribute to their own management. "Experts in laity" inform the presentation and representation of those choices.

It is not, though, clear that top-down regulation can be quite so lightly discarded. Law still has a role in the post-Foucauldian world, particularly given the emphasis placed by both Foucault and Rose in the role of professions in the construction of the modern citizen. Rose and Miller (1992), for example, discuss the way in which professions are a form of government "action at a distance," independent agents who are allies of the state rather than its agents. This is, in effect, a version of Halliday's (1987) observations of the way in which professions can solve problems of state overload identified in a different tradition of political science. However, the regulatory changes currently in process are not based on a model of alliance between the state and independent professions, representing the decentred form of governance identified by both Rose and Halliday, and which ultimately derives from Spencer's (1886) thinking. They impose state control of the licensing bodies and, through mandatory revalidation by these institutions, define all professional licences as temporary grants of authority to practice which rest on the state's goodwill towards the profession. Even the present arrangements have an interim quality: the Foster (2006) review of the non-medical healthcare professions, for instance, looks favorably on the case for a significant reduction in the number of licensing boards and proposes a further review in 2011, when some of the new structures will have operated for barely one year, to reconsider this question.

How should we understand these developments? One obvious conclusion is that the historical narrative of the rise of professions needs radically to be reappraised. In some respects, social scientists have been too ready to ally themselves with the "origin myths" that professions told about themselves. Licensing may have been preceded by organized occupational pressures demanding favourable regulation. Whether this was granted or not, however, seems to have depended, certainly in the UK context, on whether this coincided with some compelling state interest in supplying such regulation. Once that state interest changed, as in the break-up of the post-war social democratic consensus since the 1970s, the terms of licensing have been subject to unilateral revision by the state in ways that underline the fragility rather than the stability of jurisdictional monopolies. However, we still need to consider what may be involved in prompting this particular shift in state interest. Why are professions being remodelled as agents rather than partners of the state?

PROFESSIONS IN A POST-LIBERAL STATE

One way to address this may be to reflect on whether the British experience of the last thirty years has been one of marketization and liberalization or one of growing state authoritarianism. This may seem an odd formulation: surely, markets have become increasingly central to social and economic policy and state centralism has been consigned to the dustbin of history along with the state socialist regimes that gave birth to it. However, the same period has also been marked by the consistent decline of independent secondary associations, as Putnam (2000) has documented in the United States. The United Kingdom has seen similar declines in union membership and civic participation. Voluntary associations have been increasingly co-opted by the state to perform services under contracts that define their roles and constrain their ability to act independently. In effect, they become vehicles for reducing labour costs in public services rather than expressions of civic engagement. Similarly, with the important exception of the devolved administrations in the nations of the United Kingdom, local government has increasingly been regarded merely as an agency of central government, to be bypassed when it shows any inconvenient signs of independence, as in infrastructure planning or the management of schools. Alongside this, individuals in the population are increasingly surveyed, registered and documented, not solely as they cross frontiers but throughout their everyday life.

The erosion of professional autonomy is just one further element in this process. Traditionally, the licensed professions owed their primary loyalty to their clients, to help them solve problems of massive concern to them as individuals—life and death, liberty and property, the fate of their eternal souls. The new professionals are expected to owe their primary loyalty to the state that conditionally grants their licences. Some of the problems that this generates have already emerged: the growing critique of nursing practices that prioritize organizational goals over compassion and patient dignity, for example. Even the Foster (2006, 42) review concedes that the loss of professional 'buy-in' could be a challenge to any revised system of licensing boards—professionals 'working to the rules' rather than responding to the needs of their clients or patients. In his last work, Freidson (2001) saw the professions as the last defense of humane values against managed care in the United States. In the United Kingdom, one might argue that the professions could be seen as the citizen's last defense against a state that seeks increasingly to micro-manage everyday life. That defense seems increasingly threadbare.

NOTES

1. *The Doctor's Dilemma* (1911, Act 1)
2. Harold Shipman was an English general practitioner who is believed to have murdered more than 200 of his patients between 1970 and 1998. "Shipman had the reputation in Hyde of being a good and caring doctor. He was held in very high regard by the overwhelming majority of his patients. He was also respected by fellow professionals. His patients appear to have regarded him as the best doctor in Hyde. His register was full and there always seems to have been a waiting list" (The Shipman Inquiry 2002, para. 13.21).
3. Strictly, he also allowed that laws might derive from the commands of God, as far as these could be determined, or be expressions of a common morality without a specific sovereign authority. There is a useful introduction to Austin's approach and its problems in Harris (1980, 24–35).
4. The *Complementary and Natural Healthcare Council* does not have a statutory basis, but has been set up with Department of Health funding and on a similar basis of lay domination. It is being suggested that this will eventually acquire a statutory basis, although it may register rather than licence practitioners. (This means that only CNHC-registered homeopaths, for example, can describe themselves as "registered homeopaths," but those who choose not to register can continue to describe themselves as "homeopaths"; registration does not confer a monopoly.)

REFERENCES

Abbott, A. 1988. The System of Professions: An Essay on the Division of Expert Labor, Chicago, IL: University of Chicago Press.

Akerlof, G.A. 1970. The market for lemons: qualitative uncertainty and the market mechanism. *Quarterly Journal of Economics* 94: 749–775.

Austin, J. 1998. *The province of jurisprudence determined*, eds. D. Campbell and P. Thomas, with an introduction by W.L. Morison. Aldershot, UK: Dartmouth.

Buchanan, J.M. 1975. *The limits of liberty*. Chicago, IL: University of Chicago Press.

Brint, S. 2006. Saving the 'soul of professionalism': Freidson's institutional ethics and the defense of professional autonomy. *Knowledge, Work and Society* 4: 101–129.

Cain, M. 1976. The general practice lawyer and the client: Towards a radical conception. *International Journal of the Sociology of Law* 7: 331–54.

Clarke Inquiry. 2008. Report of the independent inquiry into a professional body for pharmacy. http://theclarkeinquiry.com/index.html (accessed July 1, 2008).

Clementi Report. 2004. *Review of the Regulatory Framework for Legal Services in England and Wales: final report by Sir David Clementi*. London: Department of Constitutional Affairs.

DCA. 2006. Government response to the report by the Joint Committee on the Draft Legal Services Bill, Session 2005–06 Cm 6909. http://www.official-documents.gov.uk/document/cm69/6909/6909.asp (accessed July 1, 2008).

Dingwall, R. 1986. The Jasmine Beckford Affair. *Modern Law Review* 49: 489–507.

Dingwall, R. 1999. Professions and social order in a global society. *International Review of Sociology* 9: 131–140.

Dingwall, R. 2006. Is 'professional dominance' an obsolete concept? *Knowledge, Work and Society* 4: 77–98.

Dingwall, R and P. Fenn. 1987. A respectable profession? Sociological and economic perspectives on the regulation of professional services. *International Review of Law and Economics* 7: 51–64.

Dingwall, R. and M.D. King. 1995. Herbert Spencer and the professions: Occupational ecology reconsidered. *Sociological Theory* 13: 13–24.

Donaldson Report. 2006. *Good doctors, safer patients: Proposals to strengthen the system to assure and improve the performance of doctors and to protect the safety of patients: A report by the Chief Medical Officer* (Sir Liam Donaldson). London: Department of Health.

Dubar, C. 1995. *La socialisation—construction des identités sociales et professionnelles*. Paris: Armand Colin.

Dubar, C. 2000. *La Crise des identités: l'interprétation d'une mutation*. Paris: Presses Universitaires de France.

Durkheim, E. 1992. *Professional ethics and civic morals*. London: Routledge.

Edelman, L.B. and M.C. Suchman. 1997. The legal environments of organizations. Annual Review of Sociology 23: 479–515.

Evans, R. 2008. The Sociology of Expertise: The Distribution of Social Fluency. *Sociology Compass* 2: 281–298.

Evetts, J. 2006. Short Note: The Sociology of Professional Groups. Current Sociology: 133–143.

Evetts, J. and R. Dingwall. 2002. Professional occupations in the UK and Europe: legitimation and governmentality. *International Review of Sociology* 12: 159–171.

Foster, A. 2006. *The regulation of the non-medical healthcare professions*. London: Department of Health.

Freidson, E. 1970a. *Professional Dominance: The Social Structure of Medical Care*, New York: Atherton Press.

Freidson, E. 1970b. *Profession of Medicine: A Study of the Sociology of Applied Knowledge*. New York: Dodd, Mead & Co.

Freidson, E. 1982. Kennedy's masked future (Review of *The Unmasking of Medicine*). *Sociology of Health & Illness* 4: 95–97.

Freidson, E. 1986. *Professional Powers: A Study of the Institutionalization of Formal Knowledge*. Chicago, IL: University of Chicago Press.

Freidson, E. 2001. *Professionalism: The third logic*. Chicago, IL: University of Chicago Press.

Freidson, E. 'The theory of professions: State of the art'. In *The Sociology of the Professions: Lawyers, Doctors and Others*, eds. R. Dingwall and P.S.C. Lewis, 19–37. London: Macmillan.

Friedman, M. 1962. *Capitalism and freedom*. Chicago, IL: University of Chicago Press.

Friedman, M. and S. Kuznets. 1945. *Income from independent professional practice*. General Series No. 45, National Bureau of Economic Research, New York.

Galanter, M. 1974. Why the "haves" come out ahead: Speculations on the limits of legal change. *Law and Society Review* 9: 95–160.

Harris, J.W. 1980. *Legal philosophies*. London: Butterworth.

Halliday, T. 1987. *Beyond monopoly: Lawyers, state crises and professional empowerment*. Chicago, IL: University of Chicago Press.

Hughes, E.C. 1971. *The sociological eye*. Chicago, IL: Aldine.

Johnson, T.J. 1972. *Professions and power*. London: Macmillan.

Johnson, T.J. 1995. Governmentality and the institutionalization of expertise. In *Health professions and the state in Europe*, eds. T.J. Johnson, G. Larkin, and M. Saks, 7–24. London: Routledge.

Kennedy, I. 1981. *The Unmasking of Medicine.* London: George Allen and Unwin.

Khurana, R. 2007. *From higher aims to hired hands: The social transformation of American business schools and the unfulfilled promise of management as a profession.* Princeton, NJ: Princeton University Press.

Krause, E.A. 1996. *Death of the Guilds: Professions, states, and the advance of capitalism, 1930 to the present.* New Haven, CT: Yale University Press.

Larson, M.S. 1977. *The rise of professionalism: A sociological analysis.* Berkeley, CA: University of California Press.

Lees, D. 1966. *The economic consequences of the professions.* London: Institute of Economic Affairs.

Legal Services Act 2007 (2007 c.29)

Leland, H.E. 1979. Quacks, lemons and licensing: A theory of minimum quality standards. *Journal of Political Economy* 87: 1328–1346.

Light, D. 1995. Countervailing powers: a framework for professions in transition. In *Health professions and the state in Europe,* eds. T.J. Johnson, G. Larkin, and M. Saks, 69–79. London: Routledge.

Macdonald, K.M. 1995. *The sociology of the professions.* London: Sage.

Marshall, T. H. 1939. The recent history of professionalism in relation to the social structure and policy. *Canadian Journal of Economics and Political Science* 5: 325–40.

Martin, G.P. 2008. "Ordinary people only": Knowledge, representativeness, and the publics of public participation in healthcare. *Sociology of Health & Illness* 30: 35–54.

Parsons, T. 1939. The professions and social structure. *Social Forces* 17: 457–67.

Peltzman, S. 1976. Towards a more general theory of regulation. *Journal of Law and Economics* 19: 211–237.

Posner, R. 1974. Theories of economic regulation. *Bell Journal of Economics* 5: 335–351.

Putnam, R. D. 2000. *Bowling Alone: The Collapse and Revival of American Community.* New York: Simon & Schuster.

Rose, N. and Miller, P. 1992. Political power beyond the state: Problematics of government. *British Journal of Sociology* 43: 173–205.

Rueschemeyer, D. 1983 Professional autonomy and the social control of expertise. In *The Sociology of the Professions: Lawyers, Doctors and Others,* eds. R. Dingwall and P.S.C. Lewis, 38-58. London: Macmillan.

The Shipman Inquiry. 2002. *First report: Death disguised.* (chairman Janet Smith). http://www.the-shipman-inquiry.org.uk/firstreport.asp (accessed September 27, 2008).

Sciulli, D. 2007a. Paris Visual Académie as First Prototype Profession. *Theory, Culture & Society* 24: 35–59.

Sciulli, D. 2007b. Professions before Professionalism. *European Journal of Sociology* 48: 121–147.

Smith, A. 1976. *An inquiry into the nature and causes of the wealth of nations.* Chicago, IL: University of Chicago Press.

Spencer, H. 1886. *The principles of sociology: Vol. 3.* London: Williams and Norgate.

Thurow, L. 1975. *Generating inequality.* London: Macmillan.

Tullock, G. 1982. *The economics of redistribution.* Boston: Kluwer-Nijhoff.

Waitzkin, H. 1991. *The politics of medical encounters.* New Haven, CT: Yale University Press.

Witz, A. 1992. *Professions and Patriarchy.* London: Routledge.

6 Critical Risk Management
Moral Entrepreneurship in the Management of Patient Safety

Justin Waring

INTRODUCTION

The language of risk has come to feature significantly within contemporary culture, and politics (Lupton, 1999; Power, 2007). We are constantly warned, for example, of the health risks from activities such as smoking, the risks to employment from economic downturns, and the risks to the environment from burning fossil fuels. The increased prominence of 'risk' is underpinned by the burgeoning and, seemingly, indeterminate dangers associated with technological and social change, which are the subject of fervent debate (Taylor-Gooby and Zinn, 2006). A cursory review of the print news at the time of writing (*The Guardian*, May 5, 2009) found reference to the risks of 'swine flu', extreme diets, mining in the Hindu Kush, and umemployment and economic downturn in the wake of the 'credit crunch' (Boone, 2009; Campbell, 2009; Finch, 2009; Jha et al. 2009; Meikle and Connolly, 2009; Wray, 2009). Whereas once the language of risk may have been associated with the technical and rational goal of bringing certainty to issues of uncertainty, within contemporary society this language has itself become the focus of doubt as risks have become increasingly global in character and the focus of individual action (Beck, 1992). At a time when the management of risk is common to virtually all aspects of social life, it is important to raise questions about the inherent implications for social order and power.

The management of risk has been an implicit feature of public and social policy throughout the twentieth century. This was evident in the creation of post-war welfare regimes across the Western world, which sought to address the risks of unemployment, homelessness, sickness, and poverty (Manning and Shaw, 2000). Such services were largely premised on an implicit notion of risk articulated in terms of need and embedded within the relative areas of professional expertise. As society has developed, such welfare issues have been rearticulated through a more explicit and rational language of risk (Power, 2007), while new risks have come to shape the development of public services (Taylor-Gooby and Zinn, 2006). Today, the definition and control of risks is no longer embedded within professional decision-making, but it has become an unambiguous criterion in the organization and delivery of services. This is exemplified by the growth of formal risk management practices that provide a calculable, rational, and often, bureaucratic basis for resource allocation and the reordering of services.

Without question, risk, or what might be called uncertainty, is an inevitable feature of contemporary life. Furthermore, there is clear merit in adopting practices that seek to better understand and control for risks in ways that enhance human well-being and reduce the potential for loss. Yet questions need to be asked about the dominance of management practices and their often unrecognized and implicit consequences for public services delivery. Outside mainstream management thinking, there is a well-established socio-cultural literature revealing how meanings or 'rationalities' of risk vary significantly between social and cultural groups (Lupton, 1999). These reveal how the social construction of risk can have an important role in relation to social identity, belonging, and the dynamics of power. Specifically, what one group or community regards as dangerous or 'risky' has implicit connotations for how individuals should act relation to that risk and how it should be controlled. Building on such works questions can be asked about the prevailing managerial conceptualization and application of risk as a basis for decision-making (Lupton, 1999). Risk management practices are not merely rational or technical procedures for measuring and controlling risks, but also mechanisms for identifying, labelling, and controlling behaviors or social groups that are deemed by another social group to be 'risky' (Castells, 1991).

This chapter questions the prolific application of risk management practices within the public sector and considers the often implicit implications for service organization and delivery. First, it offers a theoretical critique of the mainstream approaches to risk management by contrasting these with more socio-cultural theories, revealing how issues of morality, responsibility, and legitimacy are inherent to the control of risk. Second, it elaborates these ideas through considering the growth of clinical risk management practices within the UK National Health Service (NHS), showing how emerging techniques to reduce the risks to clinical quality have underlying implications for the control of professional practice and authority. Through this discussion, wider questions are raised about the general adoption and proliferation of risk management within the public sector and the inherent implications for social power and control.

RISK AND RISK MANAGEMENT

Risk management practices have evolved from the finance and insurance industries of early capitalism to offer a widespread and popular way of identifying and controlling (or compensating) for uncertainty and the potential for harm in many aspects of socio-economic and organizational life (Covello and Mumpower, 1985; Giddens, 1991; Taylor-Gooby and Zinn, 2006). In practice, risk management is associated with a number of key procedures that aim to reduce or control for potential harm or loss through forms of learning, intervention, and change (Power, 2007). The first is normally associated with identifying risks; the second involves determining the scale or measure of risk; the third, where possible, seeks to identify the sources of risk; and the fourth introduces interventions to control or compensate for risk. There are numerous ways these stages can be articulated, dependent upon the social or organizational setting, the role of technologies, the socio-cultural and political context, and the inherent nature of the uncertainty (Taylor-Gooby and Zinn, 2006). For example, there are significant differences in managing genetic risks to health compared to the risks of air travel. Nevertheless, a number of common procedures and techniques are often used.

In gathering information about risk, both proactive and reactive systems can be used. Proactive approaches include assessing risk through problem-based analysis for planned activities, while reporting systems can gather post-hoc information about situations of loss to provide lessons for subsequent risk identification. In the identification and measurement of risk, mainstream approaches typically utilize a probabilistic definition of risk derived from the financial industry and developed, for example, in the engineering sciences. This centers on determining the likely frequency of a situation in conjunction with the expected severity of loss or harm. This technical approach to risk (R) calculation can be summarized as seeking to ascertain the magnitude (M) and the probability (P) of exposure, e.g. $R = PM$ (e.g. Tansey and O'Riordan, 1999).

Identifying the probable sources of risk and then implementing an appropriate solution, again varies according to the particular setting and risk, but a number of strategies are common. These vary from seeking to prevent or limit risk to those that seek to control for the impact of risk. For risk avoidance, this involves removing activities or situations that are deemed to be 'risky' or risk inducing. Risk reduction involves introducing systems that work to combat or mitigate the full effect of loss, such as seat belts in the case of automobile accidents. It is also common to transfer the costs of risk to some form of insurance scheme that can provide compensation or relief in the event of loss. More generally, risk management systems themselves are regarded as proactive forms of risk reduction because they enable organizations to learn about and control risks.

Such risk management techniques have become popular, not only in high-risk industries such as aviation or petrochemicals (Reason, 1997) but also in public policy (Power, 2007). Their is associated with wider transitions in public sector management, especially the rise of New Public Management and now 'progressive governance' (Hoggett, 1996; Hood, 1991; Flynn, 2007; Newman, 2000; Rhodes, 1997). During this time, public services have been increasingly subject to government steering, target-setting, and audit, while the responsibility for performance has been devolved to a new cadre of service managers operating in a more business-like and competitive environment. Situated within wider performance management and governance frameworks, formal risk management structures and systems, like those described earlier, have been established across the public sector. This can be seen in the management of financial risks but also in the risks to service quality and effectiveness, as exemplified by the fashions for process re-engineering, quality assurance, and Total Quality Management (Hansson, 2000; Power, 2007; Wilkinson, et al., 1998). In contrast to public sector professionalism where issues of risk were often implicit and obscured within expert practice, the formal management of risk is based upon the application of explicit, rationalized, and technical systems. Furthermore, in the pursuit of cost saving and quality improvements, the prevailing managerial approach has turned upon the risks of professional practice illustrating a significant tension point within the organization of public services. This is particularly evident in healthcare where evidence suggests that the processes of care can almost be as threatening to patient wellbeing as disease or illness (Department of Health, 2000).

THINKING CRITICALLY ABOUT RISK MANAGEMENT

It is important to ask critical questions about these mainstream approaches and to offer alternative ways of thinking about risk. A number of preliminary points can be made about the prevailing risk management approach. First, the mainstream approach, as illustrated in the fields of economics or engineering, holds that risks are ontologically 'real' and amenable to objective and scientific investigation and measurement (Lupton, 1999). As shown previously, this is often linked to the use of probabilistic forms of risk calculation that seek to empirically and statistically measure a given risk so as to better inform intervention. Second, it is assumed that through first measuring risk it then becomes possible to rationally control the risk through management intervention. This can be seen in economics where it is assumed that through gathering information about financial risks relevant parties can make informed rational choices about their future investments. The mainstream approach represents an example of the 'measure and manage' orthodoxy that has come to influence public policy (Power, 2007). Third, and raising doubts about the aforementioned, the rational and objective approach to risk management remains successful where outcomes are amenable to identification, where loss and harm can be measured and where risks can controlled or mitigated (Zinn and Talyor-Gooby, 2006). It has become evident, however, that contemporary risks have become increasingly global in magnitude, open to public controversy, and those institutions, technologies, and experts historically directed towards the control of risk are now the source of new uncertainties and dangers (Beck, 1992). Accordingly, risk increasingly resides outside the scope of management intervention.

More critical ways of thinking about risk can be found within socio-cultural and sociological theory (Lupton, 1999). Sociological work often characterizes 'risk' as a modern language, semantic or rationality for defining and seeking to order what might otherwise be considered uncertainty or danger (Beck, 1992; Giddens, 1991; Luhmann, 1986). Developing this line, Beck's (1992) *Risk Society* locates the contemporary significance of risk within the context of modernity and late modernity. He describes how, within contemporary society, risks have taken on a more prominent role in shaping individual identities and social roles, while also showing that risks have become increasingly global and unmanageable in character. He suggests that if modernity can be characterized by the production of 'goods' with corresponding social divisions in terms of class, then advanced industrial societies involve the production of 'bads,' which bring with them new social divisions and inequalities. This work accounts for the growth of rationalistic risk management practices to control risk or uncertainty, but also highlights how these strategies and related technological advances are also the source of new risks (Beck, 1992). A major theme within his work is that society has become increasingly skeptical about risk expertise requiring individuals to reflexively navigate the uncertainties of contemporary life.

Of particular significance to this chapter are the cultural theories of risk associated with the work of Mary Douglas (1966, 1994; with Wildavsky, 1982). Her work shows how perceptions and judgments about risk reflect wider cultural assumptions and value systems. This means that what an individual or society selects as a risk is rarely an objective assessment or calculation, as aspired by mainstream perspectives, but rather selection reflects wider cultural, ideological, and moral systems. As such, knowledge about risks is socially constructed with social interaction and the cultural fabric of everyday life.

Douglas' work is critical of the mainstream techno-scientific approach (Lupton, 1999), especially cognitive psychological perspectives. It takes issue with that view that different perceptions of risk illustrate cognitive deficiency or error of judgment. This is often associated with the idea of a 'lay-expert divide,' where the expert is seen as scientifically determining risk hence establishing some objective 'truth,' whereas lay groups lacking this expertise fail to comprehend or accurately determine risk. Her work suggests, however, that different interpretations of risk should not be presumed to illustrate cognitive bias or misperception; rather they reflect important cultural, normative, or moral variations:

> Whilst such psychological approaches tend to focus narrowly on individual cognition and bias, this fails to reflect the fact that the subjects of psychological enquiry do not leave their "cultural bias" at the door of the experimentation booth (Douglas, 1994. 32).

All knowledge about risk is socially constructed and accordingly, the risks identified through risk management are themselves the product of particular cultural or ideological assumptions, despite claiming to be objective. Furthermore, with the inherent bias towards scientific and positivistic methods, these mainstream approaches fail to consider, and often marginalize the myriad of cultural influences that shape how individuals and groups make sense of risk and uncertainty (Weick, 1995).

Douglas' work (1994) develops this constructionist perspective to show how knowledge about risk also provides a basis for social control. She shows how the perception of risk has implicit implications for issues of responsibility, blame, and 'otherness.' That is, the way a particular group defines its risks reflects assumptions about how that risk came about, how it disrupts social order and how individuals should act to restore social order. It therefore has implicit connotations about the morality of social behavior: those who break the rules are regarded as risky, while those who conform to customary (risk reducing) behaviors are seen good citizens. In these terms, strategies to control risk, whether operating at the level of rituals and customs or in formal risk management systems are mechanisms for allocating blame and in turn controlling social behavior:

> Under the banner of risk reduction, a new blaming system has replaced the former combination of moralistic condemning the victim and opportunistic condemning of the victim's incompetence (Douglas, 1994, 16).

In this way, the social construction of risk contributes to social order and identity. Victim blaming reinforces both good and bad behaviors, punishing the latter and vindicating the former. In this sense, risks are a fulcrum of social control. In turn, how a social group gives meaning to risk established share and collective behaviors that reinforce social cohesion and promote a sense of belonging. Equally, those who interpret and react to risks differently are seen as being different, 'others' or 'outsiders' (Douglas and Wildavsky, 1982).

This has strong theoretical connections with the work of Becker, especially his studies of deviance in *Outsiders* (1966). Becker highlights how all social groups establish rules, with mechanisms to enforce them, as a way of maintaining social order. When action is perceived as infringing the rules, the perpetrators are often labelled as deviants or seen as acting 'outside' the expected norms of conduct. Becker's work develops our understanding of labelling as a mechanism of social control, but also has relevance to our understanding risk management. Specifically, any system of risk regulation, whether cultural or managerial, works to establish actions deemed to be deviant or risky. However, it is important to identify those groups who work to define and then enforce these rules. Here Becker introduces the idea of 'moral entrepreneurs' as a way of thinking about those groups that seek to establish and police 'the rules.' It is through the work of these groups that certain 'deviant' individuals are identified, labelled, and eventually defined as 'outsiders' or 'others.' Applying these ideas, mainstream risk management practices resemble expressions of moral entrepreneurship. Despite being portrayed as rational and claiming to establish objective facts, it can be argued that the risks identified through these techniques reflect particular cultural and ideological preferences. Furthermore, these activities work to establish the social 'rules' for good or low-risk behavior, while those behaviors deemed high-risk or deviant are amenable to social control and intervention. However, Becker also highlights the possibility that those who create and enforce the rules may themselves be regarded as 'outsiders' by others who have their own rules and thus question the authority and legitimacy of these moral entrepreneurs.

These critical perspectives on risk raise important questions about the prolific extension of risk management practices. In general, we are persuaded that through the technical procedures of probabilistic assessment it is possible to objectively determine and then manage risk. Yet the socio-cultural perspective highlights that knowledge about risk is inherently constructed through social interaction and reflects prevailing cultural and ideological systems (Smith, 2004). From this perspective, knowledge about risk has an implicit moral dimension about good or bad behaviors to which individuals are encouraged to conform to establish their belonging to a social group or culture, while also drawing boundary distinctions with those who do not conform. Those at the forefront of risk management can also be interpreted as 'moral entrepreneurs' because they are active in the definition and assessment of 'risky' behaviors and the development of strategies to limit their occurrence. To elaborate this perspective, the chapter examines the growth of clinical risk management practices in the UK NHS and how, in the pursuit for quality improvement and patient safety, risk management has inherent forms of moral entrepreneurship and social control.

CLINICAL RISK MANAGEMENT AND PATIENT SAFETY

The Context of Clinical Risk Management

As with other public services, health policies are caught within the wider political, institutional, and cultural preoccupation with risk (Wilson and Tingle, 1999). Over the last quarter century there has been an unprecedented desire by policy makers, managers, and clinicians to assure the quality of clinical care, culminating in major policy initiatives around clinical risk and patient safety (Department of Health 2000; World Health Organisation, 2004). However, this drive for quality improvement, risk management, and patient safety has been shaped by a range of broader social and political factors, including the growth of consumer pressures, political change, public sector reform, and the growing influence of management theory and practice (Close, 1997; Wilson, 1999).

As noted previously, the influence of public sector reforms, associated with New Public Management have been integral to the growth of clinical risk management within the NHS. These can be traced to the introduction of General Management in the early 1980s and the creation of the internal market in the 1990s (Department of Health and Social Security, 1983; Department of Health, 1989). These have been interpreted as replacing established 'diplomatic' hospital administration with more responsive and cost-conscious management (Cox, 1991; Harrison, 1988), while the purchaser–provider split replaced longstanding bureaucratic planning structures with the aim of delivering greater transparency, accountability, and efficiency through competitive contracting of services (Bartlett and Harrison, 1993). More recent NHS 'modernization' plans illustrates the rise of 'progressive governance' or 'New-New Public Management' (Dent 2005; Newman 2001; Rhodes 1997). Here, collaborative partnerships and governance systems offer an addition to devolved management or market-styled reforms through seeking to inclusively engage service providers within the delivery of public services (Pettigrew and Fenton, 2000). For the NHS, this can be seen with the introduction of managed networks in the delivery of services, the use of private–public partnerships, and the use of new performance management systems to modernize healthcare regulation (Exworthy et al., 1999; Walshe, 2003).

It is within this changing landscape that a number of different programs have been implemented to better manage the quality of NHS care (Hart, 1997). In the early 1990s, clinical audit was introduced to systematically benchmark and make more explicit the processes of peer review (Dent, 1995). Attempts have also been made to apply forms of quality assurance and Total Quality Management (Pollitt, 1993). More recently, clinical governance has provided the framework for continuously assuring the quality of professional practice and clinical care (Harrison, 2004). This involved the application of evidence-based guidelines, care pathways, and streamlined models of service delivery to guide the planning and delivery of services, matched by formal systems of local and national performance review. Of importance to this chapter, risk and risk management have featured significantly within shifts in quality improvement. For example, one prominent interpretation of clinical governance highlights 'risk avoidance' as one of the major areas for action (Scally and Donaldson, 1997).

The importance of risk management within health policy is also framed by a range of broader socio-political and economic factors. The rising costs of litigation, for example, has also promoted the need for more robust forms of risk management (Wilson and Tingle, 1999) The creation of the litigation insurance program, the Clinical Negligence Scheme for Trusts (CNST) in the mid 1990s was a major force for change, offering healthcare providers with more developed systems of risk management reduced premiums for participation in the scheme. Risk has also moved up the political agenda in the wake of major scandals in the healthcare safety as exemplified by the Bristol Inquiry (Kennedy, 2001). This has resulted in public pressure for reform and widespread regulatory change, including risk-based forms of regulation (Department of Health, 2008). Finally, evidence from around the world has revealed the enormous risks to safety patients face from the routine organization and delivery of clinical services (Institute of Medicine, 1999; World Health Organization, 2004). For the NHS, it is estimated that as many as one in ten hospital patients experience some form of error or adverse event in the delivery of care, annually claiming the lives of up to 40,000 people and costing the tax payer around two billion British pounds in remedial care (Department of Health, 2000). Together these influences have pushed clinical and patient safety to the forefront of health policy.

Managing Clinical Risk and Patient Safety

Within the current period of health service modernization, the management of clinical risk is largely articulated in terms of 'patient safety.' Safety is now ranked first among the Healthcare Commissions Core Standards for NHS care (Department of Health, 2006). With the growing evidence of clinical error and patient harm, questions have been asked about the capacity for existing systems of quality assurance, risk management, and professional regulation to effectively manage the risks to patient safety (Department of Health, 2000). In turn, policies have introduced a more robust and dedicated system of risk management and organizational learning across the NHS. This is described as the National Reporting and Learning System (NRLS) and, in common with the principles of risk management described earlier, involves procedures to identify and understand the risks to safety manifest within the organization and delivery of patient care, together with corresponding procedures to control and avoid risks (NPSA, 2003). Indicative of wider public sector reforms, policies have developed this system from the managerial techniques and experiences found in other industries, such as aviation (Department of Health, 2000).

In seeking to better identify the risks to patient safety, the NRLS introduces a new framework of incident reporting across the NHS (NPSA, 2003). In short, this can be described as a formal mechanism for documenting and communicating any event that did or had the potential to risk patient safety. It is expected that any healthcare professional, support worker, patient, or family member that experiences such an event will report the incident through electronic or paper-based communication channels thereby sharing this information with service leaders and risk managers. The type of information to be collected includes a description of the event, the possible causes, the impact on the patient, and the immediate steps taken to alleviate the risk (Department of Health 2001; NPSA, 2003).

An important corollary to the introduction of incident reporting is the promotion of a 'reporting culture' (NPSA, 2003). It is often suggested in policy that a 'blame culture' prevails within health care and discourages communication because workers believe they will be held responsible for unsafe patient care (Department of Health, 2000; Waring, 2005a). As such, a no-blame or low-blame culture has been endorsed that emphasizes incident reporting as a means of learning and stresses that individuals should not arbitrarily be held responsible for patient harm. Central to this cultural shift is the promotion of 'systems thinking' or the idea that the risks to safety are rarely the consequence of individual error, but are more often brought about by a chain of events located upstream within the wider organization and management of care (Reason, 2000). The is strongly associated with the Human Factors approach, which brings together a range of ideas from ergonomic, social psychological and management theory about human error and risk management (Reason, 1997). By adopting this systems perspectives and promoting a no-blame culture it is believed that healthcare workers will be more likely to report the risks to safety (NPSA, 2003).

Incident reporting, and the associated change in culture, enables service leaders to better identify the risks to safety manifest within the organization and delivery of care. It is expected that managers will utilize this new information to identify the significance and scale of risks. As with other forms of risk analysis, this is largely premised on determining the severity or impact on patient safety, together with the likelihood or frequency of occurrence. Through determining and cross-referencing these dimensions, based upon collected incident data, it then becomes possible to establish a more accurate measure of risk. For example, incidents with high severity and high frequency are graded high-risk or 'red.' Measuring and categorizing risks in this way enables service managers to focus their attention and scarce resources on those situations that pose the greatest risk. Once risks are identified in this way it is then expected that service leaders will apply the type of 'systems thinking' to better understand the sources of risk within the organization and delivery of healthcare (Department of Health, 2000). This is articulated as 'root cause analysis' and involves a structured investigation into the underlying risks to potential harm. In practice, it often involves asking a series of sequential 'why' questions to elaborate the chain of events underling a clinical risk (Department of Health, 2001; NPSA, 2003). Through identifying these risk factors it then becomes possible to introduce more substantial interventions to reduce the burden of risk on clinical care.

The NRLS enables service leaders to more thoroughly measure and manage the sources of risk in the organization and delivery of patient care (NPSA, 2003). It is assumed that this information will make it possible to make changes deep within the organization of care that will have a lasting and widespread impact on the delivery of services. Taking example from other sectors, this is described as applying a range of techniques that seek to make clinical practice less risky, such as formulating check lists, protocols, and standardized operating procedures to direct 'safe' practice; additional strategies include introducing monitoring devices to detect risky behavior and providing training and professional development to tackle consistent risky performance.

The NRLS can therefore be seen as comprehensive form of risk management. Engaging with frontline clinical staff to better identify risks through incident reporting; providing service managers with new ways of assessing and analysing risks; and making it possible for service providers to learn the lessons for safety and develop strategies to better manage clinical risks. Of interest here, however, are the underlying implications for the reordering of healthcare services and managerial power.

Thinking Critically About Clinical Risk Management and Patient Safety

Within policy, the patient safety reforms and the NRLS are portrayed as contributing to the reduction of clinical risk through enhanced forms of organizational learning and management intervention. Drawing upon the critical lines of thinking described earlier, the chapter now offers a reinterpretation of these systems with the aim of surfacing the inherent implications for social order and organizational control. In developing this line of analysis it also seeks to locate these implications within the wider managerial reform context, considering the impact on professional working practices and the enhancement of managerial powers.

An initial observation relates to the way in which policies, via the NRLS and local risk managers, construct or define the risks to patient safety. Illustrating the technical-scientific approach of mainstream risk management systems (Lupton, 1999) primary attention is given to defining objectively what constitutes a threat to patient safety or more precisely an 'adverse event.' One early policy definition included "an event or omission arising during clinical care and causing physical or psychological injury to a patient" (Department of Health, 2000, xii). More interesting, however, is the way in which the risks to safety are to be calculated as a function of learning and management intervention. Reflecting the probabilistic and technical model described previously, the threats to patient safety are determined in terms of their 'severity' and 'frequency.' Furthermore, the way in which the sources of risk are to be identified involves applying a quasi-technical (pseudo-scientific) form of accident investigation. This shift in thinking about clinical risks illustrates the ascendance of a supposedly rational and managerial approach to risk management, whereby the interpretation of risk no longer resides within the tacit or localized domains of professional practice, but becomes an explicit task based upon the scientific theories of 'safety science' and risk management.

In practical terms, the implementation of these new procedures, while often devolved to local clinical areas, is typically located within wider performance management and governance frameworks. This means risk management is normally led by managers far removed from the frontline of care delivery. These 'expert' managers, trained in the principles of 'safety science' are the primary actors and authority in defining and assessing the risks to patient safety through the application of the prevailing technical and rational approach. Although the NRLS relies upon the participation of clinical staff to report information, it is those who receive and analyze this information that ultimately determine what is or is not risky.

The powers accorded to risk managers goes beyond simply determining the risks to patient safety, but in line with other forms of strategic risk modification, these actors also identify and promote the required organizational or occupational changes. Specifically, by identifying the underlying sources of risk, via the application of 'root cause analysis,' risk managers become able to identify new ways of working that have the potential to reduce risk and enhance patient safety. As suggested previously, this includes checklists, service guidelines, or protocols to direct safe clinical practice. In this way, risk managers can be seen as moral entrepreneurs (Becker, 1966)—analyzing incident data to define the appropriate behaviors and rules that inform safe practice. This also means that those healthcare professionals who are found to contravene these rules can be labelled as rule breakers, deviants, or 'risky.' Developing this line of analysis, the risk control strategies developed through these systems promote expected ways of ordering healthcare services that, not only enhance safety, but also define 'good' clinical practice. Conformity to these new expectations reaffirms the authority of service leaders, but also offers a way on controlling the work of healthcare professionals through blaming those 'others' or 'risky' individuals who do not conform to the expectations for safe practice. Despite being premised on a culture of 'no blame,' questions should be raised about the scope for the NRLS to actually offer new opportunities for blaming.

When located within the NHS reform context, the significance of the NRLS to reordering clinical services and professional practice is even more pronounced. There is a well-established literature examining the impact of organizational and managerial reforms on the work, autonomy, and status of healthcare professionals. For example, General Management in the 1980s has been interpreted as "cutting a swathe" across established lines of power within the NHS (Cox, 1991) and shifting the balance of power from doctors to managers (Hunter, 1994). More recent modernization reforms have also been seen as constituting complex expressions of power over healthcare professionals, whether through the introduction of explicit guidelines to direct practice or through new forms of self-surveillance, associated with the clinical governance framework (Flynn, 2004; Harrison, 2004). Located within this context, the patient safety reforms can be regarded as a new frontier in medical/managerial relations in the NHS around the management of clinical quality and risk (Waring, 2005b). Specifically, the NRLS provides service leaders and risk managers with a way of defining unsafe and risky forms of practice, based upon their acquisition of a new legitimate knowledge base, together with the creation of systems for monitoring and then reordering clinical practice. As suggested earlier, this recasts risk managers as moral entrepreneurs, capable of establishing the rules for safe practice, but also capable of defining and blaming professional who contravene these rules and are found to be responsible for unsafe practice. As such, it provides risk managers with enhanced legitimacy and authority in the control of clinical quality, an area of managerial practice that in the past had resided almost exclusively within professional knowledge and practice (Waring, 2007).

CONCLUSION

The language of risk and the desire to manage risks more effectively has become a prominent feature of contemporary society (Lupton, 1999). According to the likes of Beck (1992) and Giddens (1991) this illustrates underlying structural changes within society typical of modernity and late modernity. Over the last twenty years, the management of risk within the organization and delivery of public services reflects this preoccupation (Power, 2007). The definition and control of risks have steadily moved from the localized and tacit domains of professional practice, to become an explicit and rationalized feature of management intervention that seeks to establish objective knowledge around clinical risk. Within the current period of health service modernization, this is most clearly found in the pursuit of patient safety. Rather than seeing this managerial system as purely an objective and instrumental method of raising quality and controlling risks, questions should also be raised about its capacity to reorder and better control the work of healthcare professionals. Research in the socio-cultural tradition highlights the way the language of risk, even when based upon explicit scientific or empirical standards, reflects particular expectations around morality, i.e. what constitutes good or bad behaviors. This is reinforced through the development of practices, customs or management strategies that seek to reduce risk through dictating particular forms of social behavior. In doing so, risk management practices can be seen as reordering the organization and delivery of clinical services in ways that reduce risk, but also remodel and control professional practice. In this way, risk management systems have the scope to identify social behaviors that fail to comply with these strategies and can serve to further blame or label these individuals as dangerous or risky. Ultimately, the development of risk management systems within healthcare can be interpreted as a further stage in the continuing efforts to better manage and control professional practice.

REFERENCES

Althaus, C. 2005. A disciplinary perspective of the epistemological status of risk. *Risk Analysis*, 25(3): 567–588.

Bartlett, W. and L. Harrison. 1993. Quasi-markets and the National Health Service Reforms. In *Quasi-markets and social policy*, eds. J. Le Grand and W. Bartlett, 68–92. London: Macmillan.

Beck, U. 1992. *Risk society: Towards a new modernity.* London: Sage.

Becker, H. 1966. *Outsiders.* London: The Free Press.

Boone, J. 2009. 'A scoop of explosives, a short fuse and a gamble with death in the Hindu Kush'. *The Guardian,* May 5th: 17.

Campbell, D. 2009. 'Beware extreme diets, cancer patients warned'. *The Guardian,* May 5: 14.

Castel, R. 1991. 'From dangerousness to risk' in *The Foucault Effect: studies in governmentality,* eds. G. Burchell, C. Gordon and P. Miller, 281–298. Hemel Hemstead: Harvester Wheatsheaf.

Close, A. 1997. Quality management in health care and health care education. In *Excellence in health care management,* eds. A. Morton-Cooper and M. Bamford, 75–112. Oxford, UK: Blackwell.

Covello, V. and J. Mumpower. 1985. Risk analysis and risk management: An historical perspective. *Risk Analysis* 5(2): 103–119.

Cox, D. 1991. Health service management—a sociological view: Griffiths and the neo-negotiated order of the hospital. In *The sociology of the health service,* eds. J. Gabe, M. Calnan, and M. Bury, 89–114. London: Routledge.

Dent, M. 1995. Doctors, peer review and quality assurance. In *Health professionals and the State in Europe,* eds. T. Johnson, G. Larkin, and M. Saks, 49–58. London: Routledge.

Dent, M. 2005. Post-New Public Management in public sector hospitals? The UK, Germany and Italy. *Policy and Politics* 33(4): 623–36.

Department of Health. 1989. *Working for patients.* London: HMSO.

Department of Health. 1998. *A first class service.* London: TSO.

Department of Health. 2000. *An organisation with a memory.* London: TSO.

Department of Health. 2001. *Building a safer NHS for patients.* London: TSO.

Department of Health. 2006. *Standards for better health.* London: Department of Health.

Department of Health. 2008. *Trust, Assurance and Safety.* London: TSO.

Department of Health and Social Security. 1983. *NHS management inquiry.* London: HMSO.

Dickson, G. 1995. Principles of risk management. In *Clinical risk Management,* ed. C. Vincent, 35–38. London: BMJ Publishing.

Douglas, M. 1994. *Risk and blame: Essays in cultural theory,* London: Routledge.

Douglas, M. 1966. *Purity and danger: An analysis of the concepts of pollution and taboo.* London: Routledge and Kegan Paul.

Douglas, M. and A. Wildavsky. 1982. *Risk and Culture: An essay on the selection of technological and environmental dangers.* Berkley, CA: University of California Press.

Exworthy, M., M. Powell, and J. Mohan. 1999. 'The NHS: Quasi-market, quasi-hierarchy, quasi-network'. *Public Money and Management* 19: 15–22.

Finch, J. 2009. 'It will be twice as bad as we fear, says Brussels' *The Guardian,* 5th May, p. 26.

Flynn, N. 2007. *Public sector management.* London: Sage.

Flynn, R. 1992. *Structures of control in health management.* London: Routledge.

Flynn, R. 2004. "Soft bureaucracy," governmentality and clinical governance: Theoretical approaches to emergent policy. In *Governing medicine,* eds. A. Gray and S. Harrison, 11–27. Maidenhead, UK: Open University Press

Giddens, A. 1991. *The consequences of modernity.* Cambridge, UK: Polity Press.

Hansson, J. 2000. Quality in health care: Medical or managerial? *Managing Service Quality* 102: 78–81.

Harrison, S. 1988. *Managing the National Health Service: Shifting the frontier?* London: Chapman and Hall.

Harrison, S. 2004. Medicine and management: Autonomy and authority in the National Health Service. In *Governing medicine*, eds. A. Gray and S. Harrison, 51–59. Maidenhead, UK: Open University Press.

Hart, A. 1997. Monitoring quality in the British Health Service—a case study and a theoretical critique. *International Journal of Health Care Quality Assurance* 107: 260–266.

Health and Safety Executive. 2006. *Five steps to risk assessment.* INDG162rev2. London: HSE.

Hoggett, P. 1996. New modes of control in the public services. *Public Administration* 74: 99–132.

Hood, C. 1991. A public management for all seasons? *Public Administration* 69: 3–19.

Hunter, D. 1994. From tribalism to corporatism: The managerial challenge to medical dominance. In *Challenging Medicine*, eds. J. Gabe, D. Kelleher, and G. Williams, 1–24. London: Routledge.

Institute of Medicine. 1999. *To err is human; building a safe healthcare system.* Washington, DC: National Academy Press.

Jha, A., Curtis, P. and Carrell, S. 2009. 'Another school shuts as UK swine flu toll rises' *The Guardian*, 5th May, p. 6.

Kennedy, I., Chair. 2001. *Bristol Royal Infirmary Inquiry—learning from Bristol.* London: TSO.

Lupton, D. 1999. *Risk.* London: Routledge

Manning, N. and I. Shaw. 2000. Introduction: The millennium and social policy. In *New risks, new welfare*, eds. N. Manning and I. Shaw, 1–19. Oxford, UK: Blackwell.

Meikle, J. and Connolly, K. 2009. 'Second patient hospitalised after seeing relief doctor who killed man on first shift' *The Guardian*, 5th Maym p. 8.

Newman, J. 2001. *Modernising governance: New Labour, policy and society.* London: Sage.

NPSA. 2003. *Seven steps to patient safety.* London: NPSA.

Pettigrew, A. and E. Fenton. 2000. *The innovating organization.* London: Sage.

Pidgeon, N. 1999. Social amplification of risk: Models, mechanisms and tools for policy. *Risk, Decision and Policy* 42: 145–159.

Pollitt, C. 1993. The struggle for quality: The case of the National Health Service. *Policy and Politics* 213: 161–170.

Power, M. 1997. *The audit society: Rituals of verification.* Oxford, UK: Oxford University Press.

Power, M. 2007. *Organized uncertainty.* Oxford, UK: Oxford University Press.

Reason, J. 1997. *Managing the risks of organizational accidents.* Aldershot, UK: Ashgate.

Reason, J. 2000. Human error—models and management. *British Medical Journal* 320: 768–70.

Rhodes, R. 1997. *Understanding governance: Policy networks, governance, reflexivity, and accountability.* Buckingham, UK: Open University Press.

Scally, G. and L. Donaldson. 1998. Clinical governance and the drive for quality improvement in the new NHS in England. *British Medical Journal* 317: 61–65.

Slovic, P. 2001. *The perception of risk.* London: Earthscan.

Smith, M. 2004. The paradox of the risk society state. *British Journal of Politics and International Relations* 6: 312–33.

Tansey, J. and T. O'Riordan. 1999. Cultural theory and risk: A review. *Health, Risk and Society* 11: 71–90.

Taylor-Gooby, P. and J. Zinn. 2006. The current significance of risk. In *Risk in social science*, eds. P. Taylor-Gooby and J. Zinn, 1–19. Oxford, UK: Oxford University Press.

Walshe, K. 1999. Medical accidents in the UK: A wasted opportunity for improvement. In *Medical Mishaps*, eds. M. Rosenthal, L. Mulcahy, and S. Lloyd-Bostock, 59–73. Buckingham: Open University Press.

Walshe, K. 2003. *Regulating healthcare*. Maidenhead, UK: Open University Press.

Waring, J. 2005a. Beyond blame: The cultural barriers to medical incident reporting. *Social Science and Medicine* 60: 1927–1935.

Waring, J. 2005b. Patient safety: new directions in the management of health service quality. *Policy and Politics* 33(4): 675–692.

Waring, J. 2007. Adaptive regulation or governmentality: Patient safety and the changing regulation of medicine. *Sociology of Health and Illness* 29(2): 163–79.

Wilkinson, A., T. Redman, E. Snape, and M. Marchington. 1998. *Managing with total quality management*. London: Macmillan Wilson.

Wilson, J. and J. Tingle. 1999. *Clinical risk modification: A route to clinical governance?* Edinburgh, UK: Butterworth-Heinemann.

World Health Organisation. 2004. *World Alliance for Patient Safety*. Geneva: WHO.

Zinn, J. and P. Taylor-Gooby. 2006. Risk as an interdisciplinary research area. In *Risk in social science*, eds. P. Taylor-Gooby and J. Zinn, 20–53. Oxford, UK: Oxford University Press.

7 Public Participation in State Governance from a Social-Theoretical Perspective

Graham P. Martin

The involvement of the public and service users in the management of public services has increasingly emerged as an ambition of governments worldwide in recent years. Efforts of this kind cast the public in the role of both citizens with a democratic franchise and consumers to be endowed with real choices about how their needs and wishes are met. Various authors highlight the tensions and contradiction faced by such efforts in practice; this chapter, however, takes a step back to ask why the views of the public, whether as citizens or service users, seem to command such attention and respect from governments across the political spectrum. Why is it that for state agencies to pay no heed to the views of the public now would be as unthinkable as it would have been for professionals and officials to accede to the whims and wishes of the public fifty years ago? And how far can the insights that might arise from such a socio-historical understanding of the rise and rise of public participation explain the challenges that such initiatives now face, and suggest ways in which these might be overcome?

To answer these questions, this chapter explores the social theories associated with the work of Ulrich Beck, Anthony Giddens, and various writers in the Foucaultian 'governmentality' tradition. Accounts of the changing constitution of society that emphasizes 'active citizenship' and 'institutional reflexivity' posit an ambiguous role for the individual citizen in relation to state authority, treading an uneasy line between prescription for policy and prescription for individual subjectivity. In the terms of governmentality, these might be seen as a means of implicating the individual into new fields of governmental power, extending the reach of particular forms of instrumental rationality rather than permitting new challenges to these. While this perspective on public participation might suggest that it is inextricably bound by a power-imbued, instrumental logic, the chapter ends by suggesting how public servants might start to slip these constraints on such initiatives.

Governments across the economically more developed world are increasingly embracing policies which grant greater power to the public in the management and delivery of public services. From large-scale questions of policy down to the micro-level interaction between individual professionals and their clients, the legitimate contribution of the public—as citizens, communities, service users and so on—is increasingly recognized. In contemporary society, state-employed officials and professionals are no longer seen as possessing the knowledge, the competence, and perhaps the trust to prosecute the public's interest on their own, without the direct input of that public. Hierarchical accountability, upwards through (in the parliamentary model) public service organizations, government ministries, secretaries of state and thence to parliament and the voting public, has thus come to be complemented by a more direct relationship between the public and public servants.

In the United Kingdom, public participation has taken manifold forms, as a particularly prominent aspect of the modernization agenda promulgated by Labour governments since 1997, in pursuit of public-service provision across government that is more responsive, accountable and sensitive to the needs of the public (Cabinet Office, 1999). Large-scale innovations in democracy, such as directly elected mayors, varying degrees of devolved government in Scotland, Wales, Northern Ireland, and London, and dalliances with ideas such as citizens' juries, have been introduced. Obligations have been placed on public service organizations, such as the National Health Service (NHS) and local authorities with social service responsibilities, to involve the public in major decisions about service provision. Efforts have been made to empower individuals in their dealings with public services and servants, through arrangements such as direct payments and individual budgets, which give clients of social services greater control over how money is spent to meet their needs. These varied forms of public involvement, then, cast the public in the role of both citizens with a democratic franchise and consumers to be endowed with real choices about how their needs and wishes are met. In these ways, public participation seeks to address two divergent aspects of the modernization agenda, reconciling democratic renewal with the improvement and reform of public services (Gustafsson and Driver, 2005). Prior to this, public involvement also had a part to play in the reforms of the Thatcher- and Major-led Conservative governments, in relation to the internal market introduced in health and social care.

In practice, however, the effects of public participation have not always lived up to these grand modernizing potentials in respect of democratization and service improvement. Academic analyses tend to find public-involvement initiatives stymied by professional resistance (Beresford and Campbell, 1994; Milewa et al., 1999; Williams, 2004); by ambiguities about role, remit, and representativeness (Barnes et al., 2003; Crawford et al., 2003; Daykin et al., 2004); and by the selective deployment of their suggestions by professionals and managers (Mort et al., 1996; Harrison and Mort, 1998; Milewa et al., 1998). Despite a concerted research effort over some years now, the evidence for the effectiveness of public- and user-involvement initiatives remains thin, albeit partly due to the intangibility of some of the suggested influences of the process (Crawford et al., 2002). The purpose of this chapter is not to consider these difficulties directly, but to take a few steps back and consider why and how public participation has become so prominent a policy in contemporary society in the United Kingdom and other countries. Why is it that for state agencies to pay no heed to the views of the public now would be as unthinkable as it would have been for professionals and officials to accede to the whims and wishes of the public fifty years ago? And how far can the insights that might arise from such a socio-historical understanding of the rise and rise of public participation explain the challenges that such initiatives now face, and suggest ways in which these might be overcome?

We begin this chapter with a brief overview of public involvement as it has developed over the last half century, focusing on health and social care and paying particular attention to the changing roles in which it has been cast. Following this, we consider one commonly posited explanatory framework for the kinds of changes in society that may have given rise to the esteem in which the public's input is now held, the 'risk society' and 'reflexive modernization,' theories of sociologists Ulrich Beck and Anthony Giddens, respectively. We then consider the social changes described by Beck, Giddens, and their followers from a somewhat different vantage point, that taken by scholars working in the Foucaultian 'governmentality' tradition. Each of these social-theoretical perspectives offers a way of understanding the changing position of the public, shedding light on how it fits in with the constitution of the state and the wider operation of contemporary society. In so doing, they help understand the reasons why public involvement has been cast in the role it finds itself playing under the direction of governments of various political persuasions, the limitations to this role, and the degree to which more open, valuable and emancipatory forms of public participation might be possible given the constraints presented by the state and society.

A BRIEF HISTORY OF PUBLIC INVOLVEMENT IN HEALTH AND SOCIAL CARE

From its inception in 1948, the NHS represented an archetypal professional bureaucracy, characterized by the relative autonomy granted to various professional groups within it, especially the medical profession (Harrison et al., 1992). As a public service organization directly accountable to the Secretary of State for Health, the NHS was subject to no local democratic accountability, save for community health services, which until the 1970s were controlled by local authorities (Hogg, 1999). When these were incorporated into the NHS in 1974, community health councils (CHCs) were set up to ensure continued local involvement in these matters, and for two decades these remained the principal formal means of patient and public involvement in health and social care, with mixed outcomes (see Hogg,

1996). Over this period, however, social and political changes were afoot which began to render CHCs marginal to the relationship between the public and the state in relation to health and social care. The rise of the 'new social movements'—organized communities of interest founded in identities other than social class, such as gender, sexual preference, and ethnicity—brought a challenge to the traditional organization of the welfare state, premised on traditional conceptions of the organization of work, the family, and society. In health and social care, it was in the field of mental health where such movements were most influential, putting forward challenges to psychiatric constructions and practices with some success (Cowden and Singh, 2007). Meanwhile, the election of the new-Right Conservative governments from 1979 brought changes to the organization of the state which rendered the model of 'community involvement' premised in the CHC anachronistic. The introduction of New Public Management (NPM) had only mixed success in the NHS on account of the entrenched power of the medical profession (Harrison and Ahmad, 2000), but this—along with the introduction of the internal market in the early 1990s—did manage to alter the fundamental organizing principles of health and, especially, social care. Through quasi-markets and NPM, public services were to be made more efficient, effective *and consumer oriented*, in a bid to move power away from professionals and towards their clients, and to reduce the paternalism and inflexibility of monopolistic state provision (Le Grand, 1997; Martin et al., 2004). Following this rhetoric, the purchasers in the market were to become 'champions of the people,' leaving CHCs somewhat redundant as the consumer orientation of the new NHS led to responsiveness, satisfaction, and the services that people wanted (Department of Health 1992; Hogg 1999).

Whatever the reality of this vision (and leaving aside the question of whether marketization was primarily about consumerism or cost reduction), the purchaser–provider split required a new function of the involved member of the public: that of consumer representative, who could elucidate for the purchasing health or local authority exactly what the public required of the services being commissioned (Milewa et al., 1998). This role of *public as consumer* has been widely criticized (Prior et al., 1995; Bauman, 1995) for the way it gives rise to:

> a fundamental conflict between the emphasis on consumer choice, aimed at achieving improvement in efficiency, effectiveness and economy along the lines of consumer satisfaction, and the politics of empowerment or liberation, aimed at giving users greater control over their lives by giving them a direct say in agencies and services (Rhodes and Nocon, 1998, 78).

By reducing citizenship to consumerism, this approach fostered for its critics essentially passive forms of involvement, failing to engage individuals in the most important aspects of public-service provision, and failing to empower them in the most important decisions. Consumerism premised involvement not on obligations to fellow citizens or the pursuit of the collective good, but on the satisfaction of individual needs, often in competition with others in a context of limited resources (Prior et al., 1995).

The election of the 1997 Labour government saw the abolition—initially—of the internal market in the NHS, and promises of democratic renewal that seemed to herald novel forms of public involvement that might prioritize citizenship over consumerism. In line with wider 'Third Way' social policy, this was about cutting between 'old Left' statism and 'new Right' marketism, fostering instead a dynamic relationship between the state and the citizen or community (Labour Party, 1995; Chandler, 2001). On this basis:

> the Conservative consumer would become a fully fledged citizen, with rights and duties in the governance of the country beyond the voting booth and the market place. This notion of the active citizen would be at the core of the government's strategy for 'democratic renewal' and the 'modernization' of public services (Gustafsson and Driver, 2005, 530).

Even before new Labour's eventual reconciliation with the internal market, however, there was something of an ambiguity about the role of the public in the communitarian and Third Way ideologies that informed its program. Critics point towards the burden that such discourses place on the individual over the state: communitarianism represents for Delanty "almost entirely a theory of citizenship as a self-empowering force" (2000, 30), with a focus on voluntarism that absolves the state of a duty to its citizens. For some, then, new Labour's approach to social policy retained the fundamentally individualistic and individualizing ethos of consumerism, recast in a communitarian and Third Way light. With the return to the internal market in the NHS during new Labour's second term, the consumerist tendencies in modernization and democratic renewal became more explicit. Alongside this inheritance from the Conservative years, several commentators have noted the ongoing influence of NPM in Labour's approach to public participation. Competing pressures of top-down management and directive targets have meant that concerns about citizenship become marginal in public involvement (Cook 2002; Rowe and Shepherd 2002). Frequently, consumerist approaches, such as feedback forms and complaints systems, have been prioritized over deliberative models aimed at promoting dialogue, development, and empowerment (Martin and Boaz 2000; Cook 2002).

Despite the rhetorical shift, then, in the philosophy and purpose of public involvement since 1997, the literature highlights continuity from the consumerist forms of participation introduced under the Conservatives. For many commentators, involvement based on consumerism and involvement based on citizenship are inherently incompatible (Croft and Beresford, 1992; Rhodes and Nocon, 1998; Cook, 2002), despite the efforts of successive Labour governments to pursue both approaches through its policies. This tension, between the individualizing tendencies of consumerism and the collectively oriented discourse of involvement based on citizenship or community membership, is a fundamental one, since it embodies a difference of understanding about what public participation is for. As we shall see in the next section, though, this ambiguity about the role of the public in relation to state decision making reflects wider ambivalence among social theorists, some of them influential in contemporary democratic–socialist political thought, about the constitution of late-modern society, and the relationship between an increasingly knowledgeable, individualized, and skeptical public and the state and other traditional sources of authority.

LATE MODERNITY, INSTITUTIONAL REFLEXIVITY AND DEMOCRACY

For most sociologists, it is axiomatic that Western society has changed fundamentally since the formation of the modern welfare state after World War II, and particularly since the mid-1970s. Writers of accounts of 'post-Fordism,' 'high modernity,' 'late modernity' and 'postmodernity' agree that the certainties of the Fordist economic order, stable for thirty years following WWII, no longer apply to contemporary society in the economically more developed world (though they often disagree on the question of causation). Concurrently, fundamental changes in the social and cultural institutions of modernity, from the family to the nation state, have occurred, such that traditional assumptions about welfare provision are also redundant. Two influential, and closely linked, accounts of this reconstitution of the fabric of modernity are the 'risk society' and 'institutional reflexivity' theses of Beck (1991) and Giddens (1991). They describe a truly modern modernity, shorn of the traditional tendencies that underpinned the earlier post-war modern era, and replete with risks and opportunities for the individual. Notably, this narrative represents not only an analysis and description of late modernity, but has also been influential in the political philosophy of the Third Way which is at the heart of the policies of post-1997 Labour governments (e.g., Giddens, 1994a; Blair, 1998). As a *prescription* for contemporary policy as well as a *description* of late modernity, then, it is of particular interest to our discussion, in the role that it posits for the individual citizen/consumer in late-modern society.

Beck and Giddens see a modernity that has reached crisis point. Scientific progress has resulted not in certainty but in plurality of knowledge; the institutions of civil society that underpinned economic and social development since industrialization have lost integrity and popular faith; industrial society has given rise to new risks that threaten the very existence of humanity, from nuclear weapons to global warming. However, in large part this crisis has arisen not from some kind of failure of the Enlightenment project, but from its success. The scientific skepticism, for example, which challenged the dominance of the Church in pre-modern society, has now been turned on science itself, so that the almost religious degree of faith in scientific progress that characterized earlier modernity is now itself subject to challenge. It is in this respect that late-modern society is characterized by 'institutional reflexivity' (Giddens, 1994b): the *traditional* deference to *modern* institutions of earlier modernity is vanquished, and so modernity itself is modernized.

The consequence for the individual is that she may no longer rely upon the old certainties of traditional society and the 'industrial modernity' of the 1950s and 1960s, and must now face for herself all kinds of risks and life-altering decisions that would previously have been made for her. Beck (1991, 128) writes of a simultaneous 'liberation' from and 'disenchantment' with the institutions on which earlier modernity rested, with "disembedding, *removal* from historically prescribed social forms and commitments in the sense of traditional contexts of dominance and support" accompanied by "the *loss of traditional security* with respect to practical knowledge, faith and guiding norms": a shift which is "both liberating and disturbing" (Giddens, 1994b, 87). A variety of responses on the part of the late-modern individual is possible, from nihilistic withdrawal to positive embracing. Here, though, the distinction between description of late-modern society and prescription for the appropriate response to that social reality becomes somewhat blurred. This is the tension in the work of Giddens and Beck between a more-or-less celebratory description of the active, reflexive citizen, ready to embrace these risks and opportunities, as a product of modernity achieved, and their parallel proposition of reflexivity as a prescription which the contemporary individual must follow to stand a chance of self-maximization and self-fulfilment.

At a collective level, what Beck in particular calls for in response to the risks and opportunities of late modernity is a democratization of modern institutions, as part of a wider project he calls 'modernity as a learning process.' The fruits of modernity are to be safeguarded by ensuring that scientific and social progress is subjected to a critically modern framework of regulation. Beck (1991, 209) calls for a "sub-politics of progress," democratizing what have traditionally been the autonomous spheres of professional experts (scientists, clinicians, engineers, etc.). Ostensibly, then, the nature of modernity results in and calls for a greater role for lay people in the governance of risks of various kinds across all parts of the state and other institutions. However, there is some ambiguity in the exact form that Giddens and Beck see this democratization as taking. As Lash (1994) and Pellizzoni (1999) point out, both accounts reserve a special place for those professional experts in the institutional reflexivity they demand. Giddens (1991) in particular seems to call for informed decision-making on the basis of dialogue between existing expert sources of authority, rather than a challenge to expertise from the inferior level of knowledge of the lay individual or collective. As Lash puts it:

> For Beck and Giddens here reflexivity involves as it were 'representative democracy' inside the new institutions with the lay public voting on competing forms of expertise. There is little room in this for the 'participatory democracy' of informal everyday lay politics and social movements (1994, 201).

The role for the lay public, then, seems more one of 'informed decision maker,' choosing between a set of options determined through this institutional reflexivity, rather than stakeholder actively participating in that process of determination.

This perhaps casts a certain light on the tension between consumerism and citizenship in the Third Way and Labour's implementation of this political philosophy since 1997. In large part, modernization of public services—to render them 'fit for purpose' in this changed contemporary society—has taken place without the direct input of the public, concentrating instead on breaking up monopolies of expertise and provision. The role of the public has thus frequently been expressed more in terms of choice than voice, perpetuating the consumerist approaches to public involvement of the Conservative years rather than contributing to the democratic-renewal agenda. Thus even as Beck and Giddens track the changing complexion of society since the 1970s and celebrate the rise of institutional and individual reflexivity, so they posit certain boundaries of expertise and authority which imply boundaries for the democratization project. State institutions are to remain relatively immune to external challenge, even if they are to be subjected to internal pluralization and challenge through marketization, challenges to professional autonomy, and so on. Rather than being the master of reflexive modernity, then, the lay citizen is cast more as the deferential consumer of the fruits of institutional reflexivity. Public participation becomes less concerned with the collectivist project of democratic renewal, and more about the individualist project of securing an effective relationship between state services and their consumers.

Furthermore, for its success this project seems to require not just a remodelling of state provision but of the individuals of late-modern society. In common with other areas of social policy, for example benefits reform and welfare-to-work programs, this becomes a matter of ensuring that those consumers fit the 'active citizen' mold, embracing the risks and opportunities that contemporary society has to offer and so responding 'properly' to social-policy interventions (Gilliatt et al., 2000; Chandler, 2001; Clarke, 2005). On this basis, both democratically- and technocratically-oriented public participation seek to act upon the population as much as the state: "both 'choice' and 'voice' embody New Labour's view of active citizens as independent agents, rather than dependent subjects waiting on the state's whims" (Clarke, 2005, 450). To this extent, public participation and contemporary social policy more generally exemplify the uneasy tension in the social theory of Beck and Giddens between prescription for policy in the face of a changed society, and prescription for society itself and the individual actors within it.

In these kinds of accounts, public involvement then seems to be less about the *empowerment* of the active citizen of reflexive modernity through a synergistic relationship with the state, and more about the transfer of responsibility from the state to the individual. From this perspective, notions of 'active citizenship,' 'risk' and so on might be seen less in terms of a substantive change in the composition of society, and more as a 'technology of government' which seeks to incline the individual towards particular dispositions and courses of action (Petersen 1997; Turner 1997; Higgs 1998), in pursuit of the modernist project of progress. In these Foucaultian terms, these discourses, drawn from the diagnosis of reflexive modernity and deployed by the state and other agents in the service of modernizing the state, modernizing society or toward any number of progressive ends, are best viewed not as the consequence of an essentially different modernity, but as a new incarnation of governmental rationality—or, in Foucault's neologism, 'governmentality.'

GOVERNMENTALITY, ADVANCED-LIBERAL SOCIETY, AND PUBLIC PARTICIPATION

In contrast to the reflexive modernization thesis—which locates the changing relationship between state, society, and individual in a largely progressive metanarrative of the 'modernization of modernity'—what is distinctive about the notion of governmentality, as framed historically by Foucault (1982, 1991; Lemke, 2001) and applied to contemporary society by numerous subsequent scholars, is its focus on the role of intersubjective power in these changes. Governmental power is a constant across all modern societies and approaches to government; it is its application that varies. Foucault (1991) traces a history of governmentality from the eighteenth century as a form of power concerned with the management of a population, which deals in the life, health, and wealth of its subjects rather than the rule of law alone. Through time, this developed into the liberal state of the nineteenth century. Ostensibly a political philosophy concerned with delimiting the legitimate boundaries of state power *vis-à-vis* the autonomous individual, liberalism in fact represented not a retrenchment of government, but a reconfiguration. Liberal government was about the complex art of ruling *through* society, by aligning, via a range of direct, and increasingly indirect, means, the needs and wishes of the individual with those of the collective (and vice versa). Liberalism, then, does not differ from statism in its ambitions for the individual and the collective, but in its methods: both in their ways seek to orient the individual subject and the collective towards modernistic ambitions of progress, efficiency and the common good. Thus for Foucault:

> The main characteristic of our modern rationality [. . .] is neither the constitution of the state, the coldest of all cold monsters, nor the rise of bourgeois individualism. I won't even say that it is a constant effort to integrate individuals into the political totality. I think the main characteristic of our political rationality is the fact that this integration of the individuals in a community or in a totality results from a constant correlation between an increasing individualization and the reinforcement of this totality (1988, 161–162).

A similar narrative is traced by the 'governmentality school' followers of Foucault of the transition (to use the terminology of reflexive modernization) from 'industrial modernity' to 'late modernity,' tracing a continuity of political rationality in the face of social change. In these accounts, the post-war welfare state represented the re-emergence of a state which sought to program society, but at arm's length, through the empowerment of state-sanctioned professionals invested with "authority to act as experts in the devices of social rule" (Rose, 1996, 40). On this basis, the welfare state did not represent a return of state interventionism so much as a new way of managing the agency of organizations and professions whose role is one of 'governing'—i.e. seeking to improve the wellbeing of individuals and collectives—in relation to the state (Rose and Miller, 1992). It follows that the rise of the 'new Right' neoliberalism in the United Kingdom from the 1970s cannot be understood as a reactionary individualistic riposte to interventionism. Rather, for Rose and Miller, it should be seen as "a reorganization of political rationalities that brings them into alignment with contemporary technologies of government" (1992, 199), In other words, the Keynesian consensus of the 1950s and 1960s, and the neoliberal reaction of the 1970s and 1980s, were at root similar political projects, to the extent that they embodied the governmentalist will to align collective and individual interests in pursuit of the modernist ideal of progress. Their differences of character were a result, first and foremost, of the need to adopt technologies of government that work best with the societies they encountered.

There are certain problems with this understanding of governmental rationality, which seems to posit political philosophy as a response to changes in the constitution of society rather than the result of, say, fundamental differences in beliefs about human motivation. Nevertheless, we can agree that the consumerism and liberalism of the 'new Right' are not simply about allowing individuals to get on with their lives as they wish unfettered by the state, but represent a governmentalist strategy striving towards particular outcomes. And indeed, this is at least in part to do with the changed constitution of late-modern society. The 'new Right' mode of governmentality is distinct from both the welfare state of industrial modernity and the liberalism of the nineteenth century because in late modernity, it must govern not through society "but through the regulated choices of individual citizens, now constructed as subjects of choices and aspirations to self-actualization and self-fulfilment" (Rose, 1996, 41). The market, then, provides the predominant logic in this governmentality, so that "it becomes the ambition of neo-liberalism to implicate the individual citizen, as player and partner, into this market game" (Gordon, 1991, 36). More specifically:

> neo-liberalism encourages individuals to give their lives a specific entrepreneurial form. It responds to stronger 'demand' for individual scope for self-determination and desired autonomy by 'supplying' individuals and collectives with the possibility of actively participating in the solution of specific matters and problems which had hitherto been the domain of state agencies specifically empowered to undertake such tasks (Lemke, 2001, 202).

In this way, the individuals that make up society are in a sense molded into appropriately rational subjects, not through the direct action of the state, let alone through coercive legal arrangements, but through the enlisting of networks of actors with greater or lesser connections to the state. Not only does advanced-liberal governmentality seek to respond to a social reality, but it seeks to shape that reality too. This is important to apprehend: in an understanding of political rationality informed by a governmentality perspective, the neoliberal construction of the constitution of the individual and society is not mere ideology, but a *powerful discourse* which produces a reality as much as responding to it.

For the individual, 'new Right' governmentality creates all sorts of new roles, casting him as consumer, rational agent, responsible citizen, and seeking to imbue him with the various competencies required for the effectiveness of this diffuse and co-optive form of rule. In this light, the active citizen of late modernity celebrated and anticipated by Beck and Giddens takes on a rather different shape. Where Beck and Giddens tend to view a certain freeing of individual agency from social structure thanks to the reflexivity of late modernity, from a governmentality perspective the boundary between structure and agency is less clear-cut. Discourses of risk, self-fulfilment, agency and the like are therefore best viewed as instruments of governmentality rather than in terms of individual autonomy (Petersen, 1997). In terms of the role of the patient, for example, the rise of the active citizen needs to be understood in the context of the changing requirements of governmental rationality rather than seen in terms of reflexive modernization alone:

> The health consumer was transformed, partly by developments in medical thought itself, from a passive patient, gratefully receiving the

ministrations of the medics, to a person who was to be actively engaged in the administration of health if the treatment was to be effective and prevention assured. The patient was now to voice his or her experiences in the consulting room if the diagnosis was to be accurate and remedies effective (Rose and Miller, 1992, 195).

More generally, the public-involvement initiatives of the Conservative years, and those following the same vein since 1997, might be understood in the same way. The marketization of public services provides a prime example. To operate effectively, markets require consumers: rational decision makers who can choose between providers on the basis of their own self-interest. In the absence of such consumers, a key market force—the aggregate of these choices—is missing, and so there is nothing to drive increased quality and effectiveness among competing service providers. Thus consumerist reforms during the Conservative years, such as the health and social care reforms of the early 1990s that set up the purchaser–provider split and required purchasers to consult with the public on its needs and wants (Department of Health 1992), can thus be characterized as

> an apparent devolution of regulatory powers from 'above'—planning and compulsion—to 'below'—the decisions of consumers. In its ideal form, this imagines a 'free market' in expertise, where the relations between citizens and experts are not organized and regulated through compulsion but through acts of choice. It addresses the pluralization of expertise, not by seeking to adjudicate between the rival claims of different groups of experts, but by turning welfare agencies—social service departments, housing departments, health authorities—into 'purchasers' who can choose to 'buy' services from the range of options available (Rose, 1993, 295–296).

Forms of public involvement that are based in citizenship rather than consumerism can similarly be understood in terms of the molding of state and society to ensure conformity with the configuration of governmental power in late modernity. For a start, any such policy presupposes that the public is willing, able, and competent to assist in the processes of government, and if it is not, must seek to create citizens who do fit this mold (Nettleton, 1997; Gilliatt et al., 2000; Hasselbladh and Bejerot, 2007). Furthermore, by seeking to draw upon the input of the individual active citizen or the wider community, public involvement can be seen to represent a shifting of responsibility and agency away from the state (Schofield, 2002; Green, 2005). Schofield identifies these governmentalist tendencies in practices of community involvement in urban regeneration schemes:

> The discourse of community is presented as one explicit solution to some of the many problems of government. Its insertion into government

relations with local people in the form of a managerial technology called community development enables the otherwise separate institutional worlds of local and national government to be aligned with the particular interests and needs of specific locales. [. . .] It is a this point, when the theoretical messages of community development become inscribed into a form of administrative technology, that the discourse of community becomes overtly governmental (2002, 675).

For governmentality scholars, then, the optimistic ideas put forward in the reflexive modernization thesis are at best a misclassification of a shift in the play of governmental power as a fundamental revision to the structures of modernity. At worst, they are a part of this reconfiguration of governmental power, providing discourses that help to enjoin people as the 'consumers' and 'active citizens' that contemporary governmentality requires.

DISCUSSION: SLIPPING THE CONSTRAINTS OF PUBLIC PARTICIPATION?

An understanding of public participation shaped by the ideas of Foucault and the governmentality scholars seems to suggest quite a negative analysis of its role and potential. Ultimately, public participation is no more than a technology of governmentality that helps to ensure that certain aspirations of modern political rationality are fulfilled, and its casts its publics accordingly. However, a couple of qualifications are required.

Firstly, it is important to note that those expounding the governmentality perspective are by no means wholly negative about what it represents and what it implies for contemporary society and politics. Numerous writers highlight the positive ramifications for the individual in late-modern society that arise from the operation of contemporary governmentality (Novas and Rose, 2000; Rose and Novas, 2005; Rabinow and Rose, 2006), following Foucault's own analysis of power as not only coercive, but also persuasive and even enabling. So Novas and Rose (2000), for example, refer to 'somatic communities' of individuals drawn together by a common genetic condition and body of knowledge, describing how they use this productively in interacting with sources of governmental authority such as the state and the medical profession. In these kinds of analyses, there is arguably something of a convergence between governmentality and reflexive modernity theses, with the power of governmentality not as inherently limiting or objectifying, but as an ambivalent fact of late-modern life which can just as easily offer self-realizing possibilities to the contemporary subject. Other writers too see potential as well as constraint in the operation of governmentality in initiatives like community engagement and public participation (Marinetto, 2003; Martin, 2008).

Secondly, a key strength of the governmentality framework is also its weakness: that it offers an integrative understanding of governmental power and authority and the will and reason of the individual subject. Governmentality can construct each shift in the behavior of the state and the psychology of the individual as exhibiting the same rationalistic inclination towards the progressive political project. Karl Popper's famous critique of Marxism—that it represented an irrefutable pseudo-science that could simply incorporate any historical eventuality as evidence for its claims—might also be applied then to governmentality. A shift away from direct state intervention from the 1970s onward is thus seen as evidence for the ongoing importance of governmental power; similarly any effort to bring the public into deliberations about public policy is a means of enjoining that public in the same ubiquitous political project.

On this basis, any effort at resistance to the managerialist public-involvement agenda is futile, since we are all engaged in the same progressivist mission anyway. Nevertheless, there is surely value in understanding how discourses of active citizenship, consumer involvement and the like, orient public-participation initiatives in certain directions, whether in terms of reducing the involvee to the rational decision-maker required by the quasi-market, or in terms of attempting to beget certain rational subjectivities in an involved public, so that it might be able to take on the self-governing role of community development, for example. By recognizing the structuring influence of these social policies and wider discourses on the practice of public involvement, the possibility of alternative approaches becomes thinkable, even if these alternatives cannot altogether escape the governmentality project in which we are all to varying extents engaged. In this way, the imperatives of contemporary political rationality might be grasped, bent, and reshaped, even if they cannot be completely broken. What forms might such a reshaped governmentality take? This rests with critical public servants, ready to reflect on the assumptions of current policies and practices, and start to think about how else public participation might be done.

REFERENCES

Barnes, M., J. Newman, A. Knops, and H. Sullivan. 2003. Constituting "the public" in public participation. *Public Administration* 81: 379–399.

Bauman, Z. 1995. *Life in fragments: Essays in postmodern morality.* Oxford, UK: Blackwell.

Beck, U. 1991. *Risk society: Towards a new modernity.* London: Sage.

Beresford, P. and J. Campbell. 1994. Disabled people, service users, user involvement and representation. *Disability & Society* 9: 315–325.

Blair, T. 1998. *The Third Way: New politics for the new century.* London: Fabian Society.

Cabinet Office. 1999. *Modernising government.* London: The Stationery Office.

Chandler, D. 2001. Active citizens and the therapeutic state: the role of democratic participation in local government reform. *Policy & Politics* 29: 3–14.

Clarke, J. 2005. New Labour's citizens: Activated, empowered, responsibilized, abandoned? *Critical Social Policy* 25: 447–463.

Cook, D. 2002. Consultation, for a change? Engaging users and communities in the policy process. *Social Policy & Administration* 36: 516–531.

Cowden, S. and G. Singh. 2007. The "user": friend, foe or fetish? A critical exploration of user involvement in health and social care. *Critical Social Policy* 27: 5–23.

Crawford, M., D. Rutter, and S. Thelwall. 2003. *User involvement in change management: A review of the literature.* London: NCCSDO.

Crawford, M.J., D. Rutter, C. Manley, T. Weaver, K. Bhui, N. Fulop, and P. Tyrer. 2002. Systematic review of involving patients in the planning and development of health care. *British Medical Journal* 325: 1263–1267.

Croft, S. and P. Beresford. 1992. The politics of participation. *Critical Social Policy* 12: 20–44.

Daykin, N., M. Sanidas, J. Tritter, J. Rimmer, and S. Evans. 2004. Developing user involvement in a UK cancer network: Professionals' and users' perspectives. *Critical Public Health* 14: 277–294.

Delanty, G. 2000. *Citizenship in a global age: Society, culture, politics.* Buckingham, UK: Open University Press.

Department of Health. 1992. *Local voices: The views of local people in purchasing for health.* London: Department of Health.

Foucault, M. 1982. The subject and power. In *Michel Foucault: Beyond structuralism and hermeneutics*, eds. H.L. Dreyfus and P. Rabinow, 208–226. Hemel Hempstead, UK: Harvester Wheatsheaf.

Foucault, M. 1988. The political technology of individuals. In *Technologies of the self: A seminar with Michel Foucault*, eds. L.H. Martin, H. Gutman, and P.H. Hutton, 145–162. London: Tavistock.

Foucault, M. 1991. Governmentality. In *The Foucault effect: Studies in governmentality*, eds. G. Burchell, C. Gordon, and P. Miller, 87–104. Hemel Hempstead, UK: Harvester Wheatsheaf.

Giddens, A. 1991. *Modernity and self-identity: Self and society in the late modern age.* Cambridge, UK: Polity Press.

Giddens, A. 1994a. *Beyond left and right: The future of radical politics.* Cambridge, UK: Polity Press.

Giddens, A. 1994b. Living in a post-traditional society. In *Reflexive modernization: Politics, tradition and aesthetics in the modern social order*, eds. U. Beck, A. Giddens, and S. Lash, 56–109. Stanford, CA: Stanford University Press.

Gilliatt, S., J. Fenwick, and D. Alford. 2000. Public services and the consumer: Empowerment or control? *Social Policy & Administration* 34: 333–349.

Gordon, C. 1991. Governmental rationality: An introduction. In *The Foucault effect: Studies in governmentality*, eds. G. Burchell, C. Gordon and P. Miller, 1–51. Hemel Hempstead, UK: Harvester Wheatsheaf.

Green, J. 2005. Professions and community. *New Zealand Sociology* 20: 122–141.

Gustafsson, U. and S. Driver. 2005. Parents, power and public participation: Sure start, an experiment in New Labour governance. *Social Policy & Administration* 39: 528–543.

Harrison, S. and W.I.U. Ahmad. 2000. Medical autonomy and the UK state 1975 to 2025. *Sociology* 34: 129–146.

Harrison, S., D.J. Hunter, G. Marnoch, and C. Pollitt. 1992. *Just managing: Power and culture in the National Health Service.* Basingstoke, India: Macmillan.

Harrison, S. and M. Mort. 1998. Which champions, which people? Public and user involvement in health care as a technology of legitimation. *Social Policy & Administration* 32: 60–70.

Hasselbladh, H. and E. Bejerot. 2007. Webs of knowledge and circuits of communication: constructing rationalized agency in Swedish health care. *Organization* 14: 275–200.

Higgs, P. 1998. Risk, governmentality and the reconceptualization of citizenship. In *Modernity, medicine and health: medical sociology towards 2000*, eds. G. Scambler and P. Higgs, 176–197. London: Routledge.

Hogg, C. 1996. *Back from the margins: Which future for CHCs?* London: Institute of Health Services Management.

Hogg, C. 1999. *Patients, power & politics: From patients to citizens*. London: Sage.

Labour Party. 1995. *Renewing democracy, rebuilding communities*. London: Labour Party.

Lash, S. 1994. Expert systems or situated interpretation? Culture and institutions in disorganized capitalism. In *Reflexive modernization: Politics, tradition and aesthetics in the modern social order*, eds. U. Beck, A. Giddens and S. Lash, 198–215. Stanford, CA: Stanford University Press.

Le Grand, J. 1997. Knights, knaves and pawns: Human behaviour and social policy. *Journal of Social Policy* 26: 149–169.

Lemke, T. 2001. "The birth of bio-politics": Michel Foucault's lecture at the Collège de France on neo-liberal governmentality. *Economy and Society* 30: 190–207.

Marinetto, M. 2003. Who wants to be an active citizen? The politics and practice of community involvement. *Sociology* 37: 103–120.

Martin, G.P. 2008. "Ordinary people only": Knowledge, representativeness, and the publics of public participation in healthcare. *Sociology of Health and Illness* 30: 35–54.

Martin, S. and A. Boaz. 2000. Public participation and citizen-centred local government: Lessons from the best value and better government for older people pilot programmes. *Public Money & Management* 20: 47–53.

Martin, G.P., K. Phelps, and S. Katbamna. 2004. Human motivation and professional practice: of knights, knaves and social workers. *Social Policy & Administration* 38: 470–487.

Milewa, T., J. Valentine, and M. Calnan. 1998. Managerialism and active citizenship in Britain's reformed health service: Power and community in an era of decentralization. *Social Science & Medicine* 47: 507–517.

Milewa, T., J. Valentine, and M. Calnan. 1999. Community participation and citizenship in British health care planning: Narratives of power and involvement in the changing welfare state. *Sociology of Health and Illness* 21: 445–465.

Mort, M., S. Harrison, and G. Wistow. 1996. The user card: Picking through the organisational undergrowth in health and social care. *Contemporary Political Studies* 2: 1133–1140.

Nettleton, S. 1997. Governing the risky self: How to become health, wealthy and wise. In *Foucault, health and medicine*, eds. A. Petersen and R. Bunton, 207–222. London: Routledge.

Novas, C. and N. Rose. 2000. Genetic risk and the birth of the somatic individual. *Economy and Society* 29: 485–513.

Pellizzoni, L. 1999. Reflexive modernization and beyond: Knowledge and value in the politics of environment and technology. *Theory, Culture & Society* 16: 99–125.

Petersen, A. 1997. Risk, governance and the new public health. In *Foucault, Health and Medicine*, eds. A. Petersen and R. Bunton, 189–206. London: Routledge.

Prior, D., J. Stewart, and K. Walsh. 1995. *Citizenship: rights, community & participation*. London: Pitman Publishing.

Rabinow, P. and N. Rose. 2006. Biopower today. *BioSocieties* 1: 195–217.

Rhodes, P. and A. Nocon. 1998. User involvement and the NHS reforms. *Health Expectations* 1: 73–81.

Rose, N. 1993. Government, authority and expertise in advanced liberalism. *Economy and Society* 22: 283–299.

Rose, N. 1996. Governing "advanced" liberal democracies. In *Foucault and political reason: Liberalism, neo-liberalism and rationalities of government*, eds. A. Barry, T. Osborne and N. Rose, 37–61. London: UCL Press.

Rose, N. and P. Miller. 1992. Political power beyond the State: Problematics of government. *British Journal of Sociology* 43: 173–205.

Rose, N. and C. Novas. 2005. Biological citizenship. In *Global assemblages: Technology, politics, and ethics as anthropological problems*, eds. A. Ong and S.J. Collier, 439–463. Oxford: Blackwell.

Rowe, R. and M. Shepherd. 2002. Public participation in the new NHS: No closer to citizen control? *Social Policy & Administration* 36: 275–290.

Schofield, B. 2002. Partners in power: Governing the self-sustaining community. *Sociology* 36: 663–683.

Turner, B.S. 1997. From governmentality to risk: Some reflections on Foucault's contribution to medical sociology. In *Foucault, health and medicine*, eds. A. Petersen and R. Bunton, ix–xxi. London: Routledge.

Williams, M. 2004. Discursive democracy and New Labour: Five ways in which decision-makers manage citizen agendas in public participation initiatives. *Sociological Research Online* 9.

8 Marketing the Unmarketable

The Vlaams Belang, a "Party Unlike Any Other"

Mona Moufahim, Michael Humphreys, and Darryn Mitussis

INTRODUCTION

The application of marketing techniques in political practice seems widespread and substantial sums of money are spent each year in political advertising, much of which goes to organizations and through channels very familiar to mainstream marketing scholars and practitioners. For example, the Conservative Party in the United Kingdom delegated their communication process to the high-profile marketing communications organization Saatchi & Saatchi (Scammel, 1996). In contemporary US presidential elections, huge sums are spent on advertising campaigns. As marketing is increasingly adopted by political parties (O'Shaughnessy, 1990), it has moving beyond influencing only tactical matters of communication and presentation, towards playing a significant role in policy formulation and long-term direction (Butler and Collins, 1996). Efforts have been made to extend political marketing as an academic discipline beyond the limitations of traditional mass marketing theory. These extensions reflect advancements in both marketing theory and political marketing practice. For example, political marketing includes studies of exchange and relationships between political entities and the way that techniques borrowed from industrial services and relationship marketing are, or could be, deployed by political marketing practitioners (e.g., Lock & Harris, 1996). The enriching of the field has also prompted discussion about the concepts and strategies that define political marketing as a separate discipline. As a consequence, political marketing is developing as a holistic concept that includes the whole behavior of the political organization and the application of marketing concepts and techniques as well as the responses of the citizen–consumer (e.g., Ingram & Lees-Marshment, 2002; Wring, 1996; Omura, 1979; Shama, 1976, among others). This broadening of both political marketing practice and the theorizing of political marketing has necessitated that political marketing emerges as an interdisciplinary subject (Henneberg, 2004), studying not just the application of marketing tools and concepts to politics but also the whole range of social theory that informs our study of postindustrial consumer society.

This chapter starts with the premise that political parties and politicians use marketing to achieve their political goals and connect with voters but, in doing so, appear to borrow marketing tools and concepts in an *ad hoc* and instrumental fashion. This article aims to highlight the marketing strategy of a Flemish extreme right party, the Vlaams Blok/Vlaams Belang (VB) as observed/extrapolated from the party's behavior in Belgium's political market. It explores in detail the marketing strategy and branding of the VB in Belgian politics. First of all, an overview of Belgian political landscape and of the VB is provided. This is followed by the analysis of the VB brand and the party's marketing strategy. A special focus is granted to the party's particular segmentation and positioning. It is argued here that the party's skilful positioning and communication contributed to the establishment of a strong political brand, which experiences success at the polls.

POLITICS IN BELGIUM: A JOURNEY
THROUGH A POLITICAL LABYRINTH

Belgium has been a constitutional monarchy since 1831. In 1993, after several revisions of the constitution, the country was transformed into a federal state. To roughly summarize a complex history, it was the strained political situation between different communities in Belgium that made the shift towards federalism a necessity. The revisions provided a new political map of Belgium and there are now five levels of competence and power: the federal state, the regions, the communities, the provinces, and the communes (or 'towns'). Belgium is characterized by its three cultural communities: the Flemish (Dutch-speaking) population in the North of the country; the Walloons (French-speaking) population in the South of the country; and a German-speaking minority in the East of the country. Brussels has been granted the status of a bilingual region. Brussels is in fact an enclave, which has a majority of French-speakers, within the Flemish territory. There are also three regions: *het Vlaams Geweest* (Flanders or Flemish Region), *la Région Wallonne* (Wallonia or Walloon Region) and *Bruxelles-Capitale* (Brussels Capital). Each of these entities has a council[1] holding legislative power and a government holding executive power, except for the Flemish Community and Region which has merged and has a common council and government. The state, the three communities, and the three regions have their own parliaments, which are authorized to legislate and constitute their government.[2]

THE VLAAMS BLOK: BIRTH AND DEATH

The Belgian extreme right party Vlaams Blok was created in 1978 from the merger of two small nationalist parties run by radical dissidents of the Volksunie, which was then the most important nationalist post-war party

(Camus, 2003; Faniel, 2003). From 1979 to 1985, the Vlaams Blok transformed itself from a minor protest group into a political party. By 1991, the Vlaams Blok had become the fourth largest party in Flanders (Mudde, 2000). The rising trend continued in 1994 when the Vlaams Blok became the largest party on the city council of Antwerp, and consequently became entitled to take part in the city's administration. However a *cordon sanitaire* (or quarantine) created by the other parties, excluded the Vlaams Blok from entering any governing coalition (Mudde, 2000; Swyngedouw, 1998). In the legislatives elections in 2000, the Vlaams Blok became the largest party in the city, with nineteen out fifty-four seats and the only opposition party (Van Der Brink, 2003). At the June 2004 regional elections, more than one Fleming out of five voted for the Vlaams Blok. It became the second largest party in Flanders, with its thirty-two seats in the Flemish government (it scored nearly 30 percent in Antwerp).

When campaigning, the Vlaams Blok focused on three major themes: firstly, the denunciation of foreigners; secondly, Flemish nationalism; and thirdly the incompetence and dishonesty of the other parties (Faniel, 2003). The VB also certainly benefited from political scandals affecting the mainstream political parties. The VB always positioned itself as an honest party caring for people's rights, and denouncing the 'diseases' of society (along with the ones responsible for those 'diseases'). The second axis of the Vlaams Blok ideology was the rejection of immigration. It has been argued that the Vlaams Blok created "a dominant ideological space" (Swyngedouw, 1998, 68) by engaging in anti-immigration agitation in sensitive neighborhoods, where crime and unemployment are high. Part of this strategy was the attribution of such problems to immigrants (Swyngedouw, 1998, 68). Thirdly, the VB campaigned for the independence of Flanders, and the separation from the Belgian state. Advocating the redrawing of the borders to include Brussels as its capital, Flanders was to become a mono-ethnic state, non-European immigrants would be repatriated and European 'foreigners' assimilated (Nollet, 2000). In 1992, Filip Dewinter argued, in the infamous seventy-point program (see Dewinter, 1991), that what was needed for the protection of Flemish identity, and the application of 'serving one's own people first' leitmotiv was a halt to immigration and the accelerated repatriation of foreigners, along with harsher regulations against criminal and illegal immigrants (Coffé, 2005). In 2004, the Vlaams Blok was disbanded to avoid further prosecution after the legal condemnation for racism of three non-profit associations linked to the VB by the *Cour de Cassation*.[3]

THE VLAAMS BELANG: THE PHOENIX ARISES

In November 2004 the Vlaams Belang was founded as a new party, with the same leaders and same structures as the Vlaams Blok. The continuity of leadership, ideology, and program has been emphasized by the Vlaams

Blok/Vlaams[4] leaders themselves: *"we are changing our name, but not our stripes"* (Frank Vanhecke, in Coffé, 2005, 217). According to Coffé (2005), the Vlaams Belang is now trying to be perceived as a nationalist right-wing party, which still has immigration, security, and anti-establishment feelings as its driving forces, but which has cut the ties with its unsavory past. If the party has softened some of its (legally) problematic stances, it still adopts a very clear view regarding immigrants and immigration; Filip Dewinter said that: *"multiculturalism leads to multi-criminality"* (in the 2005 Annual Report on Human Rights in Belgium). Filip Dewinter leaves no ambiguity about the Vlaams Belang's orientation with *"any Muslim woman wearing the headscarf will sign thereby the warrant for her repatriation"* ('Buitenhof,' Nederland 3, November 14, 2004).

When the Vlaams Belang was created, it left no doubt among observers that it would capitalize on the strengths of the Vlaams Blok. The party leaders made clear that the new party is not a toned-down version of the late Vlaams Blok. Filip Dewinter stated (in TV *Dag Allemaal*, October 26, 2004): *"We don't need a 'Vlaams Blok Light' or a 'Vlaams Blok Ultra,' but a 'Vlaams Blok Plus!' Indeed, our programme is not changing at all"* (Vanhecke, www. vlaamsblok.be, homepage). The essence of the Vlaams Blok has definitely not disappeared. This is an understandable—and very pragmatic—choice. The Vlaams Blok had managed to build a strong brand with a significantly loyal following. At every election, the market share of the Vlaams Belang increases, which indicates that the party has managed to communicate its brand's values and that it actually benefits from a high level of notoriety.

For example, Filip Dewinter sparked controversy when he said: *"'Xenophobia' is not the word I would use. If it absolutely must be a "phobia" let it be 'Islamophobia'"* (Jewish Week, October 28, 2005). Along with the 'softening' of their policies, these controlled outbursts might have been intended to avoid the alienation of the existing loyal Vlaams Blok voters. These seemingly paradoxical stances between xenophobic statements and a right-wing conservative rebirth, and the subsequent ambiguity lead to the need for a careful segmentation of the voters market and sound positioning of the party. By adopting what seem like paradoxical approaches, the Vlaams Belang seems to be aiming at both attracting a larger audience (which might be interested in its tough approach on criminality or in its call for a greater autonomy for Flanders); and at the same time reassuring the voters of the former Vlaams Blok (who were not shy about voting for an anti-immigrant party), that the party did not change and would continue defending the nation and identity of its people.

Currently, the Vlaams Belang is portrayed as, and benefits from, a positioning as an opposition party, denouncing the ills of Belgian society and the wrong-doing of the governing parties. The party is preparing itself for government, and says so:

> Electoral victories are not an objective per se. [. . .] Our story has a meaning only when we can implement the essence of our programme:

independence, a stricter immigration policy, a tough approach to crime. It is clear now that these points of our programme will not be implemented by using more and more decibels to shout original terms of abuse from within the quarantine zone. Contrary to lemmings or howler monkeys, who follow their instinct, man has the possibility of evaluating his situation, considering alternative strategies, and analysing carefully who can be opponents and who can be allies, if need be temporarily (Vlaams Belang, 2006, 3)

The Vlaams Belang presents itself here as uncompromising and honest, but willing today—for the interests of the Flemish people—to 'compromise' itself by taking part to power. It is therefore positioning itself as a governing party in waiting:

The Danish example proves that other scenarios are possible, other than quarantine zones [. . .] A shrewd Vlaams Belang is of course much more dangerous than a shouting Vlaams Belang in a quarantine zone. It is going to be a difficult but necessary exercise. We owe it not only to ourselves, but also to our children and grandchildren (Vlaams Belang, 2006, 3).

The Vlaams Belang seems to be following the footsteps of the Vlaams Blok by using strong communications, integrated marketing and precise targeting. Ostensibly, the Vlaams Belang positioning is different to the Vlaams Blok, but it is rather ambiguously sharing some common elements with the Vlaams Blok, but also some differences, at least for the public eye.

MARKETING THE VB: CREATING A POLITICAL BRAND

Since 1991, the party has employed the service of professionals to develop its advertising campaigns and create memorable slogans[5] associated with recognizable symbols (Bossemans, 2001; Vander Velpen, 1992). In 2004, Filip Dewinter announced that:

I am the head of a campaign group of 13 people. Among them, there are 3 employees of well-known advertising agencies, who are members of our party, and have helped for free to set up campaigns. Who they are, I can't say. It would cost them their jobs (in Het Belang van Limburg,[6] March 17, 2004, 4).

Throughout the last few years' campaigns, the party leaders have adopted an ambiguous position on the issue of marketing. Although party leaders have *internally* advocated the use of political marketing to their local candidates, they have *publicly* adopted an attitude of distaste for the use of 'spin doctors' by other political parties. Nevertheless, their adherence to marketing is assumed, based on the following quotation by Filip Dewinter,[7] which unambiguously illustrates the Vlaams Blok's active marketing orientation:

> Marketing comes from the study of the needs of consumers, and from this follows the production of resources which could satisfy those needs. A company must study first the needs of its consumers and adapt its production according to those needs. Political marketing broadly follows the same line of thought.

Filip Dewinter justifies the utilization of marketing strategy by explaining that:

> Political marketing is a global project with which the candidate can organize well his or her political activities. The VB is choosing without a doubt an anti-demagogic practice, with which we have so often tried to be the voice of the people.

Filip Dewinter simultaneously stresses here the importance of marketing as political instrument, and rejects the accusation of manipulation, spin and demagogic practices that could be associated with the use of marketing in politics (see Baines and Egan 2001; Scammell, 1995, Newman, 1994; Sabato, 1981).

THE VB'S MARKETING STRATEGY: THINKING THE UNTHINKABLE

Consumer marketing might provide a perspective on, and an understanding of, the processes observable in the political arena. Positioning, an important concept in marketing, arises from the desire of marketers to build a competitive advantage (Smith, 2005). Aaker and Shansby explain positioning as follows: "a product or organization has many associations which combine to form a total impression. The positioning decision often means selecting those associations to be built upon and emphasised and those associations to be removed or de-emphasised" (1982, 56). The way a brand is positioned against another helps to clarify in the customer's mind how that brand is different and, critically, better (Smith, 2005). In this way it aids the communication of differential advantage in a highly competitive and 'noisy' marketplace (Smith, 2005). Once voter segments have been identified, the candidate or party positions itself in the political marketplace (Newman, 2001). Positioning has, in fact, long been recognized as playing an important role in politics (Mauser, 1983). According to Trout and Sivkin, "all politics is perception, posturing and positioning" (1996, 79). Parties position themselves in comparison to their opponents (Smith, 2005). The positioning process begins indeed by the assessment of both the party's and the opponents' respective strengths and weaknesses (Newman,

2001). For example, Tony Blair wanted a stronger Conservative threat in 2001 to allow the New Labour agenda to be seen more clearly by comparison (Smith, 2005).

SEGMENTING THE BELGIAN POLITICAL MARKET

The VB competes in both the Flemish Region, and in Brussels' Region markets. In order to attract both French-speaking Brussels' inhabitants and Dutch-speakers, the VB has designed and distributed magazines specifically targeted at the Brussels audience, with the focus on key issues for the Brussels-Capital region, such as taxation, the important concentration of foreigners in Brussels, criminality, and so on. The brochures specially designed for Brussels are bilingual, available in both French and Dutch. In the brochure "*Immigration . . . Open your eyes!,*" the party presents its project for an independent Flanders with Brussels as capital. In this piece, the Vlaams Blok adopts a reassuring tone, by saying that Brussels would be granted a bilingual status in the new state.

The party has developed campaigns and communication materials specifically designed for Brussels alongside national documentation, denoting a careful segmentation of the national political market. For example, in Brussels campaign brochures, the Vlaams Belang carefully downplays the planned future of Brussels. Brussels' inhabitants are French-speaking, in an overwhelming majority (90 percent of the total population of Brussels), and feel neither Flemish nor Walloon, and assert an identity of their own, even if, historically, they are Flemings who were francophonized. It is important to note that the Flemish nationalist themes are not tackled in the brochures of the VB distributed in Brussels. This theme is reserved for brochures destined for Flemish audiences in Flanders, where Flanders is presented as a 'milk-cow' feeding Wallonia (Ceuppens, 2001), through the so-called solidarity transfers from the richer Flanders to the poorer Wallonia and Brussels. This indicates careful targeting and a consistent positioning of the party, furthering its interests. The party positions itself accordingly to the market (Flanders, Flemish towns, Brussels) in which it is competing.

POSITIONING OF THE VLAAMS BLOK:
FROM OUTSIDE RIGHT TO CENTRE-FORWARD

Since its inception, the Vlaams Blok has positioned itself as a nationalist, solidarist[8] party of the right. This positioning is translated through the themes adopted by the party. These are: Flemish independence; a free market; a reduction of taxes; a limitation on social security; the repatriation of guest workers; zero tolerance of criminality; and a total and unconditional amnesty for WWII collaborators (Vos [1992] in Bossemans [2001]). The party started its political career as a protest and opposition party, denouncing the ills of society. Karel Dillen, the Vlaams Blok president, in 1991 (restating the points he made in 1981) said:

> We refuse any Flemish concession. We refuse to put water in our wine. We refuse to sell our programme for a ministry portfolio. We refuse to sell our principles for anything. Do you want a real opposition on each point? Vote for the Vlaams Blok (Spruyt, 2000).

True to these words, the Vlaams Blok refused in 1991 a ministerial portfolio it was entitled to thanks to its 10.3% of the Flemish votes (Bossemans, 2001). This attitude reinforced the party's positioning as uncompromising, non-conformist and radical (Spruyt, 2000). The Vlaams Blok had already taken on the image of the 'rebel' in 1979, when the subheading of *De Vlaams Nationalist* (i.e., the Flemish Nationalist) is: "*Therefore, we are standing here as REBEL.*" In 2000, some twenty years later, the profile is similar:

> A party unlike any other. The Vlaams Blok is indeed not a compromising party, but a programme party faithful to its principles and programme, [...], for the Flemish people and the European peoples. A party, rooted in a great past, but resolutely turned towards the future (Vanhecke, www.vlaamsblok.be, homepage).

With successes at the polls, the party should have been included in governing coalitions. In 1995, the Vlaams Blok wished to participate in a right-wing, anti-socialist coalition, but the *cordon sanitaire* excluded the party. The other parties were forced into, what Gerolf Annemans, a prominent Vlaams Blok member, called, a "*monster coalition of six different parties*" (in Spruyt, 2000). The party wanted to project the image of a party that does not shy away from its responsibilities (i.e., representing the people and governing) but was excluded from power by the other parties (with the *cordon sanitaire* strategy). Adopting the underdog position could be seen as a very astute strategy, locating the Vlaams Blok as the *de facto* opposition party. The scenario was repeated in 2000, at the elections for the Antwerp city council. Although the Vlaams Blok gained a third of the votes, the liberal VLD (the other winner of the election) refused to share power with the extreme right party.

POTENTIAL WINNING RECIPE: THE INDEPENDENCE OF FLANDERS AND IMMIGRATION

The VB has managed to develop a very clear position, which might indicate a carefully thought-out strategy, or at the very least, an intuitive political conviction and direction. However, it also seems that the party has adopted an opportunistic and pragmatic approach to politics. The independence of Flanders was the original founding principle underlying the Vlaams Blok's creation, but the anti-immigrant/anti-immigration position has become the most salient theme and the most effective vote gatherer for the party. Filip Dewinter was the first to recognize the electoral potential of an anti-immigrant stance,[9] inspired by the success of the French Front National (e.g. *'Les Francais d'abord,'* i.e. 'The French first,' which inspired the party's *'Eigen Volk Eerst,'* i.e. 'Our own people First'; Coffé, 2004). In 1987, the party conducted a fierce anti-immigrant campaign in the parliamentary elections, which got them two seats in Parliament and one seat in the Belgian Senate. In 1991, at what is still known in Belgium as Black Sunday, 10.3 percent of Flemish voters, and 25 percent of voters in Antwerp supported the Vlaams Blok party (Coffé, 2004).

BRAND IDENTITY

The pragmatism of the party leaders is also evident in their recruitment of communication professionals (Bossemans, 2001; Vander Velpen, 1992). The VB was rewarded for its consistent positioning and clear, recognizable communications: the party has been winning votes at every single election (thirteenth winning the VB claims, as in October 2006). In less than thirty years, the VB has become the most popular party in Flanders. No Belgian citizen could currently ignore or confuse the party's core themes with those of the other political parties. The main themes of the VB have even become the party's *chasse gardée* (in other words, the party can claim an almost exclusive 'ownership' of these themes [Coffé, 2004]), or the *Unique Selling Proposition* (Olins, 2000) of the VB brand. Any other party calling for a clamp down on immigration or a tougher stance on crime would merely look like a pale imitation of the VB. According to Keller (2003), good positioning of a brand requires the establishment of important points of difference (POD) over the competition at the same time as turning policies where disadvantaged into points of parity (POP), such as the economy where the VB advocates liberal policies. In light of this argument, the VB's decision to concentrate on immigration becomes more understandable. The stance on immigration became their distinguishable POD at the start of the 1987 campaign. The party was successful in raising the perceived importance of immigration during the 1987 elections and since then. Butler and Collins (1996) also argue that anticipating the preferences of the electorate can be useful for challengers. If a policy can be 'branded' before its appeal is widely recognized, a party can steal a march on its opponents (Butler and Collins, 1996). Butler and Collins (1996) also note that the difficulty with this strategy, however, is retaining ownership of the idea once it is popular. The VB has clearly managed to claim ownership of some key issues (Coffé, 2004) and, in doing so, developed other PODs on crime, immigration, Flemish autonomy, and, more recently, the independence of Flanders and the end of Belgium (*"the euthanasia of Belgium" dixit*. Filip Dewinter, press conference, August 19, 2007). In short, the Vlaams Belang does not neglect those important PODs developed by the former Vlaams Blok and still capitalizes on those related issues. Other political parties have fairly unsuccessfully attempted to recover the voters they have lost to the VB, by hardening their own discourse and policies on immigration or Flemish nationalism. This arguably could well have contributed to the further legitimating of VB policies among the electorate.

'A PARTY UNLIKE ANY OTHER'

As the other Flemish political parties seem to be copying some aspects of the VB's program (in an attempt to recapture part of the electorate lost to the extreme right), the VB in contrast, has been trying to convey since its inception an image and a successful positioning of difference from, and alternative to, the mainstream. For example, the title of Franck Vanhecke's column on the Vlaams Blok's website[10] is *"A Party Unlike Any Other."* The party has tried to differentiate itself and develop a clear and unique position in the minds of voters.

According to Palmer (2002), one dimension where political marketing has replaced traditional forms of policy development is in the use of survey devices and focus groups to find out how the electorate responds to various issues and to devise policies that would fit the "existing patterns of evaluation" (Palmer, 2002, 353). In other words, the political marketer tries to find out who is persuadable, and on what grounds (Maarek, 1995). As Baines, has pointed out, "all political strategy derives from understanding the motives underlying the target groups' past voting behavior and that strategy must be competitive because there is only a limited range of options for the voter" (1999, 407). O'Shaughnessy (1990, 134) has shown that American political consultants make an issue salient, if they identify it as a weak spot in the opponent's program. This might explain why the VB is focussing heavily on the issue of the division of the Brussel-Halle-Vilvoorde (BHV) electoral constituency. The BHV-file symbolically represents the struggle between the two main linguistic communities in Belgium. Mainstream parties have failed to reach an argument about this difficult issue. Flemish parties decided to let the issue remain vague for a while because of its potential to bring down the government. The party has been extremely vocal about what they refer to as this 'new treason' to the Flemish cause using it as a symbol of the untrustworthiness and inability of mainstream parties to make difficult decisions in the interest of the Flemish people. The VB also uses the issue as another reason why French- and Flemish-speaking communities cannot coexist in a united country. This therefore presents another opportunity for the party to express its difference and to set out its differentiation strategy (i.e., remaining intractable on the topic of Flemish interest, taking a position against French-speakers, other political parties, and foreigners).

From one election to the next, from one region to another, the VB's focus has been on one particular theme, while the others themes are downplayed. For example, the 1987 campaign was fiercely anti-immigrant (Coffé, 2005). In Brussels the party downplays Flemish nationalism and secessionism, when focussing on the French-speaking voters. The VB also appeals to Brussels' voters with its strongest themes, i.e., immigration and criminality. The topics of independence of Flanders and the annexation of Brussels (and its consequent mandatory "Dutch-ization") are carefully avoided in the party's communication material for Brussels.

This strategic positioning could be attributed to a strong, coherent and consistent communication strategy. The clear evidence is that the VB's communication material is proving successful in persuading and retaining voters. The analysis of the discourse of the Vlaams Blok and the Vlaams Belang have provided examples of their persuasive discourse, and rhetorical strategies (see Moufahim et al., 2007) and arguments and these have been reinforced with evocative photographs (Moufahim and Humphreys, in press). There is also evidence here of careful orchestration of the brochures, speeches, and website so that all are 'in tune' and sending the same message, that the party's main concern is with the voters' interests.

CONCLUSION

The adoption of marketing discourse is not initially obvious in the communication of the Vlaams Belang. However, a market orientation is identifiable and manifests itself in rather subtle ways such as, careful segmentation and well-targeted segments (e.g., the respective messages for Flanders and Brussels have different focus), and consistent positioning. The new Vlaams Belang has pragmatically adopted an anti-immigration stance (electorally rewarding), and kept their original ideological core of Flemish nationalism (its origin and identity base.). They have understood voters and also attempting to manipulate their perception via, for example, raising the profile of the immigration theme from 1987's election campaigns onwards.

Coffé (2004) has shown that criminality and immigration, and to a lesser extent Flemish nationalism have become the 'unique selling points' of the party. The voters recall these two themes when asked to justify their choice for the extreme right party (Coffé, 2004). This is evidence that the party has developed a clearly defined positioning in the mind of voters. For a party that claims 'hating' spin, the VB seems to be highly effective in spinning their own position and image. A market(ing)-orientation exudes from every pore of the party's communication material. The constant call for 'referendum,' to listen to the people, to voice people's concern, and follow their opinion seems 'suspiciously' consistent with a party following a political marketing concept. The Vlaams Belang is facing a delicate situation in terms of preserving its 'unique selling points' and its loyal following (the Vlaams Blok's). The party is today adopting a somewhat paradoxical strategy: a 'softening' of problematic policies (linked to immigrants and their rights), with a reassessment of the former party's heritage. However, this is paradoxical only in appearance, if one accepts the notion of segmentation of the electoral market by the VB. The party seeks to gain a wide appeal, by stressing its Flemish nationalist and anti-establishment policies, and wishes to retain the large anti-immigrant electoral base. The outcome of such strategy is the creation of polemic in media (e.g., the statement that every woman wearing the headscarf should be sent away, or the statement made by Filip Dewinter about his Islamophobia), while the party's political program retains its newly acquired right-wing conservative flavor.[11]

Marketing can be understood as an instrument that frames and legitimates political discourse in the eyes of voters. The ability to connect with voters is a key issue for political parties and it seems that marketing discourse is mainly used strategically by parties to make their speech 'voter-friendly' and encourage the consumption of their political 'product.' Ideas in relation to marketing are part of a broader discourse: the discourse of neoliberalism makes the ideas and language of marketing acceptable, rendering them intelligible (Savigny, 2008, 74). Therefore marketing is used as a form of legitimating discourse to make politics accessible to people who have been socialized in a consumer society.

In addition, it should be noted that the discourse of marketing serves to embed the importance, even the primacy of markets as solutions to all social, economic, and political concerns (Wring and Savigny, 2008, 8). Ideas about marketing have become institutionalized, naturalized, and they become the conventional norms from which there is no alternative, and the 'common sense' way for politics to proceed (Savigny, 2008, 70). Some scholars argue that marketing practice within the political realm is inevitable. O'Cass, for example, stated "the very essence of a candidate and political party's interface with the electorate is a marketing one and marketing cannot be avoided" (1996, 38). For Butler and Collins, "political marketing is a continuous process which cannot be divorced from all other public aspects of politics" (1994, 30). And Newman (1994) reflects on whether it is conceivable for a candidate *not* to adopt a marketing perspective in contemporary politics (in Savigny, 2008, 1).

Nevertheless, our case analysis raises the question as to whether the use of marketing in politics is indeed considered 'legitimate' and acceptable by the general public or, at least, by the people the VB seeks to attract. The party seems to adopt a different approach when dealing with political marketing by other parties. On numerous occasions in the past, the party leaders fiercely denounced the use of marketing and criticized the 'spin doctors' appointed by Belgian mainstream political parties. This raises the issue of the relevance, or acceptance of marketing as a legitimate tool for 'converting' the masses, far from the spectrum of manipulation and propaganda. It is maybe an indication that today, political marketing is still perceived as a tool for mass manipulation, regardless of its claim of customer sovereignty and empowerment. Does it mean that in the political field, marketing discourse and ideology have not yet reached the full naturalization that makes it transparent and unquestioned in other aspects of modern societies? This provides a lead for further research in the area of political communication, and critical marketing, far beyond the scope of this chapter.

NOTES

1. Note that, at every level, there are different areas of allocation of powers. The federal state's jurisdiction lies in the domains of justice, social security, and money, external relations, and external commerce. The three regions deal with the matters related to their territory: planning, environment, water, energy, economic questions, transport, employment. The three linguistic communities' jurisdiction are related to the issues linked to people, such as training, culture, education, health, TV, and radio. In addition, the country is divided into ten provinces, which jurisdictions are the special schools, leisure, and roads. There are five hundred and eighty-nine communes (towns).
2. See the website of the *Missions Economiques Françaises*, http://www.dree.org/belgique/documents.asp?Rub=1&F=HTML&Num=1246
3. The highest institution of Justice in Belgium.
4. To stress this continuity, a combination of both names—"*VB*"—is used to refer indistinctively to both the Vlaams Blok and the Vlaams Belang, unless stated otherwise.
5. There were, for example, in 1991, boxing gloves and a "*Self-defence*" slogan; or in 1999, a family and "*Boss in one's land*," a broom and "Grote Kuis," i.e. "Big Cleaning Up"; in 1999, a family and "Baas in eigen land," i.e. "Boss in one's land"; a kid pointing a finger and "Thuis zijn," i.e. "at home." These slogans have always been used in combination to the well-known party slogan "Eigen Volk Eerst," i.e. "One's own people first."
6. Local Flemish newspaper (in the Flemish province of Limburg).
7. Brochure: Politieke Communicatie-Technieken, Deel 1. De persoonlijke campagne van de kandidaat. *Vlaams Blok Publications*. (Translation: Political communication techniques—Part 1: The personal campaign of the candidate)
8. '*Solidarism*' is a system where the economy should be aimed at maintaining the welfare of the whole nation and where national solidarity replaces class struggle (Mudde, 2000, 189).
9. Dewinter's ideological input is limited to the immigration theme (Mudde, 2004).
10. http://www.vlaamsblok.be

BIBLIOGRAPHY

Aaker, D. and J.G. Shansby. 1982. Positioning your product. *Business Horizons* 25: 56–62.

Baines, P. 1999. Voter segmentation and candidate positioning. In *Handbook of Political Marketing*, ed. B. Newman, 403–420. London: Sage.

Baines, P.R. and J. Egan. 2001. Marketing and political campaigning: Mutually exclusive or exclusively mutual? *Qualitative Market Research: An International Journal* 4(1): 25–34.

Bossemans, V. 2001. *De Communicatiestrategie van het Vlaams Blok. Evolutie van positionering, doelgroep en boodschap*. Unpublished dissertation, Faculteit Politieke en Sociale Wetenschappen, p. 175.

Butler, P. and N. Collins. 1994. Political marketing: structure and process," *European Journal of Marketing* 28(1): 19–34.

Butler, P. and N. Collins. 1996. Strategic analysis in political markets. *European Journal of Marketing* 30(10/11): 32–44.

Camus, J-Y. 2003. La figure de l'étranger dans le discours de l'extrême droite européenne. *Nouvelle Tribune* 33 Juin/Août Trimestriel.

Ceuppens, B. 2001. Le Vlaams Blok et le Flamand "naturel." *Critique Internationale* 10: 143–57.

Coffé, H. 2004. Can extreme right voting be explained ideologically? *Conference paper, ECPR Joint Sessions*, April 13–18 2004, Workshop No. 3.

Coffé, H. 2005. The adaptation of the extreme right's discourse: the case of the Vlaams Blok. *Ethical perspectives: Journal of the European Ethics Network* 12 (2): 205–230.

Dewinter, F. 1991. *Immigratie: de oplossing. 70 voorstellen ter oplossing van vreemdelingenproblemen.* Immigration: the solution. 70 proposals for the resolution of the foreigners' issue.

Dewinter, F. 2002. *Baas in eigen land,* Vlaams Blok publications, http://www.vlaamsblok.be/publicaties_boek_biel.shtml.

Dewinter, F. 2004. Interview reported in Dag Allenmaal, nr. 44 (October, 26, 2004).

Dewitner, F. 2004. Interview reported in Het Belang van Limburg (accessed March 17, 2004).

Dewinter, F. 2004. Interview, reported in Jewish Week News (October 28, 2004).

Dewinter, F. 2004. TV programme, Buitenhof, Nederland 3. http://www.youtube.com/watch?v=hTxDQnXKRyQ (accessed November 14, 2006).

Dewinter, F. 2007. Vlaams Belang Press Conference. August 19, 2007. Brussels, Belgium.

Faniel, J. 2003. L'extrême droite en Belgique: puissance du Vlaams Blok, (in)existence du Front National. *Nouvelle Tribune* August: 50–54.

Henneberg, S.C. 2004. The views of an advocatus dei: Political marketing and its critics. *Journal of Public Affairs* 4(3): 225–243.

Human Rights in Belgium—Annual Report (Events in 2005). http://www.hrwf.net/regliousfreedom/news/2005PDF/belgium_2005.pdf (accessed June 20, 2006).

Ingram, P. and J.P. Lees-Marshment. 2002. The Anglicisation of political marketing: How Blair "out-marketed" Clinton. *Journal of Public Affairs* 2(2): 44–57.

Keller, K. 2003. Brand synthesis: The multidimensionality of brand knowledge. *Journal of Consumer Research* 29(1): 595–600.

Lock, A. and P. Harris. 1996. Political marketing: Vive la différence. *European Journal of Marketing* 30(10/11): 14–24.

Maarek, P.J. 1992. Elections Americaines: Dans les coulisses du marketing politique. *Marketing* 43(January): 37–44.

Mauser, G.A. 1983. *Political marketing: An approach to campaign strategy.* New York: Praeger.

Moufahim, M. and M. Humphreys, M. In press. Marketing and identity: The Vlaams Belang against Turkish admission to the EU. In *Political Marketing, Cultural Issues and Current Trends*, eds. B. Newman, K. Gouliamos, and S. Hennenberg, forthcoming. Boston: The Haworth Press.

Moufahim, M., M. Humphreys, D. Mitussis, and J.A. Fitchett. 2007. Interpreting discourse: A critical discourse analysis of the marketing of an extreme right party. *Journal of Marketing Management* 23(5–6): 537–558.

Mudde, C. 2000. *The ideology of the extreme right.* Manchester, New York: Manchester University Press.

Mudde, C. 2004. "De (non)-transformatie van Vlaams Blok naar Vlaams Belang." *Samenleving en politiek: tijdschrift voor een democratisch socialisme* 11(10): 16–22.

Newman, B.L. 1994. *The marketing of the president: Political marketing as campaign strategy.* London: Sage.

Newman, B.L. 2001. Political marketing: Lessons from recent presidential elections. *Working Paper,* Yaffe Center for Persuasive Communications, Michigan Ross School of Business.

Nollet, F. 2000. L'Extrême droite en Europe et en Belgique: Etat des Lieux et stratégies. *Note du CEPESS,* February 21, 2000.

O'Cass, A. 1996. Political marketing and the marketing concept. *European Journal of Marketing* 30(10/11): 45–61.

O'Shaughnessy, N. 1990. *The phenomenon of political marketing.* London: Macmillan.

Olins, W. 2002. How brands are taking over the corporation. In *The expressive corporation*, eds. M. Schultz, M.J. Hatch, and M.H. Larsen, 320. London: Oxford University Press.

Omura, G.S. 1979. Role of attribute generality in cognitions of political candidates. *Advances in Consumer Research* 6(1): 635–641

Palmer, J. 2002. Smoke and mirrors: Is that the way it is? Themes in political marketing. *Media, Culture and Society* 24: 345–363.

Sabato, L. 1981. *The rise of political consultants—New ways of winning elections.* New York: Basic Books.

Savigny, H. 2008. *The problem of political marketing.* London: The Continuum International Publishing Group.

Scammell, M. 1995. *Designer politics: How elections are won.* London: Macmillan

Scammell, M. 1996. "The Odd Couple: Marketing and Maggie." *European Journal of Marketing* 30(10/11): 122–135.

Shama, A. 1976. The marketing of political candidates. *Journal of the Academy of MarketingScience* Fall 76, 4(4): 764–768.

Smith, G. 2005. Positioning political parties: The 2005 UK general election. *Journal of Marketing Management* 21: 1135–1149.

Spruyt, M. 2000. *Wat het Vlaams Blok verzwijgt.* Leuven: Van Halewijck.

Swyngedouw, M. 1998. The extreme right in Belgium: of a non-existent Front National and an omnipresent Vlaams Blok. In *The new politics of the right. Neo-populist parties and movements in established democracies*, eds. H.-G. Betz and S. Immerfall, 59–75. New York: St. Martin's Press.

Trout, J. and S. Sivkin. 1996. *The new positioning.* New York: McGraw Hill.

Van Der Brink, R. 2003. Frontière linguistique, Frontière politique. La Flandre redoute une poussée brune. *Le Monde Diplomatique.* http://www.monde-diplomatique.fr/2003/05/VAN_DER_BRINK/10141?var_recherche=flandre (accessed October 22, 2003).

Vander Velpen, J. 1992. *Daar komen ze aangemarcheerd. Extreem-rechts in West-Europa.* Berchem: EPO.

Vanhecke, F. 2004. http://www.vlaamsblok.be. in TV *Dag Allemaal* (accessed October 26, 2004).

Vlaams Belang. 2006. *Dertiende overrinning op rij,* Magazine Nr. 1, November 2006.

Vlaams Blok (n.d.) Politieke Communicate-Technieken, Deel 1. De persoonlijke campagne van de kandidaat. *Vlaams Blok Publications* (Translation: Political communication techniques—Part I: The personal campaign of candidate).

Vos, L. 1992. *De politieke kleur van jonge generaties.* In *Herfsttij van de 20ste eeuw. Extreem-rechts in Vlaanderen 1920–1990*, eds. R. Van Doorslaer and J. Gotovitch, 15–46. Leuven: Kritak.

Wring, D. 1996. Political marketing and party development in Britain: A "secret" history. *European Journal of Marketing* 30(10/11): 100–113.

Wring, D and H. Savigny. 2008. An ideology of disconnection: For a critical political marketing. *5th International Conference on Political Marketing*, Manchester.

9 A Critical Realist Analysis of Institutional Change in the Field of US Nursing Homes

Martin Kitchener and Bernard Leca

INTRODUCTION

While institutional analyses of organization settings including healthcare provide important advances to knowledge, two main weaknesses persist. First, studies of institutional change tend to conflate the influence of actors' motivated actions (agency) and the structures in which they are embedded (Fleetwood, 2005). Second, the uncritical acceptance of managerial explanations of motive and causality has produced accounts that fail to investigate both deeper processes at play, and the ways that organizations wield political power to shape their environment (Barley, 2007). This chapter suggests that Leca and Naccache's (2006) critical realist model of institutional analysis presents a useful basis for non-conflationary and critical studies of institutional change in healthcare fields. The potential is illustrated using an historical analysis of the development of large multifacility corporations (chains) in the US nursing home industry.

This chapter is presented in five main sections. The first outlines the problems of ontological conflation in institutional studies, and uncritical approaches to the study of: (a) consolidation in healthcare fields in general, and (b) the development of large US nursing homes chains in particular. The second section introduces critical realism as a philosophy that addresses these issues and then specifies Leca and Naccache's (2006) critical realist model of institutional analysis. Section three describes the way in which the philosophy and model were operated within a critical realist analysis of consolidation in the field of US nursing homes. Section four presents the case analysis. The chapter concludes with a discussion of the extensions to knowledge produced by this first critical realist analysis of institutional change in a field of healthcare organizations.

INSTITUTIONAL CHANGE IN HEALTHCARE: CONFLATION AND THE UNCRITICAL ORTHODOXY

While institutional analyses of contexts including healthcare have advanced knowledge of change processes, many studies are characterized by the conflation of agency and structure, and the uncritical acceptance of managerial explanations of motive and causality. This section introduces the nature of these problems in turn.

Ontological Conflation

Some of the main contributions to institutional analysis have emerged from studies conducted at the level of organizational fields defined as, "communities of organizations that partake of a common meaning system and whose participants interact more frequently and fatefully with one another than with actors outside of the field" (Scott, 1994, 207–208). Research at this level of analysis has shown that, especially in healthcare fields, dominant systems of beliefs and values (logics) perform two main functions: (1) supplying principals of organization and legitimacy, and (2) providing justification frameworks to articulate political and resource claims (Friedland and Alford, 1991; Thornton and Ocasio, 2008). Through normative, mimetic, and coercive mechanisms, actors translate logics into institutions, defined as self-reproducing recurrent patterns of behaviour and structure (Jepperson, 1991; DiMaggio and Powell, 1983). Over time, institutions acquire the moral and ontological status of taken-for-granted facts that both shape activity, and can be reproduced without actors either being aware of them, or questioning their efficiency or legitimacy (Barley and Tolbert, 1997).

Organizational analysts have shown particular concern for a specific type of institution: templates, or archetypes, that draw from a logic to specify legitimate combinations of organizational structure and action (DiMaggio and Powell, 1983; Greenwood and Hinings, 1993; Kitchener, 2002). While studies of archetypes initially concentrated on field-level inertia or isomorphism (convergence to archetypal forms), they have been criticized for conflating agency and structure, and for producing deterministic accounts of field processes. In response, institutional analysts have begun to examine relations between logics, archetypes, and actors' capacity for motivated change action (Seo and Creed, 2002; Reay and Hinings, 2005).

Central to institutional studies of field change lies the paradox of embedded agency: how institutional change (a new archetype) is possible if actors' intentions and actions are conditioned by the existing institutional logic and archetype they seek to alter (Holm, 1995). Overcoming this paradox requires developing models of change that do not reduce structure to action, action to structure, or attempt to merge the two (Archer, 1995). While the goal is to deny neither actors' freedom nor the constraining power of institutional structures, the two main attempts to deal with this issue in institutional theory have been criticized (Leca and Naccache, 2006). First, Barley and Tolbert's (1997) diachronic approach to distinguishing between agency and institutions through sequential analysis is logically unable to deal with interrelations between structure and agency at the same time, and it does not recognize the causal emergent properties of both structures and agency (Archer, 2002).

Second, explanations of institutional change as driven by institutional entrepreneurs (organized actors with sufficient resources) who are able to dissemble from existing logics (e.g., Seo and Creed, 2002) neither tackle the paradox of embedded agency, nor the issue of conflation (Emirbayer and Mische, 1998). Additionally, both of these approaches to dealing with institutional embeddedness contradict the central understanding of institutional theory that actors cannot escape institutional embeddedness (Friedland and Alford, 1991). To remain coherent with institutional theory, a model of institutional change must both: (a) allow for actors to create and change institutions without disembedding from the social world (Leca and Naccache, 2006), and (b) account for the interrelated sequencing of structures and actions and the causal emerging properties of both (Thornton and Ocasio, 2008).

Uncritical Studies of Healthcare Field Consolidation

For more than twenty years, analysts of healthcare organizations have applied institutional and other perspectives (e.g., strategic management) to study forms of field consolidation such as the growth of American physician group–hospital systems (Scott et al., 2000), and the growth of multi-facility corporations (chains) in the field of US nursing homes (Banaszak-Holl et al., 2002). Many studies start from the understanding that the currently dominant logic in US healthcare fields is accurately portrayed by Scott and colleagues' (2000) depiction of market-managerialism. This system of beliefs and values legitimates a 'market' system operated through 'rational' (value and interest neutral) management techniques aimed at achieving efficiency and quality improvements (Luke and Walston, 2003). When considered against this logic, evidence of the 'failure' of techniques such as consolidation (against the espoused managerial motives of improved efficiency and quality) is typically attributed to 'implementation problems' such as professional resistance (Bazzoli et al., 2004).

The form of uncritical research perspective outlined previously pervades the few existing studies of a process of institutional change in the US field of 16,500 nursing homes that arose, during the 1990s, from the development of large multi-facility corporations (chains). Previous studies have applied mainstream management frameworks to examine the extent to which chains realize the espoused managerial motives of improving the efficiency of acquired units through techniques including: standardization, branding, and knowledge transfer (Banaszak-Holl et al., 2002; Kamimura et al 2007). This uncritical orthodoxy has produced assertions that "public policy needs to take advantage of the ability of nursing home chains to revitalize the for-profit sector" (Mitchell et al., 2001).

The lack of critical attention given to nursing home chaining is surprising for at least three reasons. First, there have been long-standing concerns with the practices and performance of corporate health providers in the United States (Vladeck, 1980; Light, 1986). Second, health services research demonstrates significant associations between nursing home chain membership/for-profit status and outcomes including poor quality, low staffing, and high profits (O'Neill et al., 2003). Third, a new class of very large chains has attracted concern from regulators, the media, policy makers, and the public over issues including: political influence, problematic governance histories, and poor records on quality (Kitchener and Harrington, 2004). As exposure of poor quality and questionable governance have led the large chains to be dubbed 'evil empires' by the business press (Lorinc, 2003), they have also drawn concern from federal and state governments including Wisconsin where a report demanded that: "The State should have a more intimate knowledge of . . . nursing home operations as a means to afford early identification and intervention in situations where corporate fiscal and other quality problems threaten the safety and well-being of residents (Wisconsin Board on Aging and Long-Term Care, 2003, 6–8).

INSTITUTIONAL CHANGE: A CRITICAL REALIST FRAMEWORK

Critical realism presents a broad philosophy on, and for, science that is underpinned by a stratified model of reality (Bhaskar, 1989). This section argues that critical realism—through its stratified model of reality and critical perspective—has considerable promise as a means of addressing the problems of conflation and uncritical approach within studies of institutional change in healthcare fields.

Stratified Model of Reality

Critical realists consider actors' actions and structures as two separate ontologically different levels of reality that are related but not reducible, and which are characterized by: distinctive emergent properties, relative autonomy, a previous existence, ongoing interaction, and causal efficiency (Bhaskar, 1979; Archer, 2002; Sayer, 2000). To develop a model of change that accounts for both the constraints of institutional structures and agents' freedom of action, critical realists assert the need to recognize the ontological specificities of both actions and structures. This view forms the basis of a stratified model of reality that distinguishes between three domains: empirical, actual, and real.

The domain of the empirical is the arena of experienced events involving actors' sensations and perception of reality. The domain of actual includes events, whether observed or not, that happen independently of actors' experience of them. Because such things can fail to be transferred into the domain of empirical by actors (until they identify them correctly and transform them into experience), the domain of actual is the starting point of theory development by critical realists (Bhaskar, 1979). Realist explanation involves penetrating that surface level of reality to access the domain of real that consists of the structures and causal powers that generate events (Sayer, 1992). From realists' view of the world as an open system in which different casual powers may coexist, structures have causal capabilities that are transfactual—i.e. they exist whether or not they operate in the specific context under study (Archer, 2002). Thus, for realists, causal explanation centres on the ascription of causal powers to structures (Tsoukas, 1989).

Critical realists' stratified model of reality and underpinning philosophy presents four foundations for the study of institutional change in organizational fields. First, it is asserted that institutional logics predate action so that, to act, actors can use the causal powers of such structures to produce new institutions (Archer, 1995; Bhaskar, 1989). The diversity of institutional logics is a defining feature of many complex organizational fields (especially in healthcare) that allows actors to find principles to justify new archetypes and challenge existing ones (Friedland and Alford, 1991). Second, recognition of the contingent nature of the activation and effects of structures' causal powers requires the historical contextualization of analyses (Tsoukas, 1994; Archer, 1995; Mutch, 1999). In practical terms, the contingent nature of causal powers requires institutional entrepreneurs to (politically and culturally) mobilize logics that are most likely to match the interests of potential allies (Fligstein and Mara-Drita, 1996). Third, realist ontology holds that given the impossibility of closing open social systems (such as organization fields), derived social theory can only be provisional, cannot be predictive (beyond tendencies), and must be (almost exclusively) explanatory (Bhaskar, 1989). Fourth, the critical foreword of critical realism emphasizes a concern for political issues of social phenomena in healthcare fields that are underplayed within mainstream organizational perspectives (Tsoukas, 1994; Barley, 2007).

Building on these foundations, Leca and Naccache (2006) propose a framework that incorporates institutional concepts within the three domains of critical realist analysis. In the domain of empirical, researchers are first directed towards field actors' actions, perceptions, and experience. While this may provide insight into some institutions (archetypes), actors' will have restricted capacity to recognize or interpret those that are, for example, too 'taken for granted' to be identified as such. Given their training, researchers may be able to reveal and characterize the recurrent nature of those behaviors and organizational forms, and then to qualify them as institutions (archetypes). Thus, institutions should be considered in the domain of actual. As defined earlier, logics cannot be reduced to their derived institutions. Their ontological status is acknowledged as being exogenous to actors and removed from the more active struggles over resources and meaning (Lounsbury, 2003; Friedland and Alford, 1991). Thus, institutional logics correspond to structures located in the domain of real (Leca and Naccache, 2006). Depending on contextual factors and the actions of agents, it is to be expected that institutional logics will unfold in the domain of actual as institutions because the latter are framed as the results of the ways in which actors transpose these logics through scripts, rules and templates in specific contexts. This stratified model of institutional analysis is summarized in Table 9.1.

Table 9.1   A Stratified Model of Institutional Analysis

	Domain of real	Domain of actual	Domain of empirical
Institutional logics	V		
Institutions (archetypes)	V	V	
Experiences	V	V	V

Source: Leca and Naccache, 2006: 633

METHOD

Aim and Design

The aim of the analysis reported next is to apply the critical realist framework outlined previously to examine how the causal powers of an identified institutional logic (shareholder value) operates in a specific context (the field of US nursing homes), and how an institutional entrepreneur (one large chain) used them to introduce a new archetype (large chain). Following a study design principal common to critical realism and organizational field analysis (Reed, 1997; Scott et al., 2000), this analysis incorporates two vantage points (levels of analysis) provided by successive studies of related social phenomena. The first study examined historical change in the US long-term care industry that comprises a number of organizational fields including the nursing home field (Kitchener and Harrington, 2004). A central finding from that study was the emergence of a new breed of large, multi-facility nursing home corporations (chains). The second study presented a detailed case analysis of quality and cost performance in one of the largest nursing home chains, the Sun Corporation (Kitchener et al., 2008).

Analysis

This first application of critical realism to the study of healthcare field consolidation sought to draw on the domains of empirical and actual, to reveal the causal powers at work in the domain of real. The central problem for such analysis is how to establish the plausibility of the hypothesized structures and causal powers, given they are not immediately available to experience (Sayer, 1992). From their assertion of the primacy of practice over language, critical realist researchers aim to go beyond discourse analysis that, alone, is insufficient to reach the domain of actual (Laclau and Bhaskar, 1998; Archer, 2002).

This study employed a three-stage strategy of analytical 'retroduction' to explain events by postulating and identifying structures and causal powers capable of generating them (Sayer, 1992). The first stage begins in the domain of actual with the observation of connections between phenomena. The aim is to identify how such connections occur, to abstract from context-dependent data to capture the not-directly observable causal powers and structures that generate observable phenomena (Ekstrom, 1992). To do so, in the second stage of analysis, a hypothetical model was developed involving structures and causal powers located in the domain of real, which, if it were to exist and act in the postulated way, would provide a causal explanation of the phenomena in question. The final stage requires subjecting the postulated explanation to empirical scrutiny.

LARGE US NURSING HOME CHAINS: A CRITICAL REALIST ANALYSIS

The following case study analysis illustrates the way in which Leca and Naccache's (2006) critical realist model can be used to frame a non-conflationary and critical analysis of institutional change in organizational fields. Following the analytical procedures outlined above, we begin by introducing the historical context of the focal field of US nursing homes. We then describe the growth of the logic of shareholder value and identify, from previous literature, three transfactual causal powers of shareholder value logic. We round out the analysis by explaining which causal powers developed in the focal context, and how.

The Field of US Nursing Homes

The Mom and Pop Nursing Home Archetype

Prior to 1965, the US nursing home field was essentially a cottage industry of local, proprietary, 'mom and pop' providers (Kitchener and Harrington, 2004). Within a heterogeneous field that also included small chains of not-for-profit facilities, the primary sources of facility income were private payments and religious donations. The dominant organizational archetype involved medical professionals and for-profit facility owners (sometimes the same people) operating to a logic that emphasized the 'need' for 'sick patients' to receive care inside residential facilities that were locally-run, under the control of fee-for-service medical professionals who operated with limited external oversight by other stakeholders including government and families (Kitchener and Harrington, 2004). State authorization of this archetype (e.g., through facility licensing) presented medical professionals and facility operators with an early monopoly over the economic and social rewards to be gained from nursing homes (Estes and Binney, 1993).

Under the logic of 'federal involvement' that characterized mid-century US health care (Scott et al., 2000), intensive political lobbying by the nursing home industry secured significant additional government funding for nursing home care. This provided a catalyst for the corporatization and consolidation of the field (Kitchener and Harrington, 2004). Specifically, through the 1965 enactment of the federal Medicare insurance program (for the elderly) and the joint federal-state Medicaid insurance program (for the poor and disabled), government became a third-party payer for nursing home services within a market system. For nursing homes, high public demand was secured and, paradoxically, the Medicaid program became the single largest payer of US nursing home care (Light, 1986). In 1987, again following lobbying by the nursing home industry, further incentives for corporatization were presented by: (a) an expansion of the Medicare nursing home benefit, and (b) the introduction of a cost-based reimbursement system that included payment for ancillary services such as therapies (Lehman Brothers, 2004).

From the 1970s, as increased public funding flowed into the nursing home field, corporate capital intensified its search for profit using standard rationalizing techniques to produce larger bureaucratic structures. Almost immediately, it was recognized at congressional level that the emergent form of corporate development was problematic. As Etzioni reported to a congressional hearing in 1975, "this is the area of human services which is most rampant with abuse . . . what we have here is an unusual concentration of real estate manipulators and quick-buck artists" (US Congress, 1975, 18). Despite this, and largely unchallenged by researchers or government regulators, by the start of the 1990s more than half of US nursing homes were operated by corporate chains (Banaszak-Holl et al., 2002).

The Large Chain Archetype

The few studies of the growth of US nursing home chains during the 1990s have produced two important insights into this process of institutional change. First, nursing home chaining occurred primarily through a process of 5,000 acquisitions and mergers involving individual facilities or smaller chains, rather than by the building of new facilities (Banaszak-Holl et al., 2002). This occurred, in part, because many states restrict the growth of new nursing home beds. By 2001, the corporate chain was the dominant form of nursing home care with over 60 percent of all facilities reporting corporate ownership (Banaszak-Holl et al., 2002). Corporate controls on local facilities within chains minimally include a financial relationship between the corporate office and member facilities. More extensive corporate controls can include rigorous enforcement of care guidelines and staffing levels, intranets for sharing clinical information, meetings among staff from multiple sites, and the potential to share staff, training, and common contracts with suppliers, such as pharmacies, medical supply agencies, and staffing agencies (Kamimura et al., 2007).

In addition to the growth in the number of chains, a second feature of the process of institutional change during the 1990s was the emergence of a new breed of very large corporate chain. As shown in Table 9.2, the structural features of the new archetype include: large bureaucratic structures involving hundreds of nursing homes nationally, and often internationally; diversification into areas such as ancillary health service (e.g., therapy) and employment agencies; and a reliance upon government funding for approximately 70 percent of revenues. In 2001, the new nursing home archetype (the eight largest chains) operated nearly 20 percent of all nursing home beds and exerted considerable influence over the industry (Banaszak-Holl et al., 2002).

In contrast to the mom and pop nursing home archetype with its underpinning logic of locally-based care under medical control, the large corporate nursing home chain archetype can be seen as a local (field) product of the wider logic of shareholder value (Fligstein and Shin, 2006; Kitchener et al., 2008). As Table 9.3 summarizes, the two logics support different practices and organizational forms, and lead to different priorities and orientations.

Economic sociologists report that from the early 1980s, financial institutions (e.g., investment banks) frustrated with American industrial performance were successful in introducing 'shareholder value' as the dominant logic within many corporate contexts including healthcare (Zorn et al., 2005). The logic holds that the relationship between managers, boards of directors, and financial institutions involves rewarding and sanctioning managers to get them to maximize the returns on firms' assets and in doing so, raise the price of stock (Jensen and Meckling, 1976). It is asserted that if corporate boards fail to ensure the effective managerial performance they

Table 9.2   Characteristics of the Eight Largest US Nursing Home Chains, 2001

Corporation	Nursing Home Beds	Total Facilities	% of Revenue from Govt.	Total Operating Revenue	CEO Compensation
Beverly Enterprises	51,054	466	77	$2.7 billion	$3.6 million
Manor Care	41,613	299	61	$2.7 billion	$8.1 million
Kindred Healthcare	39,293	305	79	$3.1 billion[1]	$12.8 million
Mariner	38,700	326	80	$1.9 billion	$1.3 million
Integrated Health Services	34,797	300	78	$1.8 billion	n/a
Life Centers of America	28,226	213	67	$1.3 billion	n/a
Sun	27,954	229	82	$2.1 billion	n/a
Genesis	25,821	240	61	$2.6 billion	n/a

Source: Kitchener et al., 2006.

Table 9.3   Institutional Logics in US Nursing Home Field (1960s–2000s)

Characteristics	Locally-based professional care	Shareholder value
Economic system	Market capitalism	Market capitalism
Sources of identity	Local provision of care	Nursing as an investment
Sources of legitimacy	Quality of care	Share value
Sources of authority	Medical professionals Facilities owners	CEO Corporate hierarchy Public ownership
Basis of mission	Provide care to sick patients	Increase return on investment
Basis of attention	Care quality	Cost containment
Basis of strategy	Organic growth Secure high public demand	Acquisition growth Reduce costs
Logic of investment	Capital committed to firm	Capital committed to market return
Governance	Trade association, licensing	Market for corporate control, licensing
Archetypal organizational form	Single, facility, small local chain	Large chain
Event sequencing	1965. Medicare and Medicaid become third party payers 1987. Expansion of Medicare nursing home benefit and introduction of a cost-based reimbursement system including payment for ancillary services	1990s. Development of large chain archetype through 5,000 mergers and acquisitions 1998. Founding of the Alliance for Quality in Nursing Home Care

Source: Developed from Thornton and Ocasio, 2008.

are punished by equity markets through sanctions such as falling share prices and ultimately, hostile takeover (Davis and Thompson, 1994). Thus, the central tenet of shareholder value logic is that to return industries to profitability and maintain their jobs, executives must: (1) prioritize increasing returns on firms' assets in order to increase profits for stockholders, and (2) subjugate all other goals (e.g., quality) and constituencies such as consumers and employees (Fligstein, 2001).

Causal Powers of the Shareholder Value Institutional Logic

From comparative analyses of shareholder value logic in diverse fields (Fligstein, 2001), it is possible to propose three causal powers of this institutional logic that can operate independent of context. First, because firms with lots of cash, little debt, and low stock prices become merger targets, corporations expand by borrowing money to pay for acquisitions (Davis and Stout, 1992). Second, there is an intensification of attempts to constrain labor costs through lay-offs and low staffing levels (Hallock, 1998). Third, creative financial ploys are used to bolster financial reports including stock buybacks and fictitious capital formation (Westphal and Zajac, 2001; McLean and Elkind, 2003).

THE DEVELOPMENT OF THE LARGE CHAIN ARCHETYPE'S CAUSAL POWERS IN THE US NURSING HOME FIELD

Debt-Financed Rapid Growth

The first transfactual causal power of the large nursing home chain archetype (identified from the literature on shareholder value logic) is that corporations increasingly borrow money to pay for acquisitions (Davis and Stout, 1992). While industry data confirm that most large nursing home chains developed in this way, a case study of one of the largest chains (Sun) reveals detail (Kitchener et al., 2008). Over a nine-year period of debt-financed purchases in the 1990s, the chain grew to employ 80,720 persons working in 397 nursing facilities that were owned, leased, or managed across 26 states' facilities. (Kitchener et al., 2008) Additionally, Sun diversified by purchasing 1,798 ancillary service firms (e.g., pharmacies, therapy providers, and staffing agencies) and 186 international facilities in countries including the United Kingdom and Australia. Around Sun's peak in 1997–1998, its stock price of nearly $17 indicated that the purveyors of shareholder logic (financial institutions) were satisfied that corporate assets of $2.6 billion were financed by long-term debt of $1.57 billion. Additionally, the business press expressed its satisfaction with the strategy of debt-financed chaining when portraying Sun's CEO as a 'hero' who was impatient with the traditional approach to industry governance (mom and pop archetype) which he derided as 'lacking innovation' (Nakhnikian, 2000, 4).

Labor Cost Constraint and Shareholder Value

The second transfactual causal power of the large chain archetype (identified from literature on shareholder value logic) is an intensification of attempts to constrain labor costs through low staffing levels (Hallock, 1998). At the Sun chain, the CEO's desire to "cut redundancy and fat in the system" was reflected in low nurse staffing levels in the Corporation's nursing homes (Odenwald, 1996, 15). Analysis of chain-reported data for the period 2000–2003 shows that in the state of California, Sun's registered nurse staffing was 20 percent lower than the California average and 63 percent lower than the levels recommended by experts (COSHPD, 2004). Consistent with Sun's low staffing levels, Sun facilities in California reported a 95–98 percent average staff turnover rate that was nearly 20 percent higher than the state average.

Given Sun's history of low staffing, it is not surprising that average daily facility expenditures were 18 percent lower than California state averages (COSHPD, 2004). The 'benefit' to shareholders of the chain's low facility staffing is indicated by figures showing that Sun's California facilities sent a total of $30.8 million in 2001 and $35.6 million in 2002 to corporate home office for administrative services and profits (COSHPD, 2004). This represented 11 to 15.5 percent of total revenues in 2001 and 2002 respectively, ranging from 5 to 24 percent of individual facility revenues (Kitchener et al., 2008).

Creative Finance

A third transfactual causal power of the large chain archetype derived from literature on the shareholder value logic is that corporations use creative financial ploys to bolster financial reports (Westphal and Zajac, 2001; McLean and Elkind, 2003). From as early as Etzioni's congressional testimony in 1975, illustrations of this causal power within the large nursing home chain archetype abound. In 2000, five of the nation's largest chains elected to operate under bankruptcy protection, involving 1,800 nursing homes (US CMS, 2003). Evidence that member units of bankrupt large chains operating in California did not report financial losses casts some doubt on the stated 'necessity' for entire chains to enter bankruptcy, rather than selected operating divisions (Kitchener et al., 2005). Although it is acknowledged that large chains suffered financially from the 1997 introduction of a new Medicare payment system, the US General Accounting Office argued that Medicare payments were 'adequate,' and that the large chains' bankruptcies stemmed from 'poor' business strategies including 'sizeable transactions with third parties' (US GAO, 2000, 2002).

It has also been reported that two common managerial practices among large nursing home chains in the 1990s were to acquire facilities through 'creative' financing sources including the establishment of real estate investment trusts (REITS). These are separate corporate entities that own the land and/or buildings, which are leased to nursing home corporations that are sometimes related companies (Lehman Brothers, 2004). The unclear relationship between REITS and the large chains was illustrated when, following bankruptcy, Sun stopped paying rent to REITS on nursing homes that were to be divested (Killean, 2004).

Legal and Regulatory Action as a Cost of Business

While the previous three sections have explained the way that three transfactual causal powers of the large nursing home archetype and its logic of shareholder value are manifest in large nursing home chains, Kitchener and colleagues (2008) revealed an additional causal power: the treatment of legal and regulatory action as a cost of business. In the late 1990s, this issue came to the fore as one of the largest chains (Kindred) reached a $1.3 billion settlement with the government for fraud, and another (Beverly) had a corporate 'monitor' imposed by the Department of Justice (Kitchener and Harrington, 2004). Detailed analysis of the Sun chain confirmed the Corporation's view of such legal sanctions as a cost of business:

> We are a party to various legal actions and administrative proceedings and are subject to various claims arising in the *ordinary course of our business*, including claims that our services have resulted in injury or death to the residents of our facilities, claims relating to employment and commercial matters . . . in the *ordinary course of business*, we are continuously subject to state and federal regulatory scrutiny, supervision and control . . . (Sun, 2005, F-41, *emphasis* added).

As early as 1995, the implications of this view within the large nursing home archetype appeared when government inspection agencies in five states issued decertification notices to multiple Sun facilities following successive investigations of low quality, fraud, and abuse (Sun, 1996). Even though Sun entered into a corporate compliance program with the federal Office of the Inspector General (OIG), further violations and multiple lawsuits (regarding false and misleading financial reporting and improper billing) led the OIG to impose a Corporate Integrity Agreement requiring the implementation of a comprehensive internal quality improvement program and a system of internal financial controls with external oversight (US OIG, 2001). Despite this, in 2002 Sun was forced to sign a settlement agreement with the Department of Justice in eight other cases by paying $1 million in cash and signing a promissory note for $10 million (Sun, 2002).

While the aforementioned actions occurred at the national level, a similar pattern emerged at the state level of operation. In California, for example, consistent regulatory action against Sun (US GAO, 1998) intensified in 2001 when state regulators issued ten citations and 71 survey deficiencies for poor quality of care to a single facility, and Sun pleaded no contest to a felony violation of elder abuse. Subsequent targeted investigations by the California Attorney General report extensive patient neglect, false records, inadequate care, insufficient staffing, inadequate supervision, and a lack of staff training (Kitchener et al., 2008). Somewhat ironically for a chain operating under the logic of shareholder value, a series of shareholder lawsuits were also filed against Sun in the mid-1990s. In 1996, six misrepresentation complaints were filed in New

Mexico alone, and in 1997 Sun negotiated a $24 million court settlement of other shareholder lawsuits (Sun, 1998).

Political Activity

As well as identifying the treatment of legal action as a cost of business as a causal power of the large chain archetype, this study reveals a second causal power not considered within the wider literature on shareholder value: political activity. Traditionally, the American Healthcare Association (AHCA) was the primary nursing home lobby group whose 10,000 members included mom and pop facilities and the large chains. By the end of the 1990s, however, the large shareholder value chains felt that the AHCA was not working aggressively enough on their three main political concerns: (1) protecting (and increasing) the public payment rates (Medicare and Medicaid) that comprise nearly 80 percent of shareholder value chains' income, (2) limiting oversight of chaining, and (3) capping firms' liability to consumer litigation. Thus, in 1998 the large chains established the Alliance for Quality in Nursing Home Care (The Alliance).

Activities in support of the Alliance's successful campaign to oppose President Bush's proposed Medicare nursing home rate cuts included running a series of 383 TV commercials in Washington, DC, and ten print ads in *Roll Call*, a publication for Capitol Hill, that issued a dire warning of "jeopardizing quality of care" for seniors (Copelin, 2004). Such activity was orchestrated by a growing list of powerful advisers including former federal health administrator Thomas Scully, and Haley Barbour, the ex-head of the Republican National Committee (Source Watch, 2005).

Success in terms of limiting governmental oversight of chaining is illustrated by the December 2004 sale of Mariner Health Care for $1.05 billion to National Senior Care (both Alliance members). Shortly after the sale, Mariner's assets were sold to cover the transaction costs of the deal. This reduced the value of Mariner to $12 million. Critics are worried about the safety of residents under such conditions in which facility operating licenses (which are regulated) are legally disaggregated from the property ownership that is not even subjected to background checks of financial solvency or corporate responsibility (Ladd, 2005).

At the state level, Texas provides a good example of the political power exercised by the large stakeholder value chains. In the early 2000s, as part of the Alliances' campaign to restrict nursing home firms' liability to consumer litigation, a grand jury investigation held that the Alliance was the largest single contributor to a web of Republican party affiliates that were indicted for breaking political fundraising laws (Smith, 2005). After the Republican Party's election victory, nursing home liability was capped in Texas and, as hoped by the Alliance, this became a model for other states such as Mississippi, after Haley Barbour became governor (Ladd, 2005).

DISCUSSION AND CONCLUSION

This chapter has illustrated how Leca and Naccache's (2006) critical realist model provides a basis from which to develop accounts of institutional change in organizational fields that address the problems of conflation within institutional theory, and the uncritical orthodoxy of healthcare organizational research. The application of the model reported here shows how institutional entrepreneurs (corporations such as Sun) strategically used an institutional logic (shareholder value) to help create a new archetype (large chain) within a specified organizational field (US nursing homes). The present research provides an extension of the initial framework. While Leca and Naccache considered a new organization's use of a very broad logic widely diffused in contemporary societies, in our case there are two logics: one traditional which is much more limited in its diffusion—the logic of locally-based care under professional control; and one that was widely diffused outside the focal field, the shareholder value logic. Hence, this chapter contributes to the ongoing articulation between the existing research and the critical realist approach of institutionalism.

Following a critical realist framework, we identified five causal powers associated with the institutional logic of shareholder value and the way it unfolded in the specific context of US nursing homes: rapid growth of large chains through debt-financed mergers, labor cost control through low nurse staffing levels, creative financing, viewing legal sanctions as a cost of business, and intense political activity. The fact that only the first three causal powers were identified from previous studies of stakeholder value in other settings underscores critical realists' assertion of the emergent and contingent nature of causal powers. It also provides valuable insights for further research on shareholder value in other contexts. In particular it demonstrates the imperative to examine the political strategies of corporations when driven by shareholder value logic (Barley, 2007). This remains an understudied domain as the uncritical orthodoxy in healthcare analysis focuses on market strategies. In taking a critical perspective, this analysis presents a counterpoint to assertions that "public policy needs to take advantage of the ability of nursing home chains to revitalize the for-profit sector" (Mitchell et al., 2001). In sharp contrast, this analysis poses serious questions about the relationship between the public good and the large nursing homes chains that operate under the logic of shareholder value to provide care to the some of the frailest and most vulnerable members of society.

While there have been increasing programmatic calls for critical realism to be applied within organization studies, there have been few published applications within institutional analyses of field dynamics. This chapter combined the two traditions within an analysis of issues of current concern to both including: the strategic use of field logics, embedded agency, and conflation (Townley, 2002; McKinley et al., 1999). For critical realist analyses of organizational fields, an important aspect of this model is the use of institutional theory to elaborate critical realisms' previously rather abstract notion of 'structures' to comprise higher-level field logics and their derived archetypes.

For institutional analysts of field dynamics, the primary contribution of the framework presented here is a basis for developing non-conflating accounts of the permanent interrelation between agency, institutions, and institutional logics. In ontological terms this arises from an unambiguous position in which the status of actors, structures and their permanent interrelation is recognized. From this basis, the framework proposes an alternative means of addressing the paradox of institutional embeddedness. In contrast to the sequential and disemebedded approaches critiqued earlier, this framework directs attention to the ways that institutional entrepreneurs strategically select from multiple field logics according to context, and to the interests and values of the other actors whose support they seek (Leca and Nacacche, 2006). Within studies of institutional change, further development of this approach could involve, for example, analyses of interplays between different field actors' use of institutional logics. In relation to the case of US nursing homes presented here, this could involve a study of the interplay between the use of shareholder value logic by corporate executives, care workers, and consumer groups. In that form analysis, the necessity for researchers to take a reflexive stance and look beyond actors' discourses might be aided by the use of combinations of the framing analyses used in some institutional work (Creed et al., 2002), and critical discourse analysis (Fleetwood, 2005).

Reflecting on this first critical realist analysis of institutional change in a healthcare field, three issues are worthy of consideration. First, the relatively short-term and outcome-oriented research that is encouraged by the main sponsors of health services research presents limited opportunity to collect the process data and conduct the analytical retroduction required by critical realism. Until greater support is given to detailed studies of process that are conducted at multiple levels of analysis, the potential for critical realist examinations of healthcare settings may be limited to secondary research and summaries of multiple studies. Second, to incorporate the framing and critical discourse analysis within critical realist studies of healthcare fields may require healthcare researchers to collaborate with experts in those procedures. Finally, while this study has underscored the imperative to develop critical analyses of healthcare settings, for researchers embedded within a field that is dominated by uncritical orthodoxy there are safer routes to research funding, publication, and career progression.

REFERENCES

Archer, M. 1995. *Realist social theory: The morphogenetic approach*. Cambridge, UK: Cambridge University Press.

Archer, M. 2002. Realism and the problem of agency. *Journal of Critical Realism* 5: 1–20.

Barley, S.R. 2007. Corporations, democracy, and the public good. *Journal of Management Inquiry* 16(3): 201–215.

Barley, S., and P. Tolbert. 1997. Institutionalization and structuration: Studying the links between action and institution. *Organization Studies* 18(1): 93–17.

Banaszak-Holl, J., W. Berta, D. Bowman, J.A.C. Baum, and W. Mitchell. 2002. The rise of human service chains: Antecedents to acquisitions and their effects on the quality of care in US nursing homes. *Managerial and Decision Economics* 23: 261–282.

Bazzoli, G., L. Dynan, L. Burns, and C. Yap, C. 2004. Two decades of organizational change in health care: What have we learned? Medical Care Research and Review 61: 247–331.

Bhaskar, R. 1979. *A realist theory of science*. Brighton, UK: Harvester.

Bhaskar, R. 1989. *The possibility of naturalism: A philosophical critique of the contemporary human science*. Atlantic Highlands, NJ: Humanities Press.

California Office of Statewide Health Planning and Development (COSHPD). 2000–2004. Long term care facility financial data for period. Annual nursing facility cost reports. Sacramento, CA: OSHPD.

Copelin, L. 2004. Craddick downplays $100,000 exchange. Texans for Public Justice. http://www.tpj.org/page_view.jsp?pageid=696&pf=1 (accessed November, 22, 05).

Creed, D., M. Scully, and J. Austin. 2002. Clothes make the person? The tailoring of legitmimating accounts and the social construction of identity. *Organization Science* 13(5): 475–496.

Davis, G. and S. Stout. 1992. Organization theory and the market for corporate control, 1980–1990. *Administrative Sceince Quarterly* 37: 605–633.

Davis, G. and T. Thompson. 1994. A social movement perspective on corporate control. *Administrative Science Quarterly* 39: 171–193.

DiMaggio, P. and W. Powell. 1983. The iron cage revisited: Institutional isomorphism and collective rationality in organizational fields. *American Sociological Review* 48: 147–60.

Ekstrom, M. 1992. Causal explanation of social action: The contribution of Max Weber and critical realism to a generative view of causal explanation in social science. *Acta Sociologica* 35: 107–122.

Emirbayer, M., and A. Mische. 1998. What is agency? *American Journal of Sociology* 103: 962–1023.

Estes, C. and E. Binney. 1993. Restructuring the nonprofit field. In *Long-term care crisis: Elders trapped in the no-care zone*, eds. C. Estes, J. Swan, and Associates, 22–40. Newbury Park, CA: Sage.

Fleetwood, S. 2005. Ontology in organization and management studies: A critical realist perspective. *Organization* 12(2): 197–222.

Fligstein, N. 2001. *The architecture of markets: An economic socioogy of twenty-first century capitalist societies*. Princeton, NJ: Princeton University Press.

Fligstein, N., and I. Mara-Drita. 1996. How to make a market: Reflections on the attempt to create a single market in the European Union. *American Journal of Sociology* 102: 1–33.

Fligstein, N., and T-J. Shin. 2006. Shareholder value and the transformation of American industries, 1984–2001. Department of Sociology, University of Berkeley, September.

Friedland, R., and R. Alford. 1991. Bringing society back in: Symbols, practices, and institutional contradictions. In *The new insitutionalism in organizational analysis*, eds. W. Powell and P. DiMaggio, 232–63. Chicago, IL: University of Chicago Press.

Greenwood, R. and C. R. Hinings. 1993. Understanding strategic change: The contribution of archetypes. *Academy of Management Journal* 36: 1052–81.

Hallock, K. 1998. Layoffs, top executive pay, and firm performance. *American Economic Review* 88(4): 711–723.

Holm, P. 1995. The dynamics of institutionalization: Transformation processes in Norwegian fisheries. *Administrative Science Quarterly* 40: 398–422.

Jepperson, R.L. 1991. Institutions, institutional effects and institutionalism. In *The new institutionalism in organizational analysis*, eds. W. Powell and P. DiMaggio, Pp. 143–163. Chicago, IL: University of Chicago Press.

Jensen, M. and W. Meckling. 1976. Theory of the firm: Managerial behavior, agency cost, and ownership structure. *Journal of Financial Economics* 3: 305–360.

Kamimura, A., J. Banaszak-Holl, W. Berta, J. Baum, C. Weigelt, and W. Mitchell. 2007. Do corporate chains affect quality of care in nursing homes? The role of corporate standardization. *Health Care Management Review* 32(2): 168–178.

Killean, E. 2004. Here comes the sun again. *McKnight's Long-Term Care News.* July 12, p. 4.

Kitchener, M. 2002. Mobilizing the logic of managerialism in professional fields: The case of academic health center mergers. *Organization Studies* 23(3): 391–420.

Kitchener M., and C. Harrington. 2004. US long-term care: A dialectic analysis of institutional dynamics. *Journal of Health and Social Behavior* 45 (extra issue): 87–101.

Kitchener, M., C. O'Neill, and C. Harrington. 2005. Chain reaction: An exploratory study of nursing home bankruptcy in California. *Journal of Aging and Social Policy.* 17(4): 19–35.

Kitchener, M., J. O'Meara, A. Brody, H. Lee and C. Harrington. 2008. Shareholder value and the performance of a large nursing home chain. *Health Services Research* 43(3): 1062–1084.

Laclau, E., and R. Bhaskar. 1998. Discourse theory vs. critical realism. *Journal of Critical Realism* 1(2): 9–14.

Ladd, D. 2005. Haley's unholy alliance. *Jackson Free Press.* October 18, p. 3.

Leca, B., and P. Naccache. 2006. A critical realist approach to institutional entrepreneurship. *Organization* 13(5): 627–651.

Lehman Brothers. 2004. *2004 health care facilities: Long-term care industry guidebook.* January 29. New York: Lehman Brothers.

Light, D. W. 1986. Corporate medicine for profit. *Scientific American* 225(6): 38–45.

Lorinc, J. 2003. Old report. *Business Magazine.* September 5.

Lounsbury, M. 2003. The problem of order revisited: Towards a more critical institutional perspective. In *Debating organizations,* eds. R. Westwood and S. Clegg, 210–219. Oxford: Blackwell.

Luke, R. D., and S. L. Walston. 2003. Strategy in an institutional environment. In *Advances in health care organization theory*, eds. S. Mick and M. Wyttenbach, 289–323. San Francisco: Jossey Bass.

McKinley, W., M. Mone, and G. Moon. 1999. Determinants and development of schools in organization theory. *Academy of Management Review* 24: 634–648.

McLean, B., and P. Elkind. 2003. *The smartest guys in the room.* New York: Penguin.

Mitchell, W., J. A. C. Baum, J. Banaszak-Holl, W. B. Berta, and D. Bowman. 2001. Opportunity and constraint: Chain-to component transfer learning in multi-unit chains. In *Strategic management of intellectual capital and organizational knowledge: A collection of reading*, eds. N. Bontis and C.W. Choo, 144–153. New York: Oxford University Press.

Mutch, A. 1999. Critical realism, managers, and information. *British Journal of Management,* 10: 323–333.

Nakhnikian, E. 2000. Sun founder announces intention to step down. *Postacute Payment Report.* July 14, p. 4.

Odenwald, A. 1996. Andy Turner wants the government out of health care, period. *New Mexico Business Journal.* 20(4): 10. Albuquerque, NM: Mountain.

O'Neill, C., C. Harrington, M. Kitchener, and D. Saliba. 2003. Quality of care in nursing homes: An analysis of the relationships among profit, quality and ownership. *Medical Care* 41(12): 1318–1330.

Reay, T., and C.R. Hinings. 2005. The recomposition of an organizational field: Health care in Alberta. *Organization Studies* 26(3): 351–384.

Reed, M. 1997. In praise of duality and dualism: Rethinking agency and structure in organizational analysis. *Organization Studies* 18(1): 21–42.

Sayer, A. 1992. *Method in social science.* London: Routledge.

Sayer, A. 2000. *Realism in social science.* London: Sage.

Seo, M.-G., and W. Creed. 2002. Institutional contradictions, praxis and institutional change: A dialectic perspective. *Academy of Management Review* 27(2): 222–247.

Scott, W. 1994. Conceptualizing organizational fields: Linking organizations and societal systems. In *Systemrationalitat und partialintereresse [systems rationality and partial interests]*, eds. M. Hans-Ulrich Derlien, M. Uta Gerhadt and F.W. Scharpf, 203–221. Baden-Baden: Nomos Verglagsgesellschaft.

Scott, W. R., M Ruef, P. Mendel, and C. Caronna. 2000. *Institutional change and healthcare organizations: From professional dominance to managed care.* Chicago, IL: University of Chicago Press.

Smith, R. J. 2005. Delay PAC is indicted for illegal donations. *Washington Post.* September 9, Section AO3.

Source Watch. (2005). Alliance for quality nursing home care. http://www.sourcwwatch.org/index.php?title=Alliance_for_Quality_Nursing_Home_Care (accessed November 22, 2005).

Sun Healthcare Group Inc. 1996–2006. Annual report form 10-K-A. Amended report filed with the US Securities and Exchange Commission, for the prior calendar year.

Thornton, P. H., and, W. Ocasio. 2008. Institutional logics. In *Handbook of institutional analysis*, eds. R. Greenwood, C. Oliver, K. Sahlin, and R. Suddaby, 99–129. Sage: London.

Townley, B. 2002. The role of competing rationalities in institutional change. *Academy of Management Journal* 45(1): 163–179.

Tsoukas, H. 1989. The validity of idiographic research explanations. *Academy of Management Review* 14(4): 551–561.

Tsoukas, H. 1994. What is management? An outline of a metatheory. *British Journal of Management* 5: 289–301.

US Congress. 1975. *Proprietary Home Health Care.* Testimony of Amitai Etzioni before Joint Hearing before the Sub-Committee on Long-term Care of the Special Committee on Aging United States Senate, October 28. Washington, DC: Government Printing Office.

US Centers for Medicare and Medicaid Services (US CMS), Scully, T. 2003. *Health Care Industry Market Update: Nursing Facilities.* Washington, DC: CMS, May 20.

US General Accounting Office (GAO). 1998. *California nursing homes: Care problems persist despite federal and state oversight.* Report to the Special Committee on Aging, US Senate. GAO/HEHS-98-202. Washington, DC: US GAO, July.

US General Accounting Office. 2000. *Nursing homes: Aggregate medicare payments are adequate despite bankruptcies.* Testimony before the Special Committee on Aging, US Senate. GAO/T-HEHS-00–192. Washington, DC: General Accounting Office, September 5.

US General Accounting Office. 2002. *Skilled nursing facilities: Medicare payments exceed costs for most but not all facilities*. Report to congressional requestors. GAO/HEHS-03–183. Washington, DC: General Accounting Office, December.

US Office of the Inspector General (US OIG). 2001. *Corporate integrity agreement between the office of the Inspector General of the Department of Health and Human Services and Sun Healthcare Group, Inc.* Washington, DC: OIG, July 12.

Vladeck, B. 1980. *Unloving care: The nursing home tragedy*. New York: Basic Books.

Westphal, J. and E. Zajac. 2001. Decoupling policy from practice: The case of stock repurchase programs. *Administrative Science Quarterly* 46(2): 202–228.

Wisconsin Board on Aging and Long-Term Care. 2003. *Nursing homes and public policy*. Madison, WI: Wisconsin Board on Aging and Long-Term Care.

Zorn, D.F., F. Dobbin, J. Dierkes, and M. Kwok. 2005. Managing investors: How financial markets shaped the American firm." In *The sociology of financial markets*, eds. K. Knorr Cetina and A. Preda, 269–289. London: Oxford University Press.

Part III

Radical Alternatives

10 Critical Leadership Theorizing and Local Government Practice

Jackie Ford

INTRODUCTION

This chapter seeks to develop a more critical approach to researching, conceptualizing, and practicing leadership in organizations by drawing on feminist poststructuralist perspectives in an exploration of leaders and leadership in local government. Central to this more critical approach is the impact of contextual and social factors; the recognized partiality of accounts of leadership and an understanding of the complexity and intertwining of selves within work settings. This study seeks to add to the emergent theoretical and more critical debate about the lives and experiences of managers charged with the tasks of leadership in organizations, and aims to contribute to the field in two fundamental ways. Firstly, it seeks to develop a more critical approach to the study of leadership, one that is informed by an exploration of biographical narratives and interpretations of these narratives that enable an examination of gendered understandings of the selves that these managers portray. Secondly, it seeks to use ideas informed by feminist poststructural theories to explore the taken for granted assumptions and asymmetries that belie mainstream literature within this field.

THE LEADERSHIP CONTEXT

Contemporary writings on the subject of leaders and leadership refer to the burgeoning interest in both management literature and organizational policy in leadership and (to a lesser extent) on management as the means through which to enhance organizational performance in contemporary organizations (see, for example, Ford, 2007; Grint, 2000, 2005; Jackson and Parry, 2008; Sinclair, 2005). This interest is underpinned by the rising faith in the United Kingdom in leadership as a salvation to organizational struggles not only within the private sector, but also within the public sector more generally, across education (in schools and in universities), criminal justice and central government, as well as in health and local government organizations.

Since the mid-1990s, writers have depicted the emergence of a softer focussed 'New Public Management' agenda of government. Pollitt (2003, 52) describes this shift as a move away from a tough and performance-oriented model and towards a 'good neighbour' approach. This accords with the 'modernization' agenda that was introduced via Blair's 1999 white paper 'Modernising Government' (CM 4310, 1999) and has been translated into the development of models and approaches to leadership that seek to deliver this call for modernization. It has also led to the creation of a plethora of units dedicated to develop leadership initiatives. In line with such proposals, the Council for Excellence in Management and Leadership was founded in April 2000 with the remit of developing a strategy "to ensure that the UK has the managers and leaders of the future to match the best in the world" (Council for Excellence, 2002, 1).

In the National Health Service (NHS) this has been reflected in the creation, in 2001, of a Leadership Centre within the Department of Health's Modernisation Agency[1] and the subsequent development of a core set of NHS leadership qualities that sought to "set the standards for outstanding leadership in the NHS . . . which can be used to assess both individual and organizational leadership capacity and capability" (DH, 2002, 1). Central government initiatives include substantial investment in leadership development and the establishment of online resources and discussion groups that seek to promote better leadership and management in the public services. In local government, the Leadership Development Commission was established in 2002 to develop a national leadership strategy, together with 'an emerging strategy for leadership development' in 2004. This strategy has the stated aims of providing:

> A framework which will stimulate leadership development at the individual, team, local authority and national levels. It puts forward priorities that will enable leadership development within and across the sector as a whole . . . (Leadership Development Commission, 2004, 3).

This framework and set of priorities led to the launch, in mid 2004, of the Leadership Centre of Local Government, with a remit and associated resources to improve the quality of leadership in councils in England.

What has been evident in these investments and through the rising volumes of literature is the increasing confidence placed in leadership research and its development within organizational practice, and a growing belief that it will provide the means through which to ensure the long-term survival of our organizations. This apparent confidence in leadership appears to rest on a number of assumptions, the first of which is that it can be seen as a cure to the shortcomings of existing organizations generally, and managers more specifically within public services. A second assumption relates to the notion that without effective leaders, the people working within these organizations will lack direction, motivation, and inspiration. A third assumption is that leaders are rare, distant, and particularly talented individuals, and in order to try to increase the volume of such talents, special programs of development need to be created. Through such initiatives and assumptions, leadership has certainly become an authoritative discourse both in the academic literature and in organizational practice and as a consequence, it is too important to ignore, even though its definition remains unstable (Collinson and Grint, 2005; Sinclair, 2005).

A proliferation of research and publications in the field of leadership bears witness to this turn to leadership, yet as this chapter will show, despite this explosion in volume, four fundamental deficiencies are striking: the lack of clarity as to a common understanding of the concept; the lack of attention to asymmetries of power in the generally uncritical accounts; the assumed gender neutrality which belies an androcentric bias within hegemonic discourses of leadership; and the tendency to ignore complex notions of narratives of the self that warrant further attention and exploration. With a few notable exceptions, there remains a dearth of critical management and/ or qualitatively informed study within the field of leadership research and practice. The research study explored in the next section aims to address these shortcomings through an in-depth qualitative study of the biographical narratives of managers within a local government organization. The chapter is structured into four main sections. The first reviews some of the literature on men and women in organizations in a search for understanding of hegemonic discourses of gender. The second section explores the rationale for a feminist poststructuralist critique of leaders and leadership. This is followed by empirical evidence from a study of the working lives of managers within a local government organization and the final section seeks to draw conclusions and implications for the future in terms of conceptualizing, researching, and practicing leadership.

THE LITERATURE

Given the exponential explosion of literature on the topics of leaders and leadership in recent years, it would be impossible (and probably extremely dull) to attempt to present a summary and overview of the taxonomies and models exploring the transition in leadership thought. This chore has been completed admirably by a number of writers in the organization studies field and those readers interested in such reviews of the literature could find many such accounts in standard management and organizational behavior textbooks (see, for example, thorough overviews in Huczynski and Buchanan, 2007; Knights and Willmott, 2007; Linstead et al., 2004).

Rather than focus on that body of knowledge, I will instead summarize the attempts within the women in management literature to address what has been identified as the inadequate treatment of gender in leadership theorizing. Brewis and Linstead (2004, 57) categorize a range of competing perspectives on gender and its relationship to organizational theorizing. These are depicted as the *liberal feminist, radical feminist, diversity, gender in management*, and *gendering management* approaches. It is the *gender in management* approach that is most applicable to a discussion of leadership, for the majority of feminist research and theorizing in leadership is undertaken from this standpoint. Writers such as Judy Rosener (1990, 1997) argue that because men and women are socialized differently, they also manage differently. Rosener's (1990) research, subsequently developed by other writers in the United States (Denmark, 1993) and the United Kingdom (Alimo-Metcalfe, 1995) has suggested that women's style of leadership differs from that of men; that women are more likely to adopt transformational approaches which are perceived as being of greater significance in present-day organizations. Men, on the other hand, are more likely to describe themselves in ways consistent with transactional leadership behaviors, in exchange relationships in which punishment and reward are seen as prime motivators. This approach has concentrated more on how women's skills have been undervalued by placing emphasis on their (perceived) nurturing and supportive qualities and calling for an increase in the number of women managers and feminine leadership styles. As such, this prescriptive analysis can be seen as either blaming women for not being like men or for essentializing women's differences from men (Calas and Smircich, 1991, 1992). Theorizing in leadership and much of the research seems to signify that there are considerable pressures to conform to stereotypes and current fads and fashions in relation to what is perceived to be effective management and leadership in contemporary organizations (Linstead et al., 2004), and such pressures will include those of conforming to the expected gendered behaviors.

This perspective, that presumes distinct differences between men and women, has also focused on leadership as a male practice. The whole notion of leadership is arguably constructed through the leader–follower pairing, with the followers being the (subordinated) other to the leader's (dominant) position, a pairing that is informed by masculinity. In explorations of management cultures, researchers have identified a range of masculinities that are articulated and performed in organizations. Collinson and Hearn's (1994) research highlighted several subcultures associated with masculinities, which include *authoritarian, paternalistic, entrepreneurial, informal,* and *careerist*. Building on this work, Maddock and Parkin (1993) depict further masculinist cultures in which the subordination of women is concealed. They portray a 'smart macho' culture, which is motivated by highly competitive behaviors, where managers condemn those who cannot work at the same pace. Behaviors observable within this approach include a commitment to working long hours and displaying aggressive and competitive behaviors in which men are privileged as the objects of leadership and the operators of the tools of leadership (Sinclair, 1998). Judy Wajcman's study of management in five male-dominated multi-national corporations concluded that 'macho management' and traditional managerial hierarchies were still very much part of the organizational landscape, sustained by a culture of fear and uncertainty that was generated by continuous change. Wacjman argues that:

> The business context of almost continuous restructuring and job losses has greatly intensified pressures for senior managers and means that insecurity about the future is pervasive . . . The logic of survival results in heightened individualistic competition for a dwindling number of job opportunities. In this economic climate, both men and women feel the need to conform to the male stereotype of management because it is still, in practice, the only one regarded as effective (Wacjman, 1996, 345).

Wacjman is describing the material sense of job insecurity generated by prevailing economic conditions that affect the masculine practices of managers in her study.

Drawing on the poststructuralist and symbolic terms I use in my own research, I would suggest that it is not just that men and women conform to a stereotype but that the discourses of leadership offer only masculine subject positions which all managers occupy. I will show later that the smart macho cultures and discourses are central to the culture of the organization I describe in this chapter, and these cultures and discourses have become absorbed into the managers' identities as macho-leaders. As I have argued elsewhere (Ford, 2006) it is evident from critical feminist studies that (perceived) charismatic and masculine models of leadership are still featuring heavily in our organizational analyses whereby the macho, individualistic, assertive, and dominant behaviors continue to take precedence over what are regarded as the more feminine qualities such as empathy, capacity for listening, relational skills, and so on. Where the rhetoric of a more 'feminine' set of approaches is suggested, such as within post-heroic discourse, these have yet to be translated into practice (Fletcher, 2004). This can be witnessed by the target-driven, financially-motivated performance measurements that continue to dominate current assessment arrangements in UK public service organizations.

Where the vast literature on leadership presumes a homogeneous identity for the leader, gender theory helps demonstrate that there is no such homogeneity. The study I discuss here shows that the managers brought to light the coexistence within their discourses and reported managerial practices of both macho and post-heroic leadership approaches. Understandings of leadership and heroic masculinity have been so closely interwoven as to be both invisible and indivisible. Leadership theories have "pretended gender neutrality or displayed gender blindness but have inevitably imported male values and characteristics as the norm, and have been 'phallocentric'—viewing the world implicitly from a masculine point of view" (Fulop et al., 2004, 353). This privileging of men and masculinity is apparent and yet frequently unreported within management texts and practices and appears especially to be the case when leadership behavior is examined within organizational settings. Leadership discourses can thus be seen as a mechanism for masculine domination and not the neutral, objective, and unproblematic approaches that mainstream literature may suggest (Calas and Smircich, 1992; Collinson and Hearn, 1994; Fletcher, 2004; Fondas, 1997).

As explored later, analysis of the biographical narratives of these managers show how they experience anxiety when they try to extract themselves from these identities,[2] especially at a time when the rate and pace of change within local government organizations in recent years has given greater impetus to notions of heightened competition, job insecurity, and fear (Webb, 2001).

RATIONALE FOR MORE CRITICAL
DISCOURSES OF LEADERSHIP

Conducting research from critical management studies perspectives broadly and from a feminist poststructuralist perspective particularly provides opportunities to reconsider the dominant discourses and approaches to leadership. Hegemonic discourses about leadership are understood to involve strong elements of masculinity that act to strengthen male identities and thereby reproduce asymmetrical gender relations in organizational life. Connotations of leadership in the literature frequently take the form of the masculine competitive, aggressive, controlling, and self-reliant individualist and thus the question as to whether leadership is crucial in our organizations may hinge on whether we perceive a need to continue to support notions of aggressive, manipulative, logical, masculine practices. A more critical and reflexive approach to the study of leadership is needed, which pays attention to situations, events, institutions, ideas, social practices, and processes that may be seen as exercising a surplus repression of those involved as leaders. More specifically, a feminist poststructuralist approach offers a theoretical basis for analyzing the subjectivities of men and women in relation to language, other cultural practices, and the material conditions of their lives (Gavey, 1997). Drawing on this approach in my own research meant that fresh light could be shed on leadership theories. The whole sense and notion of leadership itself is both historical and subject to change, and thus universal theories on leadership are open to challenge and debate.

Feminist poststructuralist approaches have been influential in accentuating the significance of the multiple, contradictory, and fragmentary nature of subjectivity and the kaleidoscopic strands of identity open to individuals (Collinson, 2003; Kondo, 1990). They enable explorations of new, local, qualitatively informed, and contemporary analyses of leadership in organization studies in ways that mainstream (predominantly survey-based and large-scale) studies have neglected. Adopting a poststructuralist perspective encourages an analysis of the ongoing and relational acts between people, which adds a subjective counterpoint to the dominant objectivist leadership discourse. Acquiring a cultural understanding of leadership requires us to be more aware of local sense-making and meaning. A social, local, and contextually aware interpretation of leadership encourages greater recognition of what leadership means within the specific community that is using the term—at organizational, departmental, team, or individual levels.

THE RESEARCH

This study is drawn from a larger research project that sought to explore how discourses of leadership are to be found in the day-to-day biographical narratives of those in managerial roles in the council studied. In-depth interviews were conducted with twenty-five male and female managers from across the council, and the narrative data for this chapter draws from that sample. I also worked, as part of the larger study, as a development consultant with the organization and my field notes are data gathered during these opportunities for observation. Interview transcripts were analysed through close reading and rereading, resulting in the emergence of several related discursive themes that were drawn on repeatedly by the managers involved. As explored elsewhere (Ford, 2006, 2007) numerous and shifting subject positions are identifiable, as respondents drew on different, often competing, and at times contradictory discourses to construct and describe their working lives.

Analogous with Thomas and Davies (2005) and Watson's (2001) findings, there is much fluidity and multiplicity of subject positions in this study, around discourses of leadership but also around other significant projects of the (managerial) self. There are clear indications within the transcripts of both collision and slippage within and between the ways the managers constructed and depicted themselves, of the contradictory and fragmented discourses of leadership, as well as other projects of the self, including the notion of striking a balance between work and out of work issues.

A number of major themes emerged from the transcripts and discussions with managers associated with work and out of work issues, depicted as long hours working, managerial work rituals, work addiction, work supremacy, and contradictory narratives, and these are explored in some detail elsewhere (Ford, 2006, 2007). The focus of this section is the hegemonic leadership discourses that managers drew on for their leadership identities.

Leadership Discourses and the Working Lives of Managers

In relation to leadership discourses, Bresnen (1995) describes ways in which managers carry their own implicit leadership theories that inform their view of what leadership does or should entail and also of what leadership styles work best in different circumstances. In similar ways to findings reported later, the particular interpretation placed on leadership is an individualistic one that is influenced by individual's narratives of the self and informed by a wider range of experiences, including exposure to leadership development programs (Ford, 2005, 2007; Ford and Harding, 2007) and the contemporary discourses of leadership that are promulgated through the literature and through management educators and gurus. Within the interview transcripts, there is coexistence of both consistency and diversity of perspectives on leadership. In relation to people's sense of identity and the leadership discourses, shifting, contradictory and multiple discourses were discernable, which were at once compelling and coercive, fluid and constraining. These individuals had to construct themselves through ambiguity of meaning of leadership. Managers were seen to adopt the language of two discernibly different discourses of leadership that were evident in the transcripts of the managers within my study. These can be depicted as *macho* and *post-heroic* leadership discourses, and are explored next.

Macho discourses

This macho perspective seems to draw from hegemonic masculinist discourses of leadership that depict leaders who are competitive, controlling, and self-reliant individualists.

The following analysis shows how the managers in this study appear to adopt the language and rhetoric of one approach to leadership (the post-heroic approach) while at the same time practicing a macho approach, and the considerable tension and anxiety that also features within the narratives.

Stuart is a director of a corporate support function. Our discussions and his overall aim appeared to be one of presenting a post-heroic leadership approach in relation to his team and yet that does not appear to be his practiced leadership style. He suggests that on a day-to-day basis, his approach tends much towards the macho approach:

> I'm not giving much attention to [the team] because I've more or less drifted off . . . I'm so tied up in the corporate agendas now and fighting all the battles there. Em . . . so I'm less engaged with my staff than I ever have been individually, . . . any actual work that's going on with people on development is happening lower down the food chain, and I'm not really engaged with. I suspect there's not enough of it going on, but er . . . but again, we're a processed organization and a task focussed organization so . . . not a lot of time for that stuff . . .

This separation and disengagement with his staff appears to reflect his lack of interest in working more closely with colleagues in his team. These contradictions and collisions of leadership discourses and identities continue in Robert's account (another senior manager but this time of a front-line service directorate). Robert's transcripts reflect his dissonance in relation to his leadership role and these are reflected in his depictions of his accounts of the 'chastening experiences' in the recent past that have given him opportunities to reflect on his leadership practice. He describes how his previous personal assistant drew his attention to the deleterious impact of his approach to his management team and how staff would avoid face-to-face contact, preferring to engage with the personal assistant and asking her to "just slip him that piece of paper, don't tell him I'm here." He further depicts his concern at the negative experiences of staff with his former employer and this alerted him to the negative consequences of such an approach:

> . . . the organization I was then working for didn't actually care about people, if the truth was known, so if it needed to take someone out, it took them out and I saw that happen and I thought that could happen to me.

His reflections on these experiences caused him to note that he risked repeating these very same unhelpful practices in his own work. This was further exemplified in Sean's transcript, in which he argues that senior management (and he includes himself in this definition) are frequently portrayed as remote, judgemental, and transactional-focused: "do you know that one thing about senior management . . . you know you fly and squawk and shit on them, and that's the only time they ever see top management."

The accounts of these managers highlight how the dominant leadership discourse within the organization reproduces a traditional macho-management identity and practice. While the male directors sought to distance themselves from this dominant discourse, at the same time their accounts also reveal various ways in which this dominant discourse features not only as part of their own sense of who they are as managers in the organization, but also how these different leadership and organizational discourses compete with one another.

Similar discourses of macho management cultures were observable from the transcripts of both middle level managers (service heads) and front-line (principal and senior) officers. Timothy has been working as a service head for the last ten years. He depicted his approach to leadership as one that recognized the need to support and encourage staff and yet reflected that this was something he had not paid much attention to in recent years. He recognized that there was a danger of becoming so embroiled in dealing with the day-to-day pressures and demands of the job that there's a risk of neglecting the personal and interpersonal relationships. He argued that "you get so entrenched in where you . . . you have to be and the job you have to do that you tend to forget about everything else."

In a related way, Jim (a principal officer in the council) identified some of the tensions between promulgating a so-called transformational leadership style that was currently being promoted within the council and a highly effective and yet autocratic style and approach of an earlier era. He referred back to leadership behaviors of managerial colleagues with whom he had worked in the past, and notably a former boss, who he goes on to identify as highly domineering:

> So, transformational leadership . . . we didn't do transformational leadership back in [former name of organization] days, but we did do the . . . we did a leadership style—an American leadership style, which I can never remember the name of erm . . . which was very good and actually developed ideas about leadership and vision erm . . . and performance so, he was really . . . he was a great leader, yes, but, in terms of the transformational leadership program, talking about caring for your staff being 60% of the . . . something . . . importance in terms of how successful that would be with your staff—that wasn't how he operated and yet, he got significant results, so it's quite intriguing. I've other people who have not inspired me at all and that's because they were probably er . . . technocrats who'd been promoted to a level . . . one level beyond their capabilities.

Jim described how this manager was highly autocratic, "brilliant in setting direction and had a fabulous knowledge of the organization . . . but basically didn't give a toss about his staff, a very hard face . . . was a bit of a bully." This exalted manager returned at various points within Jim's transcript, especially as an exemplar in comparison to the 'useless' senior managers left within the council. He expressed a high disregard for the council's current managers, suggesting that "genuinely, I couldn't name anybody else in the authority who I would, in the last twenty years . . . who would inspire me" adding: "there's nobody at a more senior management to me that I regard as a leader."[3] Jim did actually refer to one other autocratic and uncaring leader who had left the council some years ago, and spoke in glowing terms of the successes he achieved. The sense gleaned from this discourse was one of confusion and contradiction. On the one hand, Jim argued in favor of so-called transformational (or post-heroic approaches) to leadership and caring for staff (which he claimed to be passionate about), and, on the other, he argued that the most effective leaders he has worked with were two men who were not only highly autocratic, but had no interest in the staff for whom they were responsible.

Jim refers back with nostalgia to better times within the council ten or more years ago, and this theme is also present within both Dorothy's and Jane's interview transcript. Jane has been employed within the council for the last twenty-eight years, and is a junior level manager within the training and development function. She recounts the pleasures and freedoms of designing training and education programs in the 1990s and earlier, and feels that in the last decade there has been a greater centralization of service provision and a concomitant poorer quality of delivery to the directorates. This resonates with Dorothy's experiences of twenty years ago in the council, when "we piloted programmes for the LGMB[4] at the time, particularly around personal and group effectiveness, all that's gone [. . .] you know it's gone, I still meet people who say it's the best course I ever went on and it's twenty years ago." Both Dorothy (a junior manager in a support function) and Jane depict a culture of high turnover of managers and an oscillation each time a new manager is appointed, with some progress forward, followed by several backward steps when the post holder moves on. As Jane argued: "it's felt like we've been going backwards and forwards—never getting back to the things we did manage to achieve in the 80s and 90s." She also describes the style of manager within their service group as being highly traditional:

> We seem to have had, within our own function; we seem to have had managers who've been more transactional rather than transformational—quite authoritative in some ways.

In further support of this, she presents an account of the macho-management approach of senior managers within the council, stating that the "nature of a lot of senior management who are quite erm . . . transactional and autocratic," then later in her transcript she suggests that "I suppose talking through this has made me realise that we haven't got that many transformational leaders in the council." She compares this with different behaviors of middle and more junior grades of managers:

> People at our level in the organization which is, like, junior to middle management are quite happy to meet and get things done and make changes and what it is about them up there erm . . . that they seem unwilling to share information to erm . . . share ideas, to work cooperatively, you know and they were talking about how they are in their silos, so they came from different parts of the organization, erm . . . but looking up they all had the same view that there's this silo mentality and, for some reason, the senior managers aren't open to that . . . that sharing and cooperative working, but i . . . it does still seems to be there at lower levels in the organization.

Senior managers are therefore presented as the last bastions of a more old-fashioned, traditional and macho approach to management, and also as individuals who are preventing the accomplishment of change and more cross-functional ways of working. By the same token, more junior managers perceive themselves and their colleagues as far more amenable to new ideas and approaches. However, Jane presents some worrying issues associated with this, as the lack of freedoms that are being enforced upon the middle and more junior managers is having the effect of undermining their confidence in their abilities to perform their managerial roles:

> So in the past, if I'd been working on particular projects, I would've gone to council management board with something, got approval, gone away and implemented it or I would've gone to . . . visit the chief exec's management board erm . . . on a regular basis. Erm . . . and then I was told "Ooh, no. You're only a senior. Only heads of service can do this and only principals can do that. Very narrow, rigid view . . . way of looking at things, so I was excluded from a lot of arenas erm . . . and I got told "Oh, erm . . . you . . . you can't do this." Meaning: "It's not your role or level in the organization to do this, but then, the effect of that long term can be, erm . . . I start thinking "I can't do this."

Jane suggests that the very fact of being excluded from discussions with more senior colleagues is leaving many managers at her level with doubts as to their competence to fulfill more demanding tasks. By the same token, these middle-level managers are seeing in themselves the qualities required of post-heroic leaders, and it is to this discourse that we now turn.

Post-heroic leadership discourses

The discourse on leadership that emerged from the transcripts that ran counter to the macho discourse was that summed up by post-heroic leadership, which was described as a feminine approach to leadership in which more relational, local, and shared understanding of leadership and its functions emerged in the organization. In the transcripts for the directors, the managers claimed a leadership identity as one more akin to a post-heroic approach and yet they argued vehemently that more senior management lacked such approaches in their behaviors. Post-heroic leadership discourses were depicted as at odds with the more traditional approaches to leadership that privilege individual male leaders, hegemonic masculinity, and hierarchical notions of power (represented in the foregoing macho discourses). In its place, post-heroic discourses present a more connected and team-focused identity in which the leader asserts the importance of making links with staff and showing a genuine interest in what they do.

By way of illustration, Trudie (a director of one of the front line services within the council) describes how she undertakes her work "in a hands-on way, so I went out all the time looking at services and talking to front-line managers and people using the services and whatever" to such an extent that she perceived "I was actually often the only person in the room [of senior managers] who'd talked to the people delivering the services." She depicts a model of shared leadership that is more akin to post-heroic leadership discourses, and yet what she presents in her accounts is the premium placed on masculine behaviors as the way to succeed as a director. She claims a dislike of the macho approach and yet finds it highly successful as a style to adopt in practice. She described how she had tried to use more relational and feminine behaviors in her meetings with a group of four peers with whom she worked, who were external to the council. After several months of adopting these behaviors, she perceived that she was making no progress in the discussions at all, and therefore switched her approach to a more macho one:

> I'd already decided that in certain areas we weren't really gonna get anywhere, (. . .) so we basically decided, push against open doors, do things on the ground and, basically, work round people, rather than through them and that was the sort of tactic erm. . . ¦ and as part of that, I took the role, which was, you know, every now and then, chuck my weight about and be arrogant.

This resonates with the findings from Fletcher's (2004) research, in which she indicated that the failure of the so-called female advantage depicted in Rosener and others' accounts is not necessarily owing to institutional sexism and bias. She believes that it is best understood by looking at power dynamics so as to see how femininity and notions of relational practices are played out at work. Notably, descriptions of the behavior, skills, and organizational contexts associated with post-heroic leadership are somehow presented as gender-neutral in practice, as though the organization, individuals, history, and gender are all irrelevant. This concurs with Fiske and Taylor (1991) who argue that the interpretation of events is "always contextual and is influenced by many factors including the social identity (sex, race, class, organizational title, etc.) of the actor as well as the observer" (Fiske and Taylor, cited in Fletcher, 2004, 654). Fletcher also cites Valian's work (654) in which it is suggested that gender filters on behavior are especially significant and therefore the experience of putting into practice post-heroic leadership is likely to be different for women and men. For example, men who adopt behaviors associated with post-heroic leadership may be seen to be doing something new and these behaviors are therefore accepted. Women may have more difficulties in distinguishing what they do as separate from what women are perceived as doing anyway. In relation to my research, this was brought home to me by Trudie's comments in relation to her perceived failures at adopting what she perceived as post-heroic leadership approaches. Fletcher argues that these practices by women could be construed as the invisibility act of relational behavior that suggests not calling attention to what is being done. Following this argument, when women 'intentionally' adopt post-heroic leadership behaviors, they are misconstrued and so the reciprocity embedded in post-heroic practice is rendered invisible. As Fletcher argues:

Women are expected to teach, enable and empower others without getting anything in return, expected to work interdependently while others do not adopt a similar stance, expected to work mutually in non-mutual situations and expected to practice less hierarchical forms of interacting even in traditionally hierarchical contexts (2004, 654).

This may help to explain why women are not as visible as we may expect. However, I would suggest that Fletcher's critique does not go far enough. It still oversimplifies and essentializes the differences between men and women, and presents something of the stereotypical theories in relation to gender and leadership studies. The narratives of these managers present considerably more complex and contradictory accounts, as I will explore further next.

Tensions and Oscillations in Leadership Practices

The tensions and oscillations were palpable in the transcripts and discussions with the managers. Robert was anxious to present an impression of his availability and accessibility to frontline workers:

One of the things that I attempt to do within the department is to be . . . is to . . . make sure that . . . em . . . there's not a sort of hierarchy, particularly with the manual workers, but you know like, they can come and talk to me and I can talk to them, and I don't do that in any demeaning way, I don't 'f and blind' to do it, but equally I don't want there to be any false barriers in the organization.

He refers back to the personal feedback he received from the leadership development program during which his staff reported that he was not sufficiently visible and available to them, which seemed to be at odds with the narrative of his leadership approach that is depicted in the previous excerpt. Robert's various narratives of himself, as a post-heroic leader who heads up the directorate, as an impatient manager wanting to effect changes more quickly, as the parent of a chronically ill child, all compete in his daily work and surface at different points in his narratives. Robert claims to be a post-heroic leader, and yet his team of staff remain in fear of him, as I depicted earlier in describing the chastening experiences of the lengths his staff would go to avoid face to face encounters with him. This further illustrates ways in which the managers adopt the rhetoric of post-heroic leadership while retaining the practice of macho approaches.

Analogous contradictions and tensions are evident in Alec's depiction of what he describes as an alternative approach to leadership, which he believes has emerged in recent policy diktats within the council within which there is "far more attention being paid to people's working environment and life." He voiced frustration at the tension between these subject positions, where he was feeling compelled—given the council's policies and strategy to adopt a more participative and facilitative approach rather than the (favored) command and control style that was more prevalent two or three decades ago. He describes how he has had to adapt his own approach in recent years, adding that:

> you can't instruct people to do things for you almost like people have got to be wanting to do it and you've got to manage in a way that people want to do it for their own personal satisfaction rather than being told to do it and then reluctantly doing it, because you're paying 'em.

There appears within these senior managers' accounts a desire to endorse the post-heroic discourse of a connected, feminine, and collective approach to leadership, and yet they present some reluctance, as well as oscillatory discourses and tensions in their reported practice. The continuing faith in macho discourses of leadership practice serves to illustrate much opposition in the managers' accounts of their narrative selves. These tensions emerge in both the transcripts and in my reflexive notes associated with the interviews. Part of the anxiety created appears to be associated with what Brewis and Linstead (2004) have identified as a hidden fear at the heart of managers who continue to acknowledge a preference for more macho management and leadership practices. On the one hand, this way of managing provides affirmation and security, as this masculine approach is still deemed to be representative of modern management (Kerfoot, 2000). On the other hand, sustaining this identity can in itself be an exhausting project on which individuals constantly have to work to demonstrate their abilities to expand, affirm, and maintain managerial control. Despite these tensions, research evidence affirms that striving to identify with this form of masculinity is likely to lead to employment security and material success. Put in this way, masculinity "is as seductive as it is anxiety making" (Brewis and Linstead, 2004, 79). They assert that both men and women managers in organizations are likely to be motivated to identify with masculinity, and to be "seduced by a masculinist way of being" (Whitehead, 1999, 27). Contemporary work organizations continue to encourage and nurture masculine ways of behaving and of presenting oneself as a manager.

I am not advocating here that managers adopt more 'feminine' leadership styles. Brewis and Linstead (2004, 81) urge caution in the adoption of more feminised working behaviors. They suggest that moving to a more engaged, relational, and connected approach by managers could lead to a "colonisation of the feminine with the result of *reinforcing* the edifice of maculinism." What I am doing at this point is revealing the tensions and anxieties that emerge when a 'macho, masculine' culture attempts to incorporate a 'feminine' leadership style.

One reading of the experiences of managers working in this organization case study is that there is an adoption of the language and rhetoric of post-heroic approaches, while retaining the practice of macho approaches. However, this reading does not appear to be able to explain adequately the degree of dissonance experienced by these managers—something else is going on, in as much as most of the managers within the study are reporting the coexistence within their own practices of macho and post-heroic discourses. Post-heroic models of leadership are in direct conflict with the macho leadership styles that many of these managers are arguably still practicing, and this is creating levels of conflict and anxiety. What emerges from the analysis of the transcripts is the anxiety (in a psychodynamic sense) aroused in managers who are charged with the impossible task of doing one form of leadership (a more post-heroic approach) in a context in which only another form of leadership (a macho approach) is possible.

CONCLUSIONS

These two dominant discourses of leadership discernible from the discussions with managers are examples of the implicit and explicit leadership theories carried around by managers. These tend to be highly varied and complex such that functionalist understandings such as situational and contingency models do not do them justice. It is therefore important to explore in depth the diverse effects of different social experiences and contexts that influence how leadership is conceptualized and practiced. Functionalist perspectives of leadership effectively ignore the impact of broader social relations in their consideration of the complexity of interpretations of leadership. What is increasingly significant is the need to consider the multiplicity of meanings attached to the concept of leadership and the way that the role of subjectivity and agency are underplayed (Bresnen, 1995).

What is emerging is that there are two dominant discourses, but these are asymmetrical. Macho discourses are clearly still ascendant, and there is little evidence of post-heroic approaches occurring in practice. This suggests that in studies of leadership, power and control are also relevant as well as discourse and identity. What these managers are depicting is the coexistence of competing and contradictory discourses of leadership (in symbolic senses) to the extent that considerable anxiety, fear and insecurity are experienced (in material senses). These levels of anxiety, insecurity, and fear cannot be analyzed through discourse theory alone.

Rather than the dominant leadership discourses forming the managers' subjectivities, these compete as sources of power among a number of other discourses or identities, including life outside work, gendered differences and approaches and differing career patterns that warrant further research and analysis. The interplay between the dominant discourses of leadership (notably between more traditional command/control or so-called macho approaches and more recently depicted distributive or post-heroic discourses) as well as the influence on subjectivities from other narratives such as career discourses and social/family discourse creates a multiplicity of subject positions, both within one individual and across a number of individuals. In certain respects all these discourses are in conflict, intersecting and contradicting each other. The organizational discourses of macho and post-heroic leadership compete with other organizational and personal discourses.

Understanding leadership calls not only for the consideration of social processes and cultural context. Researching, conceptualizing, and practicing leadership has become confusing, as practice within organizations lags behind developments in theory, so organizations are still informed by what academia regards as out-moded models. The result is that attempts to change (modernize) leadership styles causes anxiety in managers. Leadership theory needs to acknowledge that because it has stuck so rigidly to just one epistemological approach it has dug holes that others cannot get out of. I proffer a plea for a research agenda that aims not only to adopt a culturally sensitive and locally-based interpretive approach, that takes account of individuals' experiences, identities, power relations, and intersubjectivities, but also one that allows for the presence of a range of masculine and feminine workplace behaviors. My further entreaty is for consideration of a research agenda that will help prevent the holes getting any bigger. Greater awareness of the various discourses and subject positions that constitute leaders' subjectivities enables consideration of the multiple constraints that inhibit thoughts and actions and those oppressive discourses and subject positions that should be eradicated.

NOTES

1. These organizational arrangements have undergone structural change in recent years and responsibility for leadership development within the UK NHS context now resides with the NHS Institute for Innovation and Improvement, which was established in 2005.
2. This was also a finding from other research in which I was involved in relation to leadership training programs (Ford and Harding, 2007).
3. There is something in the order of eighty-five–ninety-five managers in more senior positions within the council.
4. This was the Local Government Management Board, which has now been replaced by the Improvement and Development Agency (IDeA).

REFERENCES

Alimo-Metcalfe, B. 1995. An investigation of female and male constructs of leadership and empowerment, *Women in Management Review* 10(2): 3–8.
Bresnen, M. 1995. All things to all people? Perceptions, attributions and constructions of leadership, *The Leadership Quarterly* 6(4): 495–513.
Brewis, J. and S. Linstead. 2004. Gender and management. In *Management and organization: A critical text*, eds. S. Linstead, L. Fulop, and S. Lilley, 56–92. London: Macmillan.

174   *Jackie Ford*

Calas, M. and L. Smircich. 1991. Voicing seduction to silence leadership.*Organization Studies* 12(4): 567–602.

Calas, M. and L. Smircich. 1992. Using the F word: Feminist theories and the socialconsequences of organizational research. In *Gendering organizational analysis*, eds. A.J. Mills and P. Tancred, 222–234. New Park, CA: Sage.

CM 4310. 1999. *Modernising Government*. London: The Stationary Office.

Collinson, D. 2003. Identities and insecurities: Selves at work, *Organization* 10(3): 527–547.

Collinson, D. and K. Grint. 2005. Editorial: The leadership agenda. *Leadership* 1(1): 5–9.

Collinson, D and J. Hearn. 1994. Naming men as men: Implications for work, organisation and management. *Gender, Work and Organisation* 1(1): 2–22.

Council for Excellence 2002. *Managers and leaders: Raising our game*. Council for Excellence in Management and Leadership.

DH. 2002. *NHS Leadership Qualities Framework*. NHS Leadership Centre, Department of health.

Denmark, F. 1993. 'Women, Leadership and Empowerment', *Pyschology of Women Quarterly* 17(3): 343–356.

Fiske, S. and S. Taylor. 1991. *Social cognition*. New York: McGraw Hill.

Fletcher, J.K. 2004. The paradox of post-heroic leadership: An essay on gender, power and transformational change. *Leadership Quarterly* 14: 647–661.

Fondas, N. 1997. Feminization unveiled: Management qualities in contemporary writings. *The Academy of Management Review* 22(1): 257–282

Ford, J. 2005. Examining leadership through critical feminist readings. *Journal of Health Organization and Management* 19(3): 236–251.

Ford, J. 2006. Discourses of leadership: gender, identity and contradiction in a UK public sector organization *Leadership* 2(1): 77–99.

Ford, J. 2007. *Managers as leaders: Towards a post-structuralist feminist analysis of leadership dynamics in UK local government*. Unpublished PhD thesis.

Ford, J. and Harding, N. 2007. Move over management: We are all leaders now? *Management Learning* 38(5): 475–493.

Fulop, L., S. Linstead, and R. Dunford. 2004. Leading and managing. In *Management and organization: A critical text*, eds. S. Linstead, L. Fullop, and S. Lilley, 324–363. London: Palgrave Macmillan.

Gavey, N. 1997. Feminist poststructuralism and discourse analysis. In *Toward a new psychology of gender: A reader*, eds. M. Gergen and S. Davis, 49–54. London: Routledge.

Grint, K. 2000. *The arts of leadership*. Oxford, UK: Oxford University Press.

Grint, K. 2005. *Leadership: Limits and possibilities*. Hampshire, UK: Palgrave Macmillan.

Huczynski, A. and D. Buchanan. 2007. *Organizational behaviour*, 6th ed. London: Prentice Hall.

Jackson, B. and K. Parry. 2008. *A very short, fairly interesting and reasonably cheap book about studying leadership*. London: Sage.

Kerfoot, D. 2000. Body work: Estrangement, disembodiment and the organizational other. In *Body and Organization*, eds. J. Hassard, R. Holliday, and H. Willmott, 230–246. London: Sage.

Knights, D. and H. Willmott. 2007. *Introducing organizational behaviour and management*. London: Thompson Learning.

Kondo, D. 1990. *Crafting selves, power, gender & discourses of identity in a Japanese workplace*. Chicago, IL: Chicago University Press.

Leadership Development Commission 2004. *An emerging strategy for leadership development in local government*. London: Employers Organization for Local Government.

Linstead, S., L. Fullop, and S. Lilley, eds. 2004. *Management and organization: A critical text*. London: Palgrave Macmillan.

Maddock, S. and W. Parkin. 1993. Gender cultures: Women's choices and strategies at work. *Women in Management Review* 8(2): 3–9.

Pollitt, C. 2003. *The essential public manager*. Berkshire, UK: Open University Press.

Rosener, J. 1990. Ways women lead. *Harvard Business Review* Nov–Dec: 119–125.

Rosener, J. 1997. *America's competitive secret: Women managers*. Oxford, UK: Oxford University Press.

Sinclair, A. 2005. Journey around leadership. *Working Paper, March 10, 2005*. Melbourne, Australia: University of Melbourne.

Sinclair, A. 1998. *Doing leadership differently*. Melbourne, Australia: Melbourne University Press.

Thomas, R. and A. Davies. 2005. Theorising the micro-politics of resistance: New Public Management and managerial identities in the UK public services. *Organization Studies* 26(5): 683–706.

Watson, T. 2001. *In search of management: Culture, chaos and control in managerial work*, revised ed. London: Thompson Learning.

Wajcman, J. 1996. Desperately seeking differences: Is management style gendered? *British Journal of Industrial Relations* 34 (3): 339–349.

Webb, J. 2001. Gender, work and transitions in the local state. *Work, Employment and Society* 15(4): 825–844.

Whitehead, S. 1999. New women, new labour? Gendered transformations in the House. In *Transforming Managers: Gendering Change in the Public Sector*, eds. S. Whitehead and R. Moodley, 1–15. London: UCL Press.

11 Individual Patient Choice in the English National Health Service
The Case for Social Fantasy Seen from Psychoanalytic Perspective

Marianna Fotaki

INTRODUCTION

Individual patient choice is the key plank of government policy in England (Department of Health, 2003; Blair, 2003; Milburn, 2003, Reid, 2003) and many other countries at present (Allen and Riemer-Hommel, 2006; Blomqvist, 2004; Vrangbæk and Bech, 2004). Being the product of a political process, policies contain a program theory, that is, assumptions about how the policy will achieve intended outcomes, and about the value of those outcomes, which are not necessarily complete, consistent or well-formulated (Fotaki et al., 2006, 25). The term 'choice' is usually taken to refer to a conscious, deliberative, mental process whose endpoint is a person's action, belief, or speech. The process of choice is also a motivational, emotional, or attitudinal process as well as being constrained by the agent's knowledge, mental capacities, and scope for choice (ibid., 27). While it is doubtful whether choice is a purely conscious deliberative process or whether it is also colored by non-rational processes (e.g., habit, information overload) or even irrational processes (e.g., unconscious compulsions), in most policy narratives choice is assumed to be a normative and highly rational process (Dixon and Le Grand, 2006; Friedman and Friedman, 1980). Thus, analytical frameworks outside political economy and narrowly conceived sociological paradigms rarely penetrate mainstream public policy analyses (Fotaki, 2006). Yet, by drawing almost exclusively on normative and positivistic perspectives, policy analyses provide an insufficient account of public policy formulation, and more specifically, of health policy implementation. My intention is to question the rational premises of policy making as an overriding factor by introducing ideas drawn from psychoanalytic theory, to suggest firstly, that public policies are a product of unconscious social fantasy and secondly, to draw attention to the implications this unrecognized function has on policy implementation.

Choice is used to explore the role of idealization, fantasy, and unconscious motivation in public policy. Namely, that policies enact and fulfill deeper imaginary strivings in society over and above what may appear to be the stated goals and objectives (Fotaki, 2006), and that this (unrecognized) imaginary function is constitutive to both their formulation and implementation. Until now postmodern social theorists have accepted that rationality alone can only partially explain the pursuits of multiple and often conflicting goals by welfare subjects (Giddens, 1994; Williams, 1999; Hoggett, 2001). Anthony Giddens (1994), for example, emphasized that the evolution of the passive recipient into a reflexive actor exercising his/ her agency in many complex ways, is the main cause behind the fundamental shift affecting public service provision. He linked the idea of *'reflexive monitoring of action'* to discursive knowledge (Giddens, 1984, 41–45), surmising that peoples' deepest engagement with the external world occurred through the unconscious, particularly during the times of dislocation and stress. Others have used Giddens ideas to argue about the role the emancipation of women and children has had in diversifying the notion of the uniform and normative subject (Williams, 1999; Fergusson, 2003). Paul Hoggett (2001) has offered a counterpoint to these views, by developing a concept of agency at the interface of rational and less rational individual motivations, delimiting the role of rationality as the supreme driver of the welfare subject's actions. He suggested specifically that destructive acting towards the self and others could be an assertion of the subject's agency under circumstances of duress and pain (Hoggett, 2001). Despite these attempts to incorporate subjectivity to explain various social policy outcomes, its impact on institutions and the influence in shaping policy-making processes has not been sufficiently theorized.

I propose to address this gap by considering policy making as a socio-symbolic process, whereby policies originate in the imaginary foundations of the individual psychic life taking the form of socially constructed fantasies. In the sections that follow, I will present an analysis of a policy specifically concerned with extending individual patient choice in the British National Health Service (NHS) during the 1990s and again, more recently, to illustrate why policies become idealistic and why this misrecognized idealization is at the root of policy failure. To argue my point, I examine important unconscious mechanisms present in today's policy conception, occurring at a distance from organizational reality and going largely unacknowledged. My aim is to bring to light factors stirring up the policy process but also disabling its realization. In doing so I will use the example of the reappearance of individual patient choice not to argue for or against its introduction into health care systems but to illustrate why and how its complex and diffuse concepts are being translated into simplistic policy pronouncements without taking into account multiple contextual realities, including diverse needs of different user groups or dynamics underlying the experience of being a patient. I will argue that this disregard disables policy effectiveness leading to disillusionment with public policy-making.

More importantly, however, I will make a case for bringing to the fore the neglected role of the unconscious motivation and fantasy permeating public and business organizations alike, as a necessary precondition for making our (social) life possible. I will therefore propose reconsidering policy making as a social activity concerned with aspirational rather than realizable goals which are not always meant to be fulfilled, but nonetheless, serve as important policy drivers. I will argue that this is precisely what keeps the choice idea alive and popular despite its vague promises and less successful outcomes whenever it is implemented. This is also why policy makers often rely on the separation of the 'good' traits of anticipated transformations, and projection of their unrealizable 'bad' aspects into external objects such as 'incompetent' managers or 'unreformable' health professionals. The splits between policy conception, and the ways they are translated in organizations, underscores the nature of defensive mechanisms (including denial, projection to the outside, and indeed, splitting), which are intrinsic to organizational dynamics (Gabriel, 1999; Hirschhorn, 1988, Brown and Starkey, 2000). My final argument will be about the need to consider the imaginary aspect of policy making as a way of overcoming these splits by bridging fantasy with reality. The notion of public policies and particularly health policy being driven by less rational forces and motives, which I advance in this study by applying psychoanalytic thinking, contributes to this aim by addressing an important gap in conventional policy analyses.

The remainder of the chapter is structured as follows. First, I outline the key premises of the proposed (psycho)-analytic framework drawing on the object relations theory. I then present a brief history of patient choice policies in the United Kingdom and its more recent re-introduction in England, contrasted with the evidence of its very moderate impact or a downright failure, as a background for illustrating my theoretical arguments. In the final section, I bring together analytical elaborations and the example discussed, to propose an alternative conception for understanding the dynamics of public health policy making.

SOCIAL DEFENSES IN PUBLIC HEALTH CARE POLICY

The notion of the ruptured subject producing its own repressions originally articulated by Sigmund Freud (Freud, 1920, 1923) is one of the core ideas of psychoanalysis. Fantasy is recognized to be the foundation of psychic life. These key tenets have been taken up differently by various schools of psychoanalytic thought including object relations theory founded by Melanie Klein in the 1930s. In her seminal work Klein was preoccupied with exploring the role of infantile fantasy as a means of protection from threatening emotions, thoughts, and images. She concluded that fantasy was vital in inducing splitting and projection of the unwanted feelings to the outside and for keeping the desired objects idealized (Klein, 1935/1986). These conceptions about individual human development were fruitfully employed by her disciples, Wilfred Bion and Elliott Jacques in theorizing about processes in social institutions and organizations.

I will now summarize briefly key ideas of splitting, projection, and idealization described by Klein and used extensively to explain organizational phenomena. I will then move to integrate the contribution of defensive mechanisms as part of the mental process with my central argument about the unrecognized role of symbolic and fantasmatic aspects of the policy making process. Although there has been some influential work on social defenses in public and private organizations (Menzies, 1960; Jacques, 1953, Bain, 1998), there is an absence of research into the role of policy formulation in supporting these defenses and their subsequent impact on organizational praxis. My aim is to argue about their pervasiveness on both institutional (policy making) and organizational (policy implementation) levels. In my theorizing about unconscious motivation and fantasy, I depart from Paul Hoggett's position about the government partly acting as the receptacle for the alienated subjectivity of citizens, with public organizations often having to contain what is disowned by the rest of the society (Hoggett, 2006). Such processes I argue, form an intrinsic experience in health care environments, dealing with inexorable facts of the human condition involving disease, decay, and dying. By counteracting and obscuring these inevitable processes, working against our well being and threatening our existence, the health system assumes the role of a specialized societal agency containing these issues and the feelings they instigate, on behalf of all of us (Obholzer, 1994). For this reason, health professionals are first and foremost the recipients of intense societal projections of omnipotence they have to act out to deflect the admission of their own and the system's limitations in dealing with what Money-Kyrle described as *'facts of life'* (Money-Kyrle, 1978, 442–449).

The notion of splitting mental functions into separate feelings of displeasure and unremitting dread occurring under the situation of stress and vulnerability originates in Melanie Klein's work (1935/1986). She developed her seminal ideas about separating ideas and subjects into good and bad *'part objects'* based on her observations of infants, surmising that they represented conflicts on a fantasy level experienced during the early developmental stages. If unresolved, these conflicts would continue into adult life leading to fragmentation and dysfunctional splitting. By contrast the adoption of the integrative, mature position indicated that individuals were capable of accepting that bad and good objects coexisted in themselves and others (Klein, 1935/1986). Klein believed that in periods of stress, adults might regress to the state of splitting and projecting bad objects to the outside, a contention that formed the forerunners of social relations (Bion, 1961). However, Klein (1935/1986) also accepted that these splits were *'of vital importance for normal development as well as for abnormal object relations'* (Klein, 1946, 103).

These ideas spawned elaborate clinical work and organizational consultancy practice to offer an interpretative key for understanding various social phenomena, for psychoanalysis was never born as a mere theoretical field. The concept of social systems supporting individual psychological defenses against anxiety generated by the work task was first recognized by Elliott Jacques in the 1950s (Jacques, 1953) in his precursory work resulting from consultancy to a failing commercial company. Isobel Menzies (1960) used psychoanalytic theory in her study of hospital nurses and identified manifestations of what she termed 'social defenses' in the form of accepted behaviors that protected nurses from the anxiety associated with their work. She described the tendency of nurses to depersonalize patients by referring to them by their (medical) condition or by organizing their work by task rather than by focusing on the patient, and to follow mindless routines by avoiding personal discretion. These 'social defenses' led to common work practices in the hospital that were not conducive to high quality care. In a more recent study, Bain (1998) noted that many of the processes described by Menzies in British hospitals in the 1960s were still prevalent in Australian hospitals in the 1990s. He suggested that defenses against anxiety remained largely unchanged in hospital systems because they have similar primary tasks arousing these defenses, which are unconsciously held, deeply ingrained, maladaptive to the task, and difficult to change. He also suggested that local changes aimed at improving care were not sustained because of the lack of concurrent changes in policy, procedures, and authority systems (Bain, 1998).

A wide range of unconscious defense mechanisms such as splitting and projective identification, denial or repression of unwanted feelings and/or uncomfortable admissions are mobilized to keep those feelings at bay. I also argue that they underpin public policy formulation and implementation. Thus the articulation of health policy frequently relies on theses pre-existing splits in order to separate the 'good' traits of pursued transformations, and on the projection of their 'bad' aspects into external objects (i.e., incompetent managers or 'unreformable' health professionals) that can be safely used as a receptacle of inner negative feelings. Such 'splitting' enables both the denial of limitations as to what can be achieved (i.e., some patients will die or patients may believe that doctors are better placed to make treatment decisions), and the repression of likely negative outcomes (i.e., some hospital services will close, some patients may not make choices that others believe to be in their best interest). Once policy makers are implicitly entrusted with formulating aspirational rather than realizable policies, managers and health professionals can dismiss policies as unworkable and continue to await a better policy that will serve to perfect the health care services they provide. This splitting between good elements, the policies themselves, and bad elements, their implementation, is particularly common and is also another powerful reason why idealization works in policy context, and how it is further reinforced by the psychological processes manifested as organizational defenses in health settings.

The dynamics described previously are perhaps nowhere more evident than in the way patient choice policy has been articulated, including the denial of the limitations to health care and in the repression of the likely negative outcomes, alongside excessive idealization of expected effects as will argue after presenting the evidence on patient choice a very few successes and many more failures. The next section presents a brief history of evidence about the effects of patient choice reforms introduced in the UK health care system and elsewhere, in relation to their proclaimed objectives, before applying the proposed analytic framework to explicate on the impossibility of policy implementation without acknowledging the role of fantasy in public policy making processes.

PATIENT CHOICE IN THE NHS: A MEANS TO AN END, A GOAL OF ITS OWN VALUE, OR A SOCIALLY CONSTRUCTED FANTASY?

Patient choice—a derivative and a tool of the market—is a popular policy pursued intermittently in the NHS in the last two decades, and other publicly funded health systems in the industrialized world more recently (Beusekom et al., 2004; Schoen et al., 2004). However, the NHS was originally designed in 1948 to give priority to collective needs rather than individual wants (Klein, 1995). Historically, the concept of choice was not on the NHS policy agenda until the introduction of the market-oriented reforms in the 1990s but even then it was not vigorously pursued. Health care policy in the 1980s and 1990s in the NHS in the United Kingdom largely focused on structural rearrangements as the means of securing improvements in the efficiency and performance of health services (Department of Health, 1989a, 1989b). Elements of choice and market competition were selectively applied in the early 1990s by some general practitioners (family doctors) holding public funds for purchasing hospital services for their patients. However, those 'quasi market' reforms resulted in lukewarm and isolated responses rather than a revolution of service provision through patient choice (Tuohy, 1999; Le Grand, 1999; Fotaki, 1999). The reasons behind this relative policy failure were various and many leading to policy makers' ambivalence towards their reforms shortly after it became evident that assumptions about market's power to transform service provision could not be easily fulfilled (Fotaki, 2001, Le Grand et al., 1998).

Similarly, choice as a market tool was introduced into many publicly planned and delivered systems in Europe in the 1990s with an aim to improve efficiency and to make services more responsive to users' needs (Williams and Rossiter, 2004), with mixed results. While its effects on improving efficiency and quality are disputable (Le Grand, 1999; Fotaki et al., 2006), there are clear indications of its negative effects on equality of access to services by different groups. The perception of inequities has led to the abolition of internal market reforms by the Labour government when it came to power in 1997 (Light, 2001). Meanwhile, studies concerning the introduction of choice and competition incentives in the United Kingdom and other countries in the 1990s, revealed that patients made little use of available choices (Fotaki et al., 2008; Williams and Rossiter, 2004), and that generally involvement in choice of doctor and treatment was particularly preferred and enacted by patients from more educated and more affluent backgrounds who had better access to information (Mukamel et al., 2004) and therefore to choice (Fotaki et al., 2006). It also turned out that many patients prefer to leave choices up to their family doctors because they don't know that they can play an active role in decision-making or otherwise have a 'doctor knows best' attitude and wish to avoid regret or responsibility for the possible failure of the chosen treatment and are reluctant to acknowledge the uncertainties of health care (Entwistle et al., 1998). Moreover, patients bring their own individual beliefs, values, and everyday experiences to the consultation—all of which can limit their ability or willingness to make choices (Fotaki et al., 2008).

Against this backdrop of complexity and relative failure with previous attempts of introducing patient choice policy in the NHS, it is baffling to see the government pursuing individual patient choice with unparalleled intensity after having abandoned the internal market only a few years earlier. The UK Government has recently reintroduced patient choice policies aimed at enabling NHS patients to participate directly in decisions about the place, time, and way treatment is provided to them (Department of Health, 2003, 2004). Individual choice is seen (yet again) as a means of achieving diverse and potentially conflicting public policy objectives, including better quality and responsiveness to users' needs, increased efficiency, and more equitable access to health services, and as a good in its own right (Milburn, 2003; Reid, 2003).

There are several reasons as to why and how this could happen. It has been argued elsewhere that the specific policy examined here illustrates the process of selective 'forgetting' and 're-evocation' of old policy archetypes including market competition, users of public services as rational utility maximizers rather than learning from experience itself (Fotaki, 2007). Another reason is that policy as a normative undertaking inevitably relies on simplistic articulations because *"a reform is a process of idea elaboration, persuasion and implementation rather than an immediate action"* (Brunsson and Olsen, 1993, 34). However, it is not perhaps a coincidence that policy articulations do not seek to distance themselves from the lack of conceptual clarity and blurring implied in the term 'choice' thus enabling its rhetorical exploitation despite or because, of the fact that choice in health care means different things to different groups of people or even to the same under different circumstances.

This chapter posits that frequent policy failures are largely due to the unrecognized role of fantasy in public policy making, which in turn leads to its interminable repetition. Therein also lays the paradox of policy making that patient choice case illustrates rather well revealing the significance of its imaginary foundations. Choice is a fantasmatic concept *par excellence* with mythological connotations (Fotaki, 2006) and universal appeal— who after all can be against choice? Policy rhetoric captures this desire attached to the signifier of 'choice' disregarding complexities involved in turning it into workable policy. Its imaginary (illusory) element is also more generally seen when public policies including health care policies are being formulated in denial of contextual reality and the issues that they are concerned with, while the chief preoccupation is with rendering legitimacy to grand schemes. Such schemes are frequently driven by unrealizable ideas. The simultaneous attainment of individual choice and equality for all as that the recent English NHS documents proclaim (Department of Health, 2003) or the elevation of the market to the role of an ultimate arbiter and a driver of improvements in health care, are good examples of how these trends are manifested. Individualistic goals of choice policy are proclaimed to achieve collective pursuits of equity, efficiency, and responsiveness to patients needs at the same time (Department of Health, 2003; Milburn, 2003, Dixon and Le Grand, 2006) while contradictions and limitations of individual choice in collectivist systems (Oliver and Evans, 2005) are glossed over and/or denied. Equity and efficiency trade-offs are well known dilemmas to health economists and the concept of societal efficiency has been the guiding principle for public policy makers. However, patient choice supersedes realistic concerns about policy implementation involving complex organizations and non uniform users of health services who have to constantly negotiate their needs against their wants. As past experience indicates, and more recent evidence confirms, patients do not seem strongly attracted to the idea of choice in health care, are reluctant to use it, and are by far more interested in obtaining information on various issues concerning their treatment (Fotaki et al., 2008; Picker Institute Europe, 2007; Schoen et al., 2004).

The overly simplistic idea for patients to choose from a range of services and for the best services to survive, derives from the mainstream economic thinking, which is *"shallow to the point of being paper thin"* as Ben Fine has described it with reference to the superficial understanding of consumption (Fine, 2002, 125). Were we to follow economic assumptions of an individual as a rational utility maximizer, and the idea of personal liberty as synonymous with the concept of consumer sovereignty, we might be led to rely on a very restrictive notion of individual autonomy. This caveat is particularly relevant to the use of health care services which are in many ways different from purchasing other consumer goods. Patients rarely enjoy free and unrestricted choice of whether to use health services at all—putting the whole idea of consumerism and choice in health care into question. Paradoxically and yet unsurprisingly, the scheme maintains also that market forces will improve efficiency and effectiveness while attaining equity and quality for all. Unsurprisingly, too, policies based on mainstream economic assumptions are formulated in denial of the fundamental existential anxieties enacted in public health care systems, invariably ignoring the consequences of those policies for real non-uniform patients, who are themselves fragmented subjects, more so in times of dislocation and stress.

Yet, this superficiality enables 'choice' to become a signifier for anchoring other less conscious meanings. In this sense, policies proclaiming a simultaneous pursuit of legitimate and important goals of equity and responsiveness via market means are underpinned by the desire for idealized health services capable of withering disease and dying. This pursuit paradoxically also provides a stark testimony to the difficulty associated with the realization of choice for all in public health system with finite resources. Thus, aside from Labour's belated enchantment with the market and competition as 'the only alternative' able to bring about prosperity and equality alike (Dixon and Le Grand, 2006), there are some intrinsic structural factors behind this policy recycling, which have to do with the inevitability of fantasy as a constitutive element of policy making and the inevitability of its failure. Ostensibly, the attraction of choice in policy makers' and allegedly also in service users' minds, overrides the evidence of previously documented failure, some of which I have presented in this study. This, I argue, is because of the underlying fantasy driving social pursuits, which goes unnoticed in conventional policy analyses. However, I do not suggest that policies are not about tackling real problems. By contrast, fantasmatic constructions are brought to life only when they are concerned with issues that matter. Yet, it is also crucial to recognize that unrealistic or rhetorical policy goals are frequently articulated in order to conceal unconscious societal strife and desire, and are then transferred to organizations to be carried out as policy implementation (Fotaki, 2006, 1726), to foster the illusion that disease and death can be mastered. The unacknowledged idealizing function of policy is strengthened further by the impossible tasks of health care to defend us against anxiety of disease and dying, which it can never fully accomplish. This absence of recognition leads to multiple splits between policy formulation and implementation. While these defenses are necessary to protect us from destructive fears of annihilation and narcissistic trauma, they also act as a dysfunctional barrier against attaining lucid awareness and ultimately against our attempts to overcome them. Moreover, the neglect of omnipotent fantasies enacted in patient choice policy results in splitting-off its likely negative outcomes. When this happens denial and repression are relied upon for cynical distancing and simultaneous glorification of the expected results i.e., patient choice will radically reform health care provision by offering personalized care to all users by increasing efficiency of services and that it will somehow meet each and every individual want at the same time.

This leads me to the central claim I make in this chapter: that the neglect of this imaginary construction of policy making leads to multiple splits and ultimately underscores its failure. Splitting involves maintenance of idealized intentions at a policy level and a projection of real (and less successful) outcome onto the NHS organizations which are held responsible for its failure. What it also means is that tacit and unspoken functions are relegated to the unconscious giving rise to all kinds of defensive policy rhetoric. These unstated functions shape organizational attitudes and behaviors of health professionals and users of services, as they are being employed to defend them against existential *and* work related anxieties inherent in health systems. It also highlights the causes of difficulty in translating value driven statements underlying public policies into organizational realities, pointing towards a need for an alternative schema for understanding policy conception and its implications for organizations and users of services.

In the final section that follows, I justify the necessity of reconsidering policy making as a socio-psychological process originating in socially constructed fantasies which are indispensable for giving rise to our various societal projects. I conclude by proposing possible ways of bridging fantasy and reality.

TOWARDS DEVELOPING AN ALTERNATIVE CONCEPTION OF PUBLIC HEALTH POLICY MAKING

So far, I have suggested that health policies fail because of mis/recognition of their unconscious and fantasmatic foundations. I have argued that public policy making expresses societal strife and desire driven by the illusory fantasy while health organizations are left in a position of a dependent subject having passively to reflect it. By maintaining the idea that health services, if better designed, can prevent suffering and dying, health policies become split from organizational reality and the reality of being a patient. Policies are thus enabled to be idealistic while responsibility for their implementation falls on health organizations. This explains also why they are frequently couched in prescriptive and rhetorical terms while glossing over and denying their likely undesirable effects for patients and organizations. I have also argued that such policies support socially structured organizational defenses, seen in rigid work practices (Menzies, 1960) and confirmed as lack of space for reflection and organizational learning (Bain, 1998). I have drawn on the object relations theory to demonstrate why and how policy has to distance itself from organizational reality in order to fulfill its idealizing function. My claim is also that this knowledge is suppressed from entering the policy formulation process as it militates against our narcissism: the indestructibility of the self. I have finally suggested that the reasons for the reintroduction of patient choice in English health care system and throughout Europe might be better understood through the psychodynamic lens highlighting the imaginary function public policy fulfils which may override or contradict its stated objectives.

Looking at the case of patient choice in the English NHS that I have used to illustrate my arguments in this study, it is clear that neither users nor health professionals saw choice as the utmost priority that the government has proclaimed (Department of Health, 2003; Blair, 2003). The research evidence available also suggested that patient choice policy is unlikely to realize the stated goals of efficiency or equity (Fotaki et al., 2008; Clarke et al., 2007), and if it is implemented it will be most likely concerned with narrowly defined and relatively unimportant issues such as choice of hospital site, time of appointment, and so on or spurious aspects of care, including the aforementioned choices together with shifting responsibility to the users of services. As I have argued elsewhere, the conflicting objectives that choice policy is proclaimed to achieve (such as equity and efficiency for example) are there to deflect from admitting the deeper defensive role that health care organizations assume (Fotaki, 2006). Thus as the pursuit of individual choice involving patients/consumers in shaping service provision continues unabated, the policy carries out other less obvious functions, of defending society from the unconscious anxiety of dying.

However, the other reason is our desire for the impossible which is also reflected in our socially constructed fantasy of choice. It is therefore important to stress that these unacknowledged imaginary and symbolic functions are indispensable to stimulate policies even if they cannot be fully achieved. Policy tends to be idealistic because it is not meant to withstand an immediate reality test but to express mythical, imaginary, and arguably unrealizable societal aspirations and longings. While patient choice overtly ignores the unconscious motivations implicit in everyday reality of the patient–doctor encounter (by assuming that rationality and utility maximization overrun patient fears and vulnerability), it takes an (unwitting) account of the fantasy that is constitutive to the human psyche. In this sense, discrepancies and discontinuities reflected in patient choice policy, as it attempts to achieve its potentially conflicting objectives (better quality and responsiveness to users' needs, higher efficiency and equity) are an expression of the contradictions of the human psyche. Thus it is quite likely that patient choice policy pursued currently in the NHS will fail again or will become concerned with issues that matter the least. And it is not unlikely that it will be resurrected again after it fails. For such is the power of fantasy.

The possibility for its 'resurrection' is explained in the second claim I advance in this chapter: that the lionization of choice would not have been possible in the absence of underlying fantasy, which is in this case signified by the freedom from the bounds of human predicament. The fantasy then becomes the stimulant and an indispensable force for driving policies forward, even if they are bound to fail. This conception focuses on the subject, which is not simply driven by rational considerations as economists would want us to believe, but by dreams, fantasies, and less obvious motives. But the fantasy is not just a desire for the promised outcome but more so for the symbol that the outcome stands for. Put differently, the search is for meaning and not for the object that signifies it. So in the case of individual choice in health, the underlying fantasy that drives this policy is the desire for the freedom (of choice), and by extension a desire for control over the uncontrollable and freedom from inexorable facts of life. Unsurprisingly, these pursuits cannot be easily (or at all) translated into workable policy objectives.

However, the recognition that policies are emebedded in fantasy does not in any case imply blank slate authorization of health policy designed without thought as to how these desirable objectives can realistically be implemented and operationalized in a multi-organization such as the NHS. Quite the opposite: the problem occurs when misrecognition of the fantasmatic and idealizing function of policy making sets in giving raise to defensive reactions and taking the form of literal splitting, of those who design policies, from operational reality. This underscores policy failure while allowing for health care organizations to be safely used as a receptacle of the inner negative feelings of disillusioned constituencies if policies fail. As a result, the splits permeate the system and various groups of professionals become subject to idealization alternating with denigration as they cascade down into organizations. Crucially, this approach also has consequences at an interpersonal micro-level, because the so conceived policy at 'a distance' cannot relate to patient requirements and so, it may still be impossible to implement it effectively.

But can policy makers purposefully integrate psychoanalytic insights by bringing them to bear on policy formation and implementation? My argument is that if policy is not to remain locked in pursuing for unattainable ideas, we need to recognize its subjective symbolic and imaginary aspects. This recognition would lead to an acknowledgement and an acceptance of the intrinsic instability and conflicting nature of the policy making processes. Such policy which is reflective of its context and of itself, would not be easily drawn into seeking simplistic 'solutions' reflecting the fantasies of the ego couched in socially acceptable terms. It would not either become the mirror showing our deepest socially sanctioned desires/fantasies taking the form of simplistic pronouncements of 'choice for all,' signifying an injunction to exercise and enjoy (choice) even if what is to be enjoyed involves the experience of being ill/being cared for. Such a consideration might be the first step enabling us to pursue more truthful and realistic policies, which could be aided involving more deeply all those concerned with their implementation: health professionals, and the intended beneficiaries, the users of services. The recognition of the fact that policy is fundamentally structured in fantasy will not however, be a substitute for meaning because in order to work policies need to ring true and to tap into real issues while involving those whom they concern. By taking into account the inevitability of fantasy in policy making and the inevitability of its failure, we can perhaps free ourselves from the tyranny of the imaginary pursuits even if it is only in these fleeting moments of lucid awareness.

CONCLUSION

This chapter drew on psychoanalytic approaches to contribute to the understanding of less tangible processes present in policy conception and organizational structures creating powerful social fantasies that have important effects on all actors in health systems. My aim was to bring together the notion of subjectivity and the idea of mental defensive processes elaborated by Klein, to unearth important dynamics that go unacknowledged in our thinking about policy making and its implications for organizations and users of services. Drawing on the concept of socially sanctioned defenses against anxiety, I highlighted the consequences of separating policy formation from health organizations entrusted with the role of specialized agencies in society, and the resulting policy failure. In exploring the limits and possibilities of one particular policy, I have also demonstrated how splitting worked in health care organizations enabling the idealization of the health task. I have also suggested how such splits might be overcome by arguing for recognition of the underlying imaginary dynamics as a starting point in a journey towards realistic policy making. This in itself is a depressing process as one must also give up the idealized objects accepting the impossibility of ever attaining them. However, only by engaging users and providers in decision making and co-production of services as self-aware subjects accepting the burden of their subjectivity and taking responsibility for their ontological predicament, without surrendering to it, and not by responsibilizing individual users of services or professionals, there is a possibility of a breakthrough in the cycle of policy repetition and failure. Therefore the path to successful policies, to be understood as truthful and authentic policies, goes through realization of unconscious motivations that underpin them by and moving toward an acceptance of the complex interaction between fantasy and reality. Finally, such a comprehensive interpretation of policy making organizational defenses and social strivings might contribute to a better understanding of the possibilities and limitations involved in developing patients' autonomy beyond normalizing 'management of expectations'.

REFERENCES

Allen, P. and P. Riemmer-Hommel. 2006. What are 'third way' governments learning? Health care consumers, choice and quality in England and Germany. *Health Policy* 76(2): 202–212.

Bain, A. 1998. Social defences against organisational learning, *Human Relations,* 51(3):413–29.

Beusekom, I., Tönshoff, S., de Vries, H., Spreng, C. and Keeler, E. 2004. *Possibility or utopia? Consumer choice in health care: A literature review.* Prepared for Bertelsmann Foundation. Santa Monica, CA: RAND Corporation

Bion, W. 1961. *Experiences in groups.* London: Tavistock Institute.

Blair, A. 2003. *We must not waste this precious period of power.* Speech given at South Camden Community College, January 23, 2003. Available at http://www.labour.org.uk/tbsocialjustice (accessed May 10, 2004).

Blomqvist, P. 2004. The choice revolution: privatization of Swedish welfare services in the 1990s. *Social Policy and Administration* 38(2): 139–155.

Brown, A. and K. Starkey. 2000. Organisational identity and learning: A psychodynamic perspective. *Academy of Management Review,* 25: 102–120.

Brunsson, N. and J.P. Olsen. 1993. *The reforming organisation.* London: Routledge.

Clarke, J., J. Newman, N. Smith, E. Vidler, and L. Westmarland. 2007. *Creating citizen-consumers: Changing publics and changing public services.* London: Sage.

Department of Health 1989a. *Working for patients.* London: HMSO.

Department of Health 1989b. *Promoting better health.* London: HMSO.

Department of Health 2003. *Building on the best: Choice, responsiveness and equity in the NHS.* London: Department of Health.

Department of Health 2004. *Choose and book—patient choice of hospital and booked appointment.* London: Department of Health.

Dixon, A. and J. Le Grand. 2006. 'Is greater patient choice consistent with equity? The case of the English NHS'. *Journal of Health Services Research and Policy* 11: 162–166.

Entwistle, V., T. Sheldon, A. Sowden, and I. Watt. 1998. Evidence-informed patient choice. *International Journal of Technology Assessment in Health Care* 14(2): 212–25.

Fine, B. 2002. *The world of consumption.* London: Routledge.

Ferguson, H. 2003. Welfare, social exclusion and reflexivity: The case of child and woman protection. *Journal of Social Policy* 32(2): 199–216.

Fotaki, M. 1999. The impact of the market oriented reforms on information and choice. Case study of cataract surgery in Outer London and County Council of Stockholm. *Social Science and Medicine* 48: 1415–1432.

Fotaki, M. 2001. *The impact of the market oriented reforms in the UK and Sweden. Case study of cataract surgery.* Unpublished thesis. London: University of London.

Fotaki, M. 2006. Choice is yours: A psychodynamic exploration of health policy making and its consequences for the English National Health Service. *Human Relations* 59(12): 1711–1744.

Fotaki, M. 2007. Patient choice in health care in the UK and Sweden: From quasi-market and back to market? A comparative analysis of failure in unlearning. *Public Administration* 85(4): 1059–1075.

Fotaki, M., A. Boyd, L. Smith, R. McDonald, A. Edwards, G. Elwyn, M. Roland, and R. Scheaff. 2006. *Patient choice and the organisation and delivery of health services: Scoping review.* Report for the NCCSDO. Manchester, UK: Manchester Business School.

Fotaki, M., M. Roland, A. Boyd, R. McDonald, R. Scheaff, L. Smith. 2008. What benefits will choice bring to patients? Literature review and assessment of implications. *Journal of Health Service Research and Policy* 13: 178–184.

Friedman, M. and R. Friedman. 1980. *Free to choose.* London: Secker and Warburg.

Freud, S. 1920. *Beyond the pleasure principle, standard edition, vol. 18.* London: Hogarth Press.

Freud, S. 1923. *The ego and the superego, standard Edition, vol. 19.* London: Hogarth Press.

Gabriel, Y. 1999. *Organisations in depth: The psychoanalysis of organisations.* Sage: London.

Giddens, A. 1984. *The constitution of society.* Cambridge, UK: Polity Press.

Giddens, A. 1994. Living in a post-traditional society. In *Reflexive modernisation: Politics, traditions and aesthetics in the modern social order,* eds. U. Beck, A. Giddens and S. Lash, 56–109. Cambridge, UK: Polity.

Hirschhorn, L. 1988. *The workplace within: Psychodynamics of organisational life.* Cambridge, MA: MIT Press.

Hoggett, P. 2001. Agency, rationality and social policy. *Journal of Social Policy* 32(1): 37–56.

Hoggett, P. 2006. Conflict, ambivalence, and the contested purpose of public organisations. *Human Relations* 59(2): 175–194.

Jacques, E. 1953. On the dynamics of social structure. *Human Relations* 6: 10–23.

Klein, M. 1935/1986. A contribution to the psychogenesis of the maniac depressive states. In *The selected writings of Melanie Klein,* eds. J. Mitchell, 115–146. New York: Free Press.

Klein, M. 1946. 'Notes on Some Schizoid Mechanisms', *International Journal of Pyscho-Analysis* 27: 99–110.

Klein, R. 1995. *New politics of the NHS.* London: Routledge

Le Grand, J. 1999. Competition, co-operation or control? Tales from the British National Health Service. *Health Affairs* 18(3): 27–39.

Le Grand, J., N. Mays, and J. Dixon. 1998. Conclusions. In *Learning from the NHS internal market: A review of the evidence,* eds. J. Le Grand, N. Mays, and J-A. Mulligan, 117–34. London: Kings Fund Publishing.

Light, D. 2001. Cost containment and the backdraft of competition policies. *International Journal of Health Services* 31(4): 681–708.

Menzies, I. 1960. A case study in the functioning of social systems as a defence against anxiety, *Human Relation,* 13(2):95–121.

Milburn, A. 2003. Choice for all. Speech to NHS Chief Executives, February 11, 2003. http://www.dh.gov.uk/en/News/Speeches/Speecheslist/DH_4000782 (accessed May 5, 2009).

Money-Kyrle, R. 1978. The aim of psychoanalysis. In *The collected papers of Roger Money-Kyrle,* eds. D. Meltzer, 442–449. Strath Tey, UK: Clunie Press.

Mukamel, D., D. Weimer, J. Zwanziger, S. Gorthy, and A. Mushlin. 2004. Quality report cards, selection of cardiac surgeons, and racial disparities: A study of the publication of the New York State Cardiac Surgery Reports. *Inquiry-the Journal of Health Care Organisation Provision and Financing* 41: 435–446.

Obholzer, A. 1994. Managing social anxieties in public sector organisations. In *The unconscious at work,* eds. A. Obholzer and V. Roberts, 170–175. London: Routledge.

Oliver, A. and Evans, J. 2005. Editorial: The paradox of promoting choice in a collectivist system. *Journal of Medical Ethics* 31: 187.

Picker Institute Europe. 2007. *The 2006 inpatients importance study.* Oxford, UK: Picker Institute Europe.

Reid, J. 2003. *Choice for all not the few.* Speech given to the Health Network on July 16, 2003. Press release: reference 2003/0267.

Schoen, C., R. Osborn, P. Huynh, M. Doty, K. Davis, K. Zapert, and J. Peugh. 2004. Primary care and health system performance: Adults experiences in five countries. *Health Affairs* (accessed September 27, 2005).

Tuohy, C. 1999. Dynamics of a changing health sphere: The United States, Britain, and Canada. *Health Affairs* 18(3): 114–34.

Vrangbæk, K. and M. Bech. 2004. County level responses to the introduction of DRG rates for "extended choice" hospital patients in Denmark. *Health Policy* 67: 25–37.

Williams, F. 1999. Good enough principles for welfare. *Journal of Social Policy* 28(4): 667–687.

Williams, J. and A. Rossiter. 2004. *Choice: The evidence. The operation of choice systems in practice: National and international evidence.* London: The Social Market Foundation.

12 From Metaphor to Reality

A Critical View of Prisons

Finola Farrant

INTRODUCTION

There are few organizations that explicitly have the infliction of pain as one of their primary functions. Prisons, however, have as their overarching aim, their ultimate purpose, the exercise of punishment. With "the deliberate infliction of suffering and hardships upon those contained within its walls" (Scott, 2007, 49) prisons are unique places (Sparks, Bottoms and Hay, 1996). Although Goffman (1961, 1968) in his analysis of 'total institutions,' and Foucault (1977/1991) in his exploration of power and control, could draw upon a range of organizational settings including mental hospitals, monasteries, factories, and schools, there is nothing so total, in constraints, in degradation, and the display of power, as the prison (Christie, 1994). A situation Foucault appears to accept when he states "the prison, much more than the school, the workshop or the army . . . is 'omnidisciplinary' . . . it gives almost total power over the prisoners; it has its internal mechanisms of repression and punishment: a despotic discipline" (1977/1991, 235–236). Despite their unique status, an understanding of prisons can resonate with issues pertinent to institutional, management, and organizational theory. For critical management theorists in particular, prisons and the related concept of the panopticon, have provided a potent metaphor for describing the repressive, disciplinary nature of managerial and organizational practices (Deetz, 1998; Papa et al., 1995; Townley, 1993). Moreover, because prisons inform us about what a society values as its core concerns, we can understand power by looking at its extremities (Foucault, 2004). Nevertheless, prisons, as real, physical institutions in which thousands of people work and thousands more are contained, have rarely been theorized within critical management studies.

Prisons have traditionally attracted significant sociological and criminological attention and a range of issues including the effects of imprisonment (Goffman, 1961, 1968, 1983; Haney, 2002; Sykes, 1958); staff–prisoner relations (Crewe, 2006; Liebling and Price, 1999; Liebling, Price, and Elliot, 1999; Edgar et al., 2003); and prison staff and management (Bryans, 2007; Crawley, 2004, 2006; Cressey, 1951, 1997; Dilulio, 1987; Jones,

2006) have been explored. Increasingly, however, penological studies have been characterized by rational, passionless terms where "moral evaluation is displaced by scientific understanding" (Garland, 1990, 186). Considerations regarding the moral and ethical dimensions of imprisonment have been superseded by a growing focus on correctional efficiency. This places individual deficits at the center of the punitive discourse and seeks to know everything about the offender. Actuarial techniques of risk management (Feeley and Simon, 1984; Simon, 1988) are used to develop standardized, packaged responses that can apply a technique, or strategy, to groups of offenders to deal with their 'criminogenic needs.' All of which are based on the belief that efficiency, management, and cost-effectiveness will somehow help to depoliticize criminal justice debates (Farrant, 2006).

It is the aim of this chapter to make prisons concrete, real, physical institutions. Rather than operating as an allegory for contemporary working and management practices, prisons as actual organizations are considered. Alvesson and Deetz (2006) suggest that critical management theory highlights how managerial values have reduced the capacity to meet human needs. How managerialism has impacted on the prison service (and therefore, by default, on prisoners) forms the backdrop to this chapter. In relation to context, it is somewhat ironic that as critical theory took hold in management studies from the late 1970s onwards, and disillusionment grew with the management discourse of rationalization and control; simultaneously, management discourse and practices became increasingly promoted as the answer to criminal justice policies and practices. In particular, the development of New Public Management (NPM) techniques have had a significant impact on the prison service. Raine and Willon (1997) identify a number of elements in NPM including an emphasis upon financial efficiency; expecting more for less money; greater standardization in policies and practices which curb autonomy and reduce idiosyncrasies; reorganization into stronger hierarchies; and, increased target setting and performance monitoring. This new managerialism can be detected in a range of public services (see, for example, Learmouth and Harding 2004 on the impact of NPM on health services) and led to radical changes in the style of prison management which started in the 1980s and continues through today. Representing a pragmatic, technological, and future-oriented approach, it emphasizes strategic planning, service delivery, efficiency and value for money; and, characterized by strong centralized direction, it is neither apolitical nor ideologically free, but has a tendency towards instrumentalism and quantification (McEvoy, 2001).

Early penological studies with their interest in the micro-level of interaction that goes on in the prison (Goffman, 1961, 1968, 1983) and the 'pains of imprisonment' (Sykes, 1958) have therefore given way to the managerialist discourse of targets, key performance indicators, and cost effectiveness. As managerialism creeps into the criminal justice system as a whole, and the prison service in particular, the time is ripe to consider prisons through a critical management lens. There is, however, a clear tension in exploring prisons in this way. If the central goal of critical theory in organizational studies is, as Alvesson and Deetz (2006) contend "to create societies and work places which are free from domination" (259), then prisons, which are premised upon punishment, fear, control, and power are organizations that will never achieve this goal. Where then, does this leave analysis of the prison? There are two possible ways forward. Firstly, through recognition that prisons are places of work which can, along with any other organization or working environment, be open to examination, and, secondly, that the consequences for those both detained and those who work in them are important, as prisons reflect broader social patterns and values. Analysis of prisons therefore tells us something about the society which sanctions their terms. If we wish to create societies and workplaces free from domination, then societies free from prisons may be the ideal place to start.

Consequently, this chapter sets out to examine the extraordinary nature of the prison institution, recognizing that while it is an institution like no other, analysis of the inner world of the prison, and its symbolic value in wider society, exposes the interplay of power and powerlessness, of conflict, loyalty, and alienation (Crewe, 2007). Adopting a critical theoretical approach legitimizes, or even demands, a non-objective view of the organizational processes within which power is exercised (Alvesson and Willmott, 2003). Applying such an approach to the world of the prison, their role as places of punishment is explored in the first instance; this is followed by consideration of their role as a place of work. The historical development of the prison as the main site of punishment is presented in the first section. The work of Sykes (1958) and Goffman (1961) is discussed in regards to their contribution to understandings on power and institutional order and the micro-level of interaction that goes on in prison. Beyond this, consideration is also given to the exercise of collective prisoner power. The Strangeways riots that occurred in Manchester in 1990 and the impact of The Woolf Report that followed in their wake, are used to provide an example of the role of collective power in prison protests and riots. The second section of the chapter discusses prison as a place of work. Recognition is given to the imbalance in research and theory in relation to the impact of prison on prisoners and staff. While there has been a great deal written about prisoners, prison staff, if not wholly neglected, have not attracted anywhere near the same attention. A coherent theoretical viewpoint about prison staff is lacking. Some studies, for example, argue that relations between staff and prisoners should be impersonal and that the prison regime should be run along militaristic lines. Other research looks at the emotional labor involved in prison work, decision-making, power, and the impact of gender.

Three themes inform each account and are drawn together in the conclusion. First, that prisons are institutions suffused with the exercise of power and control. Second, the asymmetrical power relations which define the 'total institution' are explicated and recognition given to how, even in institutions premised on power and control, resistance can still be found. Finally, the identity work undertaken by both prisoners and prison staff is explored, with particular reference to the changed context ushered in by NPM.

It is important to note that this chapter is generally based on those institutions that hold men, and although some of the issues examined are relevant to women's prisons, this is not always the case. The focus is on men's prisons as these are the vast majority of institutions in England and Wales—126 out of 140 prisons, men make up nearly 95 percent of the prison population, while prison officer staff are predominantly male.

PRISONS AS PLACES OF PUNISHMENT

The history of the prison is somewhat shorter than maybe first imagined. Prisons as places of punishment rather than confinement were devised approximately 200 years ago. The American war of independence curtailed transportation, and imprisonment as a way of dealing with crime came to be a central plank of sentencing policy (Soothill, 2007). By the final quarter of the eighteenth century the prison building was already dominating the penal and physical landscape. These first prisons were designed as 'places of real terror' (Evans, 1982, 169), frequently built in the center of cities and towns; the prison architecture itself aimed to instil a sense of fear. It was not long, however, before prisons attracted attention from reformers with a desire to rehabilitate offenders rather than to simply punish them. However, this apparent duality between reform and punishment has been questioned. Instead, both punishment and rehabilitation can be seen as equally associated with power relations, economic motives, and the operation of state power to regulate and control various sections of the community (Foucault, 1977/1991; Rusche and Kirchheimer, 1968; Melossi and Pavarini, 1981). Nonetheless, when people are imprisoned, a powerful message is communicated both to them and their fellow citizens: there are certain people who are unfit to live among us (Lippke, 2007).

As Foucault (1977/1991) argued, the exercise of power is pertinent to every practice of punishment or sanctioning. The prison, as the ultimate sanction in our society, is therefore the site in which the exercise of power is at its most brutal and is inextricably linked to knowledge and resistance (Foucault 1972, 1977/1991). Mathiesen (1965) argued that a legitimate distribution of power and authority in prisons is impossible and that attempts to discover one simply become rationalizations for the persistence of the 'prison solution', to what are in fact a range of social problems. Unsurprisingly then, the issue of power and domination has been the focus of much prison research. The effect of power, or lack of it, on prisoners has proved a particularly fruitful area of study (Clemmer, 1940; Cohen and Taylor, 1972; Mathiesen, 1965; Sykes, 1958; Toch, 1977).

Gresham Sykes's *The Society of Captives* (1958) is traditionally regarded as the seminal text on prisons, and retains contemporary credibility having recently been judged the most influential book on prison studies in the twentieth century (Reisig, 2001). Sykes identified power and institutional order as key areas of consideration in prison research. He argued that prison staff did not assert total dominance over prisoners, despite the potential for them to do so; instances of struggle for control, and examples of resistance, could be found in the numerous violations of regulations committed by prisoners. Although prison staff could coerce prisoners into obedience through force this was seen as a potentially dangerous, as well as an inefficient way of getting things done. Instead, certain members of the prison community—prisoner leaders—were co-opted by staff and became informally involved in the maintenance of order.

It was not only prisoners who compromised prison order. Staff, according to Sykes, struggled to maintain formal boundaries and to systematically enforce rules. The first reason for this was that working in such close proximity and so regularly with prisoners made it difficult to remain distant, therefore more informal relationships between staff and prisoners developed. Secondly, staff were dependent on prisoners to maintain the smooth running of the prison because of their involvement in a range of routine tasks. Negotiation and compromise between prison staff and prisoners were key for order to be maintained. Rules were not too strictly enforced as informal arrangements between staff and those prisoners who acted as prison leaders helped reduce the likelihood of disorder. Sykes concluded that order functioned through the prisoner hierarchy, and that the inmate code which included such things as, being tough, not grassing on another inmate, not siding or showing respect to prison officers, all operated to ameliorate the harshness of prison life.

Nevertheless, the defining characteristic of imprisonment for Sykes was deprivation, what he termed as the pains of imprisonment. These involved the deprivation of liberty, goods and services, heterosexual relations, autonomy, and security. Experienced by prisoners as a set of threats and attacks on their own being, one of the ways prisoners could try to diminish the pains of imprisonment was to form a cohesive set of rules and behaviors to abide by. The social solidarity between prisoners and the operation of the inmate code was therefore explained as a cultural mechanism for alleviating these pains, and of asserting some power over a situation in which they appeared to have little.

Drawing upon and developing Sykes' work, Erving Goffman (1961, 1968) argued that prison was just one among a number of 'total institutions.' Defined as "a place of residence and work where a large number of like-situated individuals, cut off from the wider society for an appreciable period of time, together lead an enclosed formally administered round of life" (1968, 11), Goffman encouraged consideration of the ways in which structural properties of institutions impact upon, and alter, the identities of their occupants. For example, the admission process into a total institution is described as a 'civic death'—a series of social and psychological attacks which undermine a person's sense of self. In prison, the exercise of power was seen as involving a range of instances which ultimately lead to the 'mortification of self'. Examples of this included the dispossession of property; dispensing with referring to people by their name; restrictions on clothing and other bodily adornments; strip and other types of searches; verbal deference; restrictions on communication; lack of control over when and what to eat, when to get up, and what to do during the day; access to showers; and reliance on staff to allow access of movements around the prison. Power in prisons, according to Goffman, operates at the very micro-level of interaction that occurs between prisoners and prison staff. Things that are minor and taken for granted in the outside world, become the focus of attention and the site of control and resistance in the total institution.

As Foucault indicated (1977/1991), the use of timetabling and spatial organization are key means by which prisons can regulate and discipline their members—both those contained and those who work there. Nevertheless, Goffman argues that despite being socially and physically separated from the outside world in a closed environment where the inmate could be completely controlled by an authority, prisoners still sought some control over their environment and some kind of independent self-concept. Individual forms of resistance can be seen in relation to the development of alternative forms of communication between prisoners, such as prison language and terminology; in breaches of prison rules; and in attempts to control and manipulate the physical body (Jewkes, 2005; Wahidin and Tate, 2005).

Power is also exercised by prisoners at a collective level, most dramatically in the form of riots (Crewe, 2007). Arguably, the most drastic and publicly notorious event in the modern history of prisons in England and Wales was the occupation and siege of Strangeways Prison in Manchester in 1990 and the subsequent wave of disturbances across the prison estate that followed in its wake. During the riot at Strangeways, 147 staff and 47 prisoners were injured. There was one fatality among the prisoners, and one prison officer died from heart failure. Much of the original prison was damaged or destroyed during the riots. Following such high profile unrest, the Woolf Report (1991) was commissioned to diagnose the causes and potential remedies for such disturbances. Lord Justice Woolf identified the primary cause of the disturbances as a widely shared sense of injustice among prisoners (Sparks, Bottoms, and Hay, 1996). This brought to attention the issue of legitimacy in the maintenance of order in prisons. The acquiescence or resistance of prisoners to the authority and power exercised upon them was seen to be a variable matter dependent on whether prisoners see the behaviour of staff as "justifiable, comprehensible, consistent, and fair or, alternatively, unwarranted, arbitrary, capricious, and overweening" (Sparks, Bottoms, and Hay, 1996, 16). The Woolf Report considered issues relating to management and leadership and argued that there needed to be a clear division of responsibility between prison governors, area managers, central prison service managers, and government ministers. He suggested that there had been a 'vacuum of visible leadership' which had contributed to the riots and the failure to contain them; and that the role of director–general of the prison service should have the authority necessary to run the prison service effectively.

In response to these criticisms, and in a climate amenable to changes in management style, the prison service became an executive agency in 1993. Taking hold across the public services, the NPM ushered in centralized objectives, uniformity and standardization, and the privatization of prisons. Brought in on the basis that they would drive up standards in public prisons, there are currently eleven private prisons in England and Wales. According to the prison service's league table of prisons, ten of the eleven are in the bottom quarter of performers, with Peterborough prison, privately managed for three years, coming bottom with a poor record for organizational effectiveness, decency, and reducing reoffending (Gourlay, 2008). Although prison privatization remains something of a contentious issue (though less so than it has been), it can be seen as crystallizing the dichotomy between a managerialist approach and the expectations of a publicly run organization, especially when tasked with inflicting pain on citizens on behalf of the state. In managerialism, the best prison is the one that most efficiently and correctly performs its allocated tasks. This contrasts with the view that recognizes the moral and constitutional dilemmas of imprisonment—that the exercise of power in imposing painful deprivation is a unique kind of 'public obligation' (Sparks, Bottoms, and Hay, 1996, 22).

The ways in which prisoners assert and resist power can be defined to a significant degree by the ways in which power is imposed upon them (Crewe, 2007). As most prison studies have shown, while power is clearly an integral part of the prison institution, prisoner resistance also features strongly. Many of the operations of the prison have control of resistance in mind and seek to establish order through various tactics including: the provision or denial of early release, home leave, release on temporary licence, and extra spending money; the use of the incentives and earned privileges schemes; and access to in-cell television or other leisure activities—all of which are focused on individual rather than collective concerns, on the assumption that prisoners are more likely to comply with the demands of the institution if good behaviour results in material benefits (Crewe, 2007).

PRISONS AS PLACE OF WORK

Prisons have provided fertile ground for research. Nevertheless, the empirical and theoretical focus has tended to be on prisoners and the impact of the prison environment upon them, rather than on prison staff. Ostensibly, every aspect of a prisoner's life involves some element of domination by prison staff. How this power is exhibited and manifests itself in relation to the running of prisons, and the impact of holding such levels of power, control, and knowledge over other human beings is increasingly forming part of penological studies. Not that this area has been completely neglected. Even in the classic prison studies of Sykes and Goffman some of these issues had been considered. For example, Goffman (1968) suggested that there are peculiar difficulties associated with the "people work" performed by staff in total institutions. Many prison officers spend more time with prisoners than with their own families and such proximity has a way of breaking down stereotypes and building relationships. Officers may therefore come to view the prisoners in their charge as "reasonable, responsible creatures who are fitting objects of emotional involvement" (Goffman, 1961, 82). It seems likely, therefore, that those who work inside the prison system become habituated to the extraordinary conditions, bizarre relationships, and the intense emotional atmosphere that makes up their daily working environment (Page, 2006).

Research on prison officers has examined prisoner–staff relationships (Dilulio, 1987; Goffman, 1961; Liebling and Price, 1999; Sykes, 1958); decision-making processes by prison officers (Liebling et al., 1999); the emotional work involved in becoming a prison officer (Crawley, 2004, 2006); and prison officer training (Arnold, 2005). Dilulio (1987) argues that officers are "arguably the key actors in any prison setting" (3) and acknowledges that prison workers experience unique emotional stresses. Prison officers and prisoners are seen as dependent upon each other within the prison organization. However, he goes on to argue that improvements within prison regimes require officers to be more 'impersonal' in their relations with inmates. The prison officer's role should be a:

> Tight, stable, uniform routine of monitoring inmate movement, frisking inmates, searching cells, and so on. Officer training would take place in an abbreviated 'boot camp' where this routine would be memorized and practiced, physical training and self-defence arts would be mastered, and the basic principles of security management, from key control to riot control would be learned (Dilulio, 1987, 239).

It would appear that for Dilulio the problem with prisons is that they are not rational enough. A more militaristic, controlled environment is needed. In fact it has been argued that the prison service management structure in England and Wales is one which is very much based on a military line management style (Jones, 2006).

Cressey (1951, 1997) has studied prisons over many years and was one of the first people to specifically consider the role of prison officers. He argues that there is no equivalent to the prison officer in the business or industrial world, but goes on to suggest that the job is little more than to stand guard and that the failure of prison organizations to set about being productive with prisoners mirrors the way in which officers are themselves not used productively by their managers. The bureaucratic, routine nature of prison work makes for what appears to be a dull and largely unrewarding job.

The role of power, and the power relations between prisoners and prison staff, has been explored by a number of more recent British studies (Crawley, 2004, 2006; Crewe, 2006; Liebling and Price, 1999; Liebling, Price, and Elliot, 1999). Generally, these studies have suggested prison officers can exert considerable power over prisoners, although how officers are subject to control themselves may also be considered (Edgar et al., 2003; Hepburn and Crepin, 1984; Valentine and Longstaff, 1998). The nuances and complexities of prison work and the emotional aspects of working in prison are at the forefront of Crawley's (2004) study *Doing Prison Work*. Liebling, Price, and Elliott's explorations on staff and prisoner relationships place the staff–prisoner relationship at the heart of the prison system and stable prison life (Liebling and Price, 1999; Liebling, Price and Elliott 1999). In these latter studies, in order to neutralize the anticipated antipathy of prison staff, and to show that the researchers were interested in what the prison officers had to say, an 'appreciative' methodology was adopted, the aim of which was to allow the prison officers to concentrate on the best aspects of their work and the situations in which they functioned particularly well. This, the authors thought, would counter previous studies on prison staff, which they believed had been superficial and overly critical (1999). The use of power in relation to the role of discretion during decision-making is examined. Although the power dynamic involved in the staff–prisoner relationship is not ignored, it is argued, however, that for most of the time power is, as Sykes (1958) had argued, 'held in reserve'. What 'goes on' in prisons is seen as happening primarily through the staff–prisoner relationship. Decisions prison officers make are seen as part of a network of relationships within the context of complex and embedded relationships with prisoners, other staff and managers. In contrast to previous studies that have highlighted how prison staff exert power, Liebling et al. argue that prison officers may in fact under, rather than over, use their power.

> Prison officers spend a great deal of their time and energy negotiating "peaceful co-existence" with and between prisoners. They avoid conflict, resolve tensions; they humour and challenge (Liebling et al., 1999, 90).

Nevertheless, even in this type of appreciative study, it is concluded that "through control, routine, indifference to the human spirit, or the damage done, prison, constrains language and imagination" (ibid., 91). Liebling returns to some of these themes in *Prison and Their Moral Performance* (2004). This highlights how the practice of managerialism is an exercise in domination. Power is wielded over an expendable workforce whose own needs and desires can be legitimately denied. The key elements that shape the working personality of the prison officer are seen to be authority and danger. Prison officers must assert authority almost constantly as the interactions between prisoners and staff frequently relate to the minutia of prison life, which is exactly where prisoners can assert some level of resistance. So, for example, flashpoints of power and control frequently revolve around meal times, the quality of food, when showers can be taken, and in many of the other routine aspects of prison life.

One element of prison work which is frequently neglected is the emotional impact on prison officers of the work that they do. As a way of seeing the social world of the prison officer, the sociology of emotions provides an invaluable insight into the "complex intertwining of bureaucracy, rationality, dramaturgy and emotion in prison" (Crawley, 2004, xiv). It is not only the day-to-day work of the prison officer that is important. Prison officer training, the arrival of the new recruit into a prison, and the impact of their work upon their family lives are all significant. Based on in-depth interviews with staff, focus groups with prison officers' families, and lengthy observation of prison officers' work, how staff are involved in constituting the organization is explored by Crawley (2004, 2006). The emotional aspects of the prison and prison work are acknowledged:

> Prisons are emotional arenas. In consequence, working in prisons demands a performative attitude on the part of staff, and (often significant) engagement in emotion work and the employment of a range of emotion work strategies (Crawley, 2004, xii).

CONCLUSION

Prisons provide a closed, intimate, extreme, and unusual setting for critically considering issues relating to work and identity. Inside the prison walls the exercise of power, and the responses to that power, shape and construct prisoner and prison officer identities. One of the key features of the power dynamic between prisoners and staff is that of violence. The use or threatened use of force in prison is omnipresent. One survey found that one in five men in prison had been hit, kicked, or assaulted in some other way, in the month before the study (O'Donnell and Edgar, 1998). Moreover, many autobiographical accounts by prisoners are replete with examples of violence at the hands of prison staff.

> In the detention centre it seemed that the purpose of the prison officers was to subject the 'trainees' as we were termed, to a rigorous regime of unrelenting 'discipline' which often included violence (James, 2006, 19).

Such examples of violence illustrate how power can be brutally enacted within the prison environment. Foucault (1977/1991) showed that the practices of punishment reflect the dominant forms of social and political control and involve the power to threaten, coerce, suppress. Significantly, he also cultivated a deep suspicion toward claims that contemporary society had humanized the forms of punishment by abandoning corporal brutality in favor of a prison system that controls the time and movements of prisoners and operates to 'transform' (or render docile) the individual. The disciplinary nature of surveillance exemplified by the panopticon—where the expectation of surveillance would eventually lead to self-discipline has provided an evocative metaphor for those interested in critically examining contemporary work practices. Nonetheless, the reality of the prison organization is one in which increasing numbers of individuals find themselves confined and in which large numbers of people work. Considering the prison as a place of punishment and work is therefore important if criminologists are to "decode and eventually unravel existing power relations" (Cheliotis and Liebling, 2006, 311) particularly at a time when managerialist discourses have been embraced by the prison service.

Rather than existing as neutral bureaucratic entities, prisons are formed in and through a matrix of gender, race, class, and sexuality, which reproduces individuals, ideas, and inequalities along all these dimensions. Indeed, gender, ethnicity, class, and sexuality are essential components of all organizations (Martin and Collinson, 2002). It is organizational studies and critical management theory which have explored identity work to a significantly greater extent than criminological studies (Sveningsson and Alvesson, 2003). Yet, criminal justice organizations produce and reproduce identity and understandings of self. Furthermore, the symbolic importance of the prison spills out beyond the confines of the prison walls. It is an institution at once both familiar and strange. Prison is something few of us will ever have direct experience of, yet is familiar to us through media-mediated images and stories, and as part of the discourse on crime, justice, and punishment which puts the prison at its center (Farrant, 2006). Although organizations operate to construct identity, individuals bring their own identities, interests, and desires into the organization. However, in an environment such as the prison, the impact on a person's identity—whether as prisoner or officer can be significant:

> I realised I had developed a prison persona: hands in pockets, a slow uncaring walk, shoulders hunched, scowling and grumpy; a woman of few words but always a curse at the ready. It had happened in just two or three days. There I was, Wyner, prison number EH 6524: scared but not going to show it; ready for anything but behaving as if I didn't give a shit. My defences were up, and I knew I needed them, but also I feared that the real "me" had been destroyed. Would I ever get her back again? (Wyner, 2003, 23)

I came into this job thinking of prison officers as rough, strict and treating everyone like dirt. I thought I'd be the one to treat prisoners well. But it didn't work out like that. They just thought I was soft. The only thing they responded to was being hard. I was as cynical as the rest of them within twelve months (prison officer cited in Crawley, 2004, 213).

The construction of a 'front' within prison or the performance required as a prisoner or prison officer is increasingly being explored in prison research. How the prison is gendered at a number of levels, from the pre-conceptions and experiences of officer recruits, in training, in ideas about working with male or female prisoners, conceptions of prison officers and prisoners as gendered beings have been considered (Britton, 2000). For example, in one study of male prisoners and female staff, the significance of 'femaleness' over professional identity and practices, is considered as part of the discourses of sexualization and chivalry evident in men's prisons (Crewe, 2006). This suggested that prisoners' life experiences, and the nature of imprisonment, had a significant influence on the relationships that developed between male prisoners and female officers. The high emotional charge that characterizes many of these relationships reflects a complex set of issues around incarceration, masculine self-identity, power, and desire. Moreover, this becomes more extreme in men's prisons due to their "hypermasculine" culture and hierarchies of domination. Most penological studies, however, treat the gender of their subjects (whether offenders or officers) as incidental despite the very maleness of the vast majority of penal institutions (Jewkes, 2005). Similar territory is explored in relation to women in prison and the aging process. In their study on this issue, Wahidin and Tate (2005) examine how women prisoners have become public property, but can seek to reinscribe their identities in order to preserve a sense of self. Strategies of subversion are therefore used to challenge, negotiate, or maintain power relations.

Crewe (2007) discusses some of the dangers inherent in prison research becoming co-opted into managerialist agendas. However, the special nature of the prison makes visible issues of universal interest in relation to adaptation, distress, endurance, and social organization. The prison provides a concrete illustration of issues relating to power, inequality, order, and conflict. They provide a potent symbol of the state's power to punish. Prisons are distinct sites of power and powerlessness, of pain, and deprivation. They are extraordinary, atypical organizations. However, the uses we make of prisons and the conditions we consider acceptable within them, are issues that provide clues to societal views and values, the operation of power and control, work and identity, in a vast array of contexts. Moreover, if we are to seriously try to create societies and work places which are free from domination, prisons should be the first places we turn to try and make that a reality.

204   *Finola Farrant*

REFERENCES

Alvesson, M. and S.A. Deetz. 2006. Critical theory and postmodernism: Approaches to organizational studies. In *The Sage handbook of organization studies*, eds. S.R. Clegg, C. Hardy, T. Lawrence, W.R. Nord, 191–217. London: Sage.
Alvesson, M. and H. Willmott. 2003. *Studying management critically*. London: Sage.
Arnold, H. 2005. The effects of prison work. In *The effects of imprisonment*, S. Maruna and A. Liebling, 394–420. Cullompton, UK: Willan.
Britton, D.M. 2003. *At work in the iron cage: The prison as gendered organization*. New York: New York University Press.
Bryans, S. 2007. Prison governors: Managing prisons in a time of change. Cullompton, UK: Willan.
Christie, N. 1994. *Crime control as industry*. London: Routledge.
Clemmer, D. 1940. *The prison community*. Boston: Christopher Publishing Company.
Cohen, S. and L. Taylor. 1972. *Psychological survival*. Harmondsworth, UK: Penguin.
Crawley, E. 2004. *Doing prison work*. Devon, UK: Willan.
Cressey, D.R. 1951. Epidemiology and individual conduct: A case from criminology. *Pacific Sociological Review* 3: 47–58.
Cressey, D.R. 1997. Prison organization. In *Handbook of Organizations*, eds. J.G. March, 1023–1070. Jaipur, India: Rawat Publications.
Crewe, B. 2006. Male prisoners' orientation towards female officers in an English prison. *Punishment and Society* 8(4): 5–421.
Crewe, B. 2007. The sociology of imprisonment. In *Handbook on Prisons*, eds. Y. Jewkes, 123–151. Cullompton, UK: Willan.
Deetz, S. 1998. Discursive formations, strategized subordination, and self-surveillance: An empirical case. In *Foucault, management and organizational theory*, eds. A. McKinlay and K. Starkey, 151–172. London: Sage.
Dilulio, J. 1987. *Governing prisons*. New York: The Free Press.
Edgar, K., I. O'Donnell, and C. Martin. 2003. *Prison violence: The dynamics of conflict, fear and power*. Devon, UK: Willan.
Evans, R. 1982. *The fabrication of virtue: English prison architecture, 1750–1840*. Cambridge, UK: Cambridge University Press.
Farrant, F. 2006. Knowledge production and the punishment ethic: The demise of the probation service. *Probation Journal* 53(4): 317–333.
Feeley, M. and J. Simon. 1994. Actuarial justice: The emerging new criminal law. In *The Futures of Criminology*, ed. D. Nelken, 173–201. London: Sage.
Foucault, M. 1972. *The archaeology of knowledge*. New York: Pantheon Books.
Foucault, M. 1977/1991. *Discipline and punish: The birth of the prison*. Harmondsworth, UK: Penguin.
Foucault, M. 2004. *Society must be defended: Lectures at the College De France 1975–76*. London: Penguin.
Garland, D. 1990. *Punishment and modern society*. Oxford, UK: Oxford University Press.
Goffman, E. 1961. On the characterisics of total institutions: Staff-inmate relations. In *The prison: Studies in institutional organization and change*, ed. D. Cressey, 15–67. New York: Holt, Rinehart and Winston.
Goffman, E. 1968. *Asylums: Essays on the social situation of mental patients and other inmates*. Harmondsworth, UK: Penguin.
Goffman, E. 1983. The Interaction Order. *American Sociological Review* 48: 1–17.

Gourlay, C. 2008. Private prisons prove poor performers. http://www.timesonline. co.uk/tol/news/uk/article3215684.ece (accessed January 30, 2008).

Haney, C. 2002. The psychological impact of incarceration: Implications for post-prison adjustment. http://aspe.hhs.gov/hsp/prison2home02/haney.pdf (accessed January 29, 2008).

Hepburn, J.R. and A.H. Crepin. 1984. Relationship strategies in a coercive institution: A study of dependence among prison guards. *Journal of Social and Personal Relationships* 1(2): 139–157.

James, E. 2006. Life inside. In *Humane prisons*, ed. D. Jones, 19–28. Abingdon, UK: Radcliffe Publishing Ltd.

Jewkes, Y. 2005. Men behind bars: "Doing" masculinity as an adaptation to imprisonment. Men and Masculinities 8: 44–63.

Jones, D. 2006. Psychopathological considerations of prison systems. In *Humane prisons*, ed. D. Jones, XX–XX. Abingdon, UK: Radcliffe.

Learmonth, M. and N. Harding. 2004. *Unmasking health management*. New York: Nova Science Publishers.

Liebling, A. 2004. *Prisons and their moral performance*. Oxford, UK: Clarendon.

Liebling, A. and D. Price. 1999. *An exploration of staff-prisoner relationships at HMP Whitemoor*. Prison Service Research Report No. 6. London: Home Office.

Liebling, A., D. Price, and C. Elliott. 1999. Appreciative inquiry and relationships in prison. *Punishment and Society* 1(1): 71–98.

Lippke, R.L. 2007. *Rethinking imprisonment*. Oxford, UK: Oxford University Press.

Martin, P.Y. and D. Collinson. 2002. Over the pond and across the water: Developing the field of "gendered organizations." *Gender, Work & Organization* 9(3): 244–65.

Mathiesen, T. 1965. *The defences of the weak*. London: Tavistock.

McEvoy, K. 2001. *Paramilitary imprisonment in northern Ireland: Resistance, management and release*. Oxford, UK: Oxford University Press.

Melossi, D. and M. Pavarini. 1981. *The prison and the factory: Origins of the penitentiary system*. London: Macmillan.

O'Donnell, I. and K. Edgar. 1998. *Bullying in prison*. Oxford, UK: Centre for Criminological Research.

Page, K. 2006. First impressions. In *Humane Prisons*, ed. D. Jones, 11–18. Abingdon, UK: Radcliffe Publishing Ltd.

Papa, M.J., M.A. Auwal, and A. Singhal. 1995. Dialectic of control and emancipation in organizing for social change: A multitheoretical study of the Grameen Bank in Bangladesh. *Communication Theory* 5: 189–223.

Raine, J. and M.J. Willson. 1997. Beyond managerialism in criminal justice. *The Howard Journal* 36(1): 95–121.

Rusche, G. and O. Kirchheimer. 1969. *Punishment and social structure*. New York: Columbia University Press.

Scott, D. 2007. The changing face of the English prison: A critical review of the aims of imprisonment. In *Handbook on Prisons*, ed. Y. Jewkes, 49–72. Cullompton, UK: Willan.

Simon, J. 1988. The ideological effect of actuarial practices. *Law and Society Review* 22: 772–800.

Soothill, K. 2007. Prison histories and competing audiences, 1776–1966. In *Handbook on Prisons*, ed. Y. Jewkes, 27–48. Cullompton: Willan.

Sparks, R., A. Bottoms, and W. Hay. 1996. *Prisons and the problem of order*. Oxford, UK: Clarendon Press.

Sveningsson, S. and M. Alvesson. 2003. Managing managerial identities: Organizational fragmentation, discourse and identity struggle. *Human Relations* 56(10): 1163–1193.

Sykes, G. 1958. *The society of captives: A study of a maximum security prison.* Princeton, NJ: Princeton University Press.

Toch, H. 1977. *Living in prison: The ecology of survival.* New York: NY Free Press.

Townley, B. 1993. Foucault, power/knowledge, and its relevance for human resource management. *Academy of Management Review* 18: 518–545.

Valentine, G. and B. Longstaff. 1998. Doing porridge: Food and social relations in a male prison. *Journal of Material Culture* 3(2): 131–152.

Wahidin, A. and S. Tate. 2005. Prison (e)scapes and body tropes: Older women in the prison time machine. *Body & Society* 11(2): 59–79.

Woolf, Lord Justice. 1991. *Prison disturbances: April 1990.* London: HMSO.

Wyner, R. 2003. *From the inside.* London: Aurum.

13 Queer(y)ing Voluntary Sector Services
An Example from Health Promotion

Nancy Harding and Hugh Lee

Our aim in this chapter is to introduce queer theory (QT) as a way of thinking about voluntary services delivered within the public sector. Our aim, ultimately, is the improvement of the services delivered. What QT does is 'queer' or make odd, or unusual, the ways in which we customarily think about voluntary and public sector services and the ways in which they are delivered. By queering voluntary sector services we show how they, like public sector services in general, can fall into the trap of homogenizing service users, and thus fail to deliver appropriate services.

The chapter explains what QT is and demonstrates the advantages of introducing it as a means of analyzing public and voluntary sector services. It uses sexual health promotion (SHP) as a case study to illustrate the value of this method of analysis.

INTRODUCING QT

Queer Theory (QT) emerged as a result of the footwork and hard slog made by feminist theorists in showing how women are discriminated against. However, a critique made against feminism in particular, but one that applied equally to men and masculinities (which had turned a feminist eye upon men), was that these perspectives presumed all women were similar just because they were women, and all men were similarly united by the single fact of their being men. Although feminism in particular claimed to be anti-essentialist, in that it rejected whole-heartedly the idea that there is anything 'given' that makes a person into a woman, it still presumed there was something about being a woman which united all women. Black women, working class women, women from ex-colonial powers and lesbian women argued forcefully that, in assuming this 'universal' woman, theorists ignored the wide variety of ways of being a woman. Theorists were therefore charged with having been supportive of a privileged form of womanhood—white, heterosexual, middle class women from developed economies (Alsop et al., 2002).

Meanwhile, stimulated in part by the liberatory potential of the work of the French academic, Michel Foucault, a highly political gay liberation movement emerged in the 1980s in both the United States and Western Europe. Where feminism has radically changed women's lives so that few women expect to spend their lives 'chained to the kitchen sink,' gay rights is bringing about remarkable changes in the lives of people who do not conform to what is known as 'the heterosexual matrix.'

Gender theory in general, and QT in particular, therefore bring together academic theory and political practice. Gender theorists have done this firstly through identifying how people are subordinated and suppressed by things so taken-for-granted and so familiar we hardly know they are governing us. Then they show that there is nothing 'natural' about the norms, practices, ways of thinking and ways of being that suppress 'minorities.' Through illustrating the constructed nature of the norms through which we are governed and controlled, it becomes possible to change those norms and the institutions which support them. Knowledge, therefore, is the vital step to bringing about changes.

This way of thinking, of 'queering' the taken for granted, that is, of looking at something that appears normal and seeing how queer, or odd, it is, can be applied not only to gender and sexuality, but to numerous other areas of our lives. One example is food: Elspeth Probyn (1993, 1999) has done sterling work in queering the ways in which food is understood and consumed in the Western world in the twenty-first century. With regard to the workplace, Parker (2002) has argued the merits of using QT in organization studies, and a number of authors are experimenting with its use in the understanding of organization and management (Brewis, Hampton and Linstead, 1997; Harding, 2003; Bowring, 2004), and in public administration (Lee, Learmonth, and Harding, 2008).

Our intention in this chapter is to show further the relevance of using QT to analyze public and voluntary sector services. This requires looking at them as if, rather than being normal, they are odd, or queer. As soon as we start thinking about what we regard as normal we find how peculiar the 'normal' is, leading us to ask: why are things this way? So 'queer' here does not refer to sexuality, but to ways of recognizing and exploring (queer[y]ing) the things we take for granted as 'normal' in our working and nonworking lives. To queer something therefore refers to exploring how norms or rules so govern identities and actions that we hardly recognize these modes of governance.

QT'S THEORETICAL ROOTS

QT's roots are to be found in the work of Michel Foucault (1979, 1986, 1992) and to a lesser extent perhaps that of Jacques Derrida (1976/1997). Their ideas have been developed notably by Eve Kosovsky Sedgwick (1991) and Judith Butler (1990, 1993, 1996). Sedgwick and Butler question the essentialist, given nature of categorizations such as straight/gay, heterosexual/homosexual and, indeed, male/female. These are binary opposites; pairs which permeate how we think about and construct our social worlds. In such pairs, one is superior, the other inferior. The superior relies upon the inferior half of the coupling for its existence (for example, how could we know there were such a thing as daylight if there were no such thing as darkness?). The inferior part of the pair is suppressed and subordinated by the dominant term's struggle for survival (Petersen, 1998; Roseneil and Seymour, 1999; Jagose, 1996). Thus women have been regarded as inferior to men, homosexuality to heterosexuality, and followership to leadership.

QT's initial focus, as noted, was upon gender and sexuality (Jagose, 1996; Butler, 1990, 1993, 1996; Sedgwick, 1991). Gender and sexuality are conventionally regarded as fixed, stable categories determined largely by biology. Feminism argued that gender is a social construction (Oakley, 1972), that is, gender is something that is *learned*, with biology determining the behaviors that are achieved. QT goes further, in that it argues that biology, too, is socially constructed (Butler, 1993). The *materiality* of the body (i.e., its physical status) is not denied, but QT argues that the ways in which we understand our bodies is through our social worlds. In different epochs and different cultures, bodies are understood (and therefore experienced) very differently.

QT therefore goes beyond social constructionism for it shows that what are constructed are *regulatory fictions*, or stories we tell ourselves as a culture and which regulate how people within that culture behave. Regulatory fictions both establish order and provide the rules, or norms, through which we organize ourselves to ensure order is maintained. They make such ordering and organizing appear natural and right. What is important here is QT's argument that these regulatory fictions are just that—fictional. They have no authenticity. QT, like most poststructuralist theories, turns accepted ways of thinking on their heads. Where we traditionally think that something exists and that it can be described using language, poststructuralism argues that it is language that brings into being those things that exist. QT's use of these insights leads to the argument that there is no "core" (such as biology) that produces gender; rather there is this language about biology, and it provides a language through which we can understand our bodies and which thus allows gender to be constructed.

This makes comprehensible Judith Butler's famous theory that 'there is no gender behind the expressions of gender' (see the previous discussion) for identity is performatively constituted by the very "expressions" that are said to be its results (Butler, 1990). By this she means that it is not gender that dictates how people should behave (for example, women should sit with their legs neatly together while men should sit in ways that take up lots of space). Rather it is the very *doing* of these gendered behaviors, behaviors that conform to the norms of how a person with the relevant genitalia should behave, which construct gender.

So QT shows how there is no choice but to adopt a recognizable identity and to perform that identity according to the name that one is called (or called to), but it also shows how tentative, how preliminary, how insecure, is that identity. It argues that in becoming a self, or enacting an identity, one aspires to act according to the norms which govern that identity. However, these norms are ideals which have no existence in the material world and so are, by definition, unattainable. For more on this impossibility of there being any essential or fixed identity see Lee (2006) from which the data for this chapter is largely taken.

We will now turn to our case study to show the value of QT in analyzing public and voluntary sector services. Through queering one particular service, we show how norms that govern identity operate in that service, and in so doing alienate its particular clientele.

THE CASE STUDY

To illustrate how to use QT we are drawing on a case study of SHP for men who have sex with men (MSM). The major form of promoting safe sex amongst MSM in the UK is a magazine-style publication called "eXposed!" that has been produced and distributed biannually since 2001 by a coalition of homosexual men's organizations. For the study we interviewed twelve MSM about their thoughts about this publication. We asked them to look at one of the issues, and talk through their thoughts, feelings and opinions as they read the magazine.

To help the reader, we will describe the issue used in the fieldwork. This issue is typical in style, content, and layout of all the issues published since 2001. Its content is highly sexualized.

The front cover of this representative edition introduces the sexualized nature of the content as a whole. It shows a young, muscular man naked from the waist down. The picture cuts off just above the base of the penis leaving his pubic hair visible. Down the left side are the words, "gay sex—how much would you reveal?" and in the bottom right corner, "PLUS YOUR CHANCE TO WIN ONE OF 25 NEW PROWLER VIDEOS OR DVDs." Finally, in small print on the left side of the front page is the eighteen certificate logo and the words "CAUTION! Explicit material for gay men only." The central visual feature of every page emphasizes an omnipresent pleasure theme, including: bare torsos; two men in passionate embrace; images of men having anal sex. There is no respite from eroticism and an implied invitation to sexual arousal. Paradoxically, however, alongside these sorts of images are short sections of text, often in very large font sizes, warning readers of the dangers of unprotected sex.

We interviewed twelve men aged between twenty-two and eighty-four, drawn from occupations including students, chefs, scientists, priests, teachers, call-center workers, who had all identified themselves as gay or MSM.

We have used pseudonyms rather than their own names. Participants were asked to read the edition of "eXposed!" summarized above and talk about what they saw as they looked at or read the literature, and what they felt about it.

Interviewees typically said they thought they had been asked to read a 'toned-down' version of commercial, semi-pornographic magazines such as *Gay Times* or *Bent* and they said they had not realized that its purpose was SHP. They all commented on how the format is distracting and confusing at times, and how the mixture of image and text is problematic for them. They experienced dissonance between the words that discussed the dangers of HIV and the pictures that represented 'perfect' (and by implication healthy) male models. They were also critical of the sexualized nature of the content. For example, one interviewee we call Alex, a twenty-six-year-old postdoctoral researcher in a long-term relationship with a man with whom he was buying a house, while looking at the images said:

> I like aspects of this I like the fact that it's sort of trying to to put you in the position of if you has HIV you might not always act as though you've got HIV . . . But I this, the problem I have with this and I don't know how you would get around it to be honest is the problem I have with a lot of the HIV adverts in gay magazines and that's that they're obsessed with sex. I know it's to do with sex but I mean *why do you need that?*

Thus for Alex, images and text conflict and undermine one another. He is ambivalent about the format, both likes and dislikes some of the ways in which the information is presented, but questions the need for the sexualized nature of the images. In his ambivalence and his uncertain response, Alex is perhaps both attracted to and offended by the images.

ALEX'S AMBIVALENCE—
QUEER(Y)ING WHAT IT IS TO BE QUEER

We will first say something more about QT so as to allow us to better understand the ambivalence with which Alex responded to the SHP literature we had asked him to read. QT, as we use it, is a set of political or politicized practices and positions which explore and are critical of normative (how things should be) knowledge and identities (Lee, Learmonth and Harding, 2008). This means that QT has powers both to explain and to bring about changes.

The first thing to say is that QT has been developing for about twenty years as a theoretical perspective having important explanatory power in the arts, humanities, and social sciences (Doty, 1993; Seidman, 1997). It offers two major advantages: firstly, it helps cast new light on behaviors and activities formerly seen as unproblematic and well understood; secondly it can contribute towards political and emancipatory projects. It complements the work of theorists who link poststructuralism explicitly to political action, such as Derrida (1994), Laclau and Mouffe (2001) and Young (2004) and thus to emancipation. QT exhorts us to interrogate taken-for-granted assumptions about what is 'normal.' We rarely think about 'normality'—we are surrounded by it, like fish are surrounded by water, and its omnipresence means we do not even notice it is there. However, QT argues that for there to be normality there must be that which is abnormal, or queer, and people who are regarded as abnormal or queer are unequal, and their oppression or exploitation is either unnoticed or regarded as acceptable. Those who fail to achieve or uphold the norms which govern identities and practices, and which subordinate some while controlling the dominant identity, thus are regarded as inferior. Those so regarded live lives that are, in Judith Butler's words (1993, 1998, 2004) abject.

QT is a poststructuralist perspective so it encourages what Hall (2003, 10) refers to as "diverse reading strategies and multiple interpretative stances." By this is meant that we should 'queer' how we read so that we see beyond the 'straightforward,' get a better understanding of how texts and practices work, and thus learn how to resist 'regimes of the normal' (Warner, 1993, xxvi). By 'regimes of the normal' is meant those notions of normality which govern and manage people's activities and expressions of selfhood (Hall, 2003, 15). These include, importantly, 'normal business in the academy' (Warner, 1993, xxvi), so QT can be used to explore how academic understanding serves, albeit unknowingly, in the constitution and maintenance of oppressive practices. QT (or indeed queer theories), seeks to trouble what we regard as normal, and helps us understand how we oppress ourselves, unconsciously or unknowingly, even as we participate (again unconsciously or unknowingly) in the oppression of others.

As noted above, QT evolved in part out of feminist and gender studies (Peterson, 1998). Feminism challenged institutions and knowledges initially through "adding in" the study of women, and followed this by offering a fundamental rethinking of every category of analysis within the social and political sciences, arts, and humanities. Gender studies 'added in' lesbian and gay studies, alongside the study of heterosexual men in 'men and masculinities.' QT, however, does more than "add in" the study of lesbians and gay men to political and social analysis: it firstly aims to make analyses queerer through exploring "all those whose lives transgress heteronormative assumptions . . . and then theorizing from their lives" (Budgeon and Roseneil, 2004, 129). It then goes on to challenge *all* categories of 'the normal.'

It may therefore seem odd that we are using SHP, and especially a version of SHP that uses raunchy images and text to address MSM, for it would seem that this method of communicating with MSM is designed to speak directly to them. However, QT shows that SHP has provided an image of what it is to be a 'normal' gay man (note—not the more broadly defined MSM), and the norms encompassed in this 'normal' gay man are so narrowly defined, and so unattainable by the vast majority of men, that gay men looking at the images are made to be feel abnormal.

QT demonstrates how dominant regimes depend upon their subjugated opposites, their other, to know and sustain themselves. In other words, a privileged "inside" could not exist without a demeaned "outside" (Fuss, 2001). For example, if the world was peopled only by men they would not know themselves as men, they would not be an intelligible category, for there would be no opposite, no women, against whose difference men could define themselves. In QT "heterosexual" can only be an intelligible category when there is also the linked category "homosexual"; in leadership theory the 'leader' can be intelligible only through the linked category of 'follower' (Ford, Harding, and Learmonth, 2008). The hierarchy of dominant/subordinate terms is maintained by repressive means that historically have involved exclusion (for example, of women, homosexuals, and people of color) from public life. They are denied civil rights, disenfranchised, and suffer other forms of exclusion and abuse. The subjugated other is 'symbolically degraded' (Fuss, 2001, 353) in contrast to the symbolic purity of the dominant construct, and so the subjugated other is defiled and dominated.

Practices ascribed to the inferior part of the binary are regarded as polluting, those of the superior part as pure: it is this ascription that allows the superior to know itself as superior, as unpolluted. Homosexuals, for example, are "individuals for whom shame and guilt are at the core of their sense of self" (Fuss, 2001, op cit.). However, those in the dominant, unpolluted category are also controlled, restricted, compelled to live by norms. As Seidman (2001) writes: "regimes of heteronormativity not only regulate the homosexual but control heterosexual practices by creating a moral hierarchy of good and bad sexual citizens" (Seidman, 2001, 354).

This is what explains Alex's ambivalence. He is being shown an image of the normative homosexual, someone who is young, fit, hedonistic, and attractive. SHP thus constructs 'the' gay man as a specific type of person and thus a normative category that must be achieved by all who would identify as gay. Alex is gay, but when he looks at these images he cannot identify with them so he cannot be gay. What therefore is his identity? It would seem he does not have one.

Alex's ambivalence is thus one of being assaulted by the knowledge that he is not good enough to be gay, so he suffers from a loss of identity. He was not alone in this response: indeed he is typical of all twelve men interviewed. Many responded initially with enthusiasm to the public health information we showed them, but after some thought found their enthusiasm turning to disquiet.

Pat, for example, initially felt these messages applied to him but later denied that they did. In so doing he, like all the men interviewed, shows the heterogeneity of the audience: there is no 'typical' MSM or gay man. Pat, although sexually active, does not fit the image portrayed in eXposed of the gay man as always youthful, fit, virile, and seeking sex. An older man, not as sexually active as those portrayed in the images, he feels excluded from the audience for SHP:

> . . . my my sort of sexual encounters have decreased over the years, not for any particular reason but erm . . . [I]f I wanted to have any sort of decent sex I would be quite pleased to get to know somebody first and perhaps a longer process (. . .) So a lot of these messages I've felt detached from (. . .) so I think I have to say that the . . . it doesn't, personally it doesn't say a lot to me personally. I agree with a lot of what it says but I can't claim that close connection with any of these because I because of my situation I have felt detached.

The SHP material therefore provides readers with an image of attractive, sexually active men who seem to have little need to work or any interest in anything other than clubbing, cruising, and showing off their amazingly fit and lean bodies. Readers are initially attracted by the images and then turn to talking about how they, personally, are not like the men portrayed. They are offered a norm of what a gay man should be, but they do not and cannot approximate to that norm.

Alex and Pat articulate very clearly for us QT's requirement that we recognize and then challenge norms, discourses, and practices that serve to subjugate some to the benefit of others. As gay men, they cannot identify with the gay men that those in authority, SHP experts, deem they should be like.

QT theorizes from the lives of any categories of people whose lives are in various ways unliveable (Butler, 2004), in that it puts into question *any* activities regarded as 'normal' and examines how the maintenance of 'the normal' makes many people feel 'abnormal.' What is defined as 'normal' is seen to exclude those who do not or cannot conform, who are thus 'abnormal,' for the normal cannot exist unless it has an abnormal by which it knows itself.

THE HOMOGENEOUS HOMOSEXUAL

Tim, a twenty-two year old university student, exemplifies the gay man who feels he is excluded because he does not fit into categories that supposedly represent what it is to be a gay man. The image of 'the gay man' is of men who 'have sex for kicks, for fun,' is not how he sees himself:

> I mean it's it's shallow it's not important but and . . . I suppose, many gay men think sex or I get the impression that many gay men might think sex falls into the you know yeah, something you do you know for

kicks for fun er . . . to go along with the whole being out on the scene having fun you know and that sort of thing.

Jay, a thirty-seven year old chef who lives with his male partner of ten years and keeps in touch with a daughter from a brief, teenage heterosexual relationship, similarly shows the heterogeneity of homosexuality. He contrasts the images in the magazine with what *he* regards as 'normal':

> When you first flick through and you see pictures it's like them, you know, back of *Gay Times* and that where they're advertising sex things, call this mobile number and that. But, why did they have to [put all this sex in]? Why can't they just show normal people in their normal working, you know, in a suit or whatever, or dressed as a chef, with a chef in, or whatever they do, instead of having them all naked.

These interviews show the *heterogeneity* that exists among MSM, and the *homogeneity* of the image of 'the' gay man. As Dollimore (1991) writes, the term 'homosexuality' is not an essential identity but:

> a cluster of things with more or less specific cultural locations, but with a history which is wider, more diverse, and more complex than the essentialist or even the constructionist view allows. It includes cultures, institutions, beliefs, practices, desires, aspirations, and much else, and changes across all of these. Hence 'homosexual' . . . is always provisional and context-dependent (1991, 32).

The homogeneous homosexual represented in the images is rejected by these readers, who resist the inherent stereotyping.

These interviews show that readers resent the implication that gay men or MSM are rampantly sexual: they are not like that, they say, and they wish to see representations of men who are like them, who are 'normal.' If these men are speaking on behalf of other MSM then we must conclude that these SHP materials (re)present a homogeneous homosexual—an image of 'the gay man' as a stereotype—who exists not so much in the material world as in the imagination of the producers of the literature.

QUEERING PUBLIC AND VOLUNTARY SECTOR SERVICES

It is only recently in much Western culture that homosexuality has ceased to be regarded as abnormal (Butler, 2008). Heterosexuality had required homosexuality as its abnormal Other (f, 1991), so that gay men and lesbian women were regarded as abject and inferior. The changes that have taken place in Western culture since the gay liberation movement started its campaigns would seem to have normalized homosexuality (Butler, 2008). SHP would thus seem, in its open portrayal of the sex lives of MSM, to be benefiting from the freedoms given by the normalizing of homosexuality. However, our queer reading of SHP shows that norms and normalizing regimes have not disappeared. Rather they have been replaced by the norms and normalizing regimes that govern what it is to be gay and who it is who can be regarded as gay. The person who is gay must be young, beautiful, sexually active, and sexually promiscuous. Any man who has sex with men who cannot approximate that norm is therefore rendered abject. We have interviewed twelve men and none of them feel they belong in that category. They are thus made to feel odd, to feel queer, to feel ambivalent about their identities. Alan Sinfield (1998) has summarized the position thus:

> Gay papers are full of someone quite different from me: a youngster who drinks spirits, wears designer clothes, goes to new clubs, takes out life insurance, goes abroad for his holidays, and does a lot of phone sex. He is conjured up not because he represents us, any more than colour supplements represent people who read newspapers on Sunday, but because he may have some money to spend. It is bad enough reading about this fantasy figure; now I am accused of being him" (1998, 16).

We contend that, in many parts of the public and voluntary sector, managers and professional staff are working with norms (of the patient, the family, the student, the householder, and indeed the manager and the professional worker) that govern identity. Such norms are unattainable, but extremely powerful. If our contention is right, then in all the organizations encompassed in the phrase 'public and voluntary sector,' there will be managers and staff suffering from personal crises because they feel they are not good enough, for they cannot achieve the norms that govern their identities as doctors, as managers, as social workers, as health promotion experts. In designing and delivering services they will, however, be constructing an image, a normative ideal, of the persons who will be delivering and the persons receiving that service. Services will thus be designed for nonexistent people to be delivered by nonexistent people. At every step of the way actors will be unable to conform to the expectations placed upon them. Our contention, of course, requires further study to discover its accuracy. We therefore suggest the need for more research using QT, and suggest its merits to the readers of this book.

QT, we contend, is a tool for assisting in anticipating the potential effect of our proposed actions. It acknowledges that we cannot escape from the norms that govern our existence, but insists we ensure that those norms do not render some, or indeed all, abject.

REFERENCES

Alsop, R., A. Fitzsimons, and K. Lennon, 2002. *Theorizing gender.* Oxford, UK: Blackwell.

Bowring, M.A. 2004. Resistance is *not* futile: Liberating Captain Janeway from the masculine–feminine dualism of leadership. *Gender, Work and Organization* 11(4): 381–405.

Brewis, J., M.P. Hampton, and S. Linstead. 1997. Unpacking Priscilla: Subjectivity and identity in the organization of gendered appearance. *Human Relations* 50(10): 1275–1304.

Budgeon, S. and S. Roseneil. 2004. Editors' introduction: Beyond the conventional family. *Current Sociology* 52(2): 127–134.

Butler, J. 1990. *Gender trouble.* London: Routledge, Chapman & Hall.

Butler, J. 1993. *Bodies that matter.* New York: Routledge.

Butler, J. 1996. Imitation and gender insubordination. In *The material queer: A lesbigay cultural studies reader*, ed. D. Morton, 180–192. Boulder, CO: Westview Press.

Butler, J. 2004. *Undoing gender.* New York: Routledge.

Butler, J. 2008. Sexual politics, torture, and secular time. *The British Journal of Sociology* 59(1): 1–23

Derrida, J. 1976/1997. *Of grammatology.* Baltimore, MD: John Hopkins University Press.

Derrida, J. 1994. *Specters of Marx: The state of debt, the work of mourning, and the new international.* New York: Routledge.

Dollimore, M. 1991. Sexual dissidence: Augustine to Wilde, Freud to Foucault. Oxford, UK: Oxford University Press

Doty, M. 1993. *Firebird.* New York: Harper Collins.

Ford, J., N. Harding, and M. Learmonth. 2008. *Leadership as identity: Constructions and deconstructions.* London: Palgrave.

Foucault, M. 1979. *The history of sexuality*, vol. 1. London: Allen Lane.

Foucault, M. 1986. *The history of sexuality,* vol. 2. Harmondsworth, UK: Viking.

Foucault, M. 1992. *The history of sexuality,* vol. 3. London: Penguin.

Fuss, D. 1991. Inside/out: Lesbian theories, gay theories. London: Routledge.

Fuss, D. 2001. Theorizing hetero- and homosexuality. In *The new social theory reader: Contemporary debates*, eds. S. Seidman and J.C. Alexander, 347–352. London: Routledge.

Harding, N. 2003. *The social construction of management: Texts and identities.* London: Routledge.

Jagose, A. 1996. *Queer theory.* Melbourne: Melbourne University Press.

Laclau, E. and C. Mouffe. 2001. *Hegemony and socialist strategy: Towards a radical democratic politics.* London: Verso.

Lee, H. 2006. *Que(e)rying sexual health promotion.* University of Leeds: Unpublished Ph.D. Thesis.

Lee, H., N. Harding, and M. Learmonth. 2008. Queer(y)ing public administration. *Public Administration,* 86(1): 149–168.

Oakley, A. 1972. *Sex, gender and society.* London: Temple Smith.

Parker, M. 2002. Queering management and organization. *Gender, Work and Organization* 9(2): 146–166.

Petersen, A. 1998. *Unmasking the masculine: "Men" and "Identity."* In *A sceptical age.* London: Sage.

Probyn, E. 1993. *Sexing the self.* London: Routledge.

Probyn, E. 1999. An ethos with a bite: Queer appetites from sex to food. *Sexualities,* 2(4): 421–431.

Roseneil, S. and J. Seymour, J. 1999. *Practising identities: Power and resistance.* New York: St. Martin's Press.

Sedgwick, E.K. 1991. *Epistemology of the closet.* New York: Harvester Wheatsheaf.

Seidman, S. 1997. *Difference troubles: Queering social theory and sexual politics.* Cambridge, UK: Cambridge University Press.

Seidman, S. 2001. From identity to queer politics: Shifts in normative heterosexuality. In *The new social theory reader: Contemporary debates*, eds. S. Seidman and J.C. Alexander, 353–361.. London: Routledge.

Sinfield, A. 1998. *Gay and after.* London: Serpent's Tail.

Warner, M. 1991. Introduction: Fear of a queer planet. *Social Text* 9(4): 3–17.

Young, R.J. 2004. *White mythologies: Writing history and the west.* London: Routledge.

14 The Contribution of Existentialist Thinking to Public Services Management

John Lawler

INTRODUCTION

Existentialist thinking has a particular contribution to make to critical analyses of contemporary organizations and to those in public sector service in particular. While it is considerably less fashionable than it might have been three decades ago (Eyre, 2002), there are a number of central themes which have resonance with other contemporary approaches. Perhaps because of this, there are signs of a renewed interest in this line of thinking and how it relates to other strands of critical thinking. While existentialist thinking might differ from other contemporary approaches in some important respects, there are nevertheless some similar themes (Reynolds, 2005; Martinot, 2006). As with other approaches, existentialist thinking presents us with new perspectives to explore and challenges taken-for-granted assumptions of the nature of public service organizations.

Existentialist thinking represents a continuing line of enquiry going back centuries, according to some authors (e.g., Barrett, 1990) way before the label 'existentialist' was applied to it. The breadth of authors contributing to this approach varies in extent, depending on the view of whichever commentator is charting the development. As with other modes of thinking and philosophical standpoints—most notably, postmodernism—existentialism is seen as ranging beyond the abstractions of philosophy, to a lived philosophy which sees expression in other forms, most notably the arts and within the arts, most notably again within literature, art, and music. Many authors are seen to be existentialist writers: some of philosophical texts such as Kierkegaard and Jaspers; some of more general literature such as Dostoyevsky and Camus; and some who combine both, most notably Sartre and de Beauvoir. Of the many authors attributed the term 'existentialist,' few have willingly accepted the label. This in itself might demonstrate something of existential thinking: the limitations and determinations due to categorization. Such categorization is anathema to existential thinking as it precludes freedom to become something other. Given that existential thinking has such a range of contributors, and that together these writers cover a wide range of issues, how do we start to outline the themes of such thinking and discuss why they might be appropriate to the consideration of public service organizations and their management?

If we reconsider the matrix developed by Burrell and Morgan (1979) to categorize sociological strands of thought, existentialist thinking is seen there as constituting a subjective theory occupying a position encompassing some elements of stability and some of radical change. This gives an indication of its foundations. It is concerned with subjective views of the world, expectedly given that it is a philosophy with a particular concern with and for individual consciousness, but it is also concerned with 'intersubjectivity,' the appreciation of the individual's world view in relation to that of others. There are eminent commentators (e.g., Cooper 1999) who reject the notion that existentialism represents a subjective philosophy on the grounds that its primary focus is on 'being in the world'—individuals and their worlds are inextricably and symbiotically related. To this extent, this approach transcends the objective–subjective dualism. Thus to focus exclusively on the subjective is to misinterpret existentialism. The subjective view though, is very important. From Kierkegaard's perspective (1992), the truth of human existence is presented through the subjective experience of the world: this is significant—not the subjective experience per se but subjective experience of and in the world. We cannot view individuals outside their historical and material circumstances. We are part of our world and our world, of us. So which of the many themes of existentialist thinking are relevant for our purposes here? Major themes include absurdity, freedom, anxiety, existence, being, consciousness, bad faith, authenticity (Solomon, 1972; Blackham, 1961; Friedman, 1991). The primary focus here will be the issues of freedom and choice, especially as they appear relevant to social policy issues such as service user empowerment and choice within the managerial context. The next section will elucidate some elements of existentialist thinking before going on to consider developments of empowerment and choice, especially in relation to service in the context of social care. The subsequent section will examine such developments in the light of the themes elaborated.

Much of the development of thinking in relation to organizations, especially that which serves the managerial agenda, can be characterized as taking an objective, positivist approach, the Functionalist Paradigm, according to Burrell and Morgan (1979). Thus scientific management and management science came into being through the examination of work practices and organization using a rational, scientific approach, developed in and borrowing from other disciplines, most notably the natural and physical sciences. Through this approach activities can be scrutinized and broken down into their isolated and separate components. Thus F.W. Taylor's approach was to fragment processes into their essential elements and redesign and reconfigure these activities so that the particular work could be carried out in the most efficient manner. In a similar way the activities of managers have come under scrutiny, including approaches such as those of Mintzberg (1973), to highlight the different roles one person, as manager, might be required to fulfill. Latterly more detailed approaches to management activities have led to the identification of different, separate but related, components of managerial work which are then identified as requiring particular skills for their completion. The result of such processes is the development of competency frameworks for management (Bolden et al., 2003). In similar vein, approaches to leadership have sought to isolate particular components of effective leadership, be they individual character traits, or behaviors, or personal qualities. Thus the object under investigation is broken down to its essential parts. Perhaps less attention is then given to how those elements are effectively reconstituted in the role (except perhaps to account for this as being part of the 'art' of management [Starkey, 1998] or leadership [Grint, 2000]). An existentialist view of management and leadership would take a quite different approach, almost a contradictory one.

ONTOLOGY

Existentialist thinking has a particular approach to ontology. Much traditional philosophy has at its base the notion of reality as something which *is* whereas existentialist thinking and its ontology focus more on the uncertainty of *becoming*. Traditional philosophical ontology transcends individual experience and is founded on certain enduring principles. Existentialist thinking focuses more on reality as being defined by what things (namely people) *do* rather than what they *are*. Thus we have a focus on continual becoming rather than simply being. The existentialist notion of 'being-in-the-world' (Sartre, 1953, Heidegger, 1977) reflects the way in which the individual is always located in the world; we are never an entity separate from the world and our material and historical circumstances. In the 'essence and existence' distinction, which we examine later in the chapter, essence is seen to be the naming of a thing: it is *what the thing is*. Thus it has certain characteristics and not others; it belongs to a certain category of being because of those characteristics. It if had different characteristics, it would give it a different essence and belong to a different category of being. Existence on the other hand denotes *that* a thing is. Existences are transient and ephemeral whereas essences are enduring and universal; for example, all beings in a certain category have the same essential characteristics. Traditionally, existences are seen as providing instances or examples of universal essences. Thus in traditional thinking the objective and universal category of being is privileged over the individual and subjective view. However, existentialist thinkers such as Kierkegaard regard the subjective experience as paramount and that this view always incorporates the future potentialities of the individual. The individual always has the possibility to choose, to develop, and is always *becoming* rather than just *being*. In this way human experience cannot be reduced to generalized objectified categorization. We as individuals always must face the challenge of going beyond a fixed and present condition of being.

Sartre makes the distinction between 'being in itself,' 'being for itself' and 'being for others' (Sartre, 2002). These are not different elements of a person but abstractions which highlight the place of consciousness in existentialist thinking. Being in itself is a nonreflective, non-self-aware state. In some ways it describes what *is*. A table might provide an example of this. It exists as a table but cannot choose to be otherwise—it exemplifies being in itself. In the human context, being in itself represents a nonaware, nonreflective mode of being. Being *for* itself is a mode of being which represents a self-conscious, reflective being, aware of itself in the world, of what it is and what it might become through how it acts in the world. Traditional views of essence and universality do not account for this notion of becoming and individual reflective being. Existentialist thinking does not see human consciousness as a predefined predetermined object. We have a bodily, historical and material facticity but we are able to transcend this by who we choose to become. As we do not exist as some entity separate from the world, we have no essence transported through life. Through consciousness and action we define ourselves—what we choose to be is our project in life. Hence we are self-determining.

ESSENCE AND EXISTENCE; CHOICE AND FACTICITY

There is something of an aphorism which is seen to characterize existentialist thinking, namely that 'existence precedes essence' (Hatab, 1999a). This summarizes existentialist thinking in relation to the prime characteristics of human being, as opposed to the being of inanimate and non-self-conscious beings—namely human beings. The prime distinction between humans and other sentient beings is that humans are the only beings for whom being itself is an issue (Heidegger, 1977). Humankind continues to explore important considerations of what it is to be human and to continue the search for meaning in life and, in some cases, beyond it. In this respect our mortality is a constant factor in our lives as we struggle to make sense of life itself.

To elaborate slightly: how can existence precede essence? In the context of management, the reverse is often demonstrably the case—essence precedes existence. In the case of Taylor, as noted previously, his view of organization was that the planning and execution of tasks should be separated. Thus the manager's role was to devise the best means of executing the job, or to plan the job, which the worker then carried out. The manager identified the essence of the work and brought this into existence through directing the worker. In relation to human life, previous thinking about individuals is that there essence is preordained, that commonalities in 'human nature' determine certain aspects of our being which then come into existence through and throughout our lives. Existentialist writers recognize that despite the restrictions of when and where we are born and despite our genetic inheritance and our exposure to many different environmental influences throughout our upbringing, our lives are not predetermined. The notion of an essential quality of an individual from this perspective is fundamentally restrictive. If we believe our genetic make-up or our upbringing or our current work and other social/situational factors make up our essence and *determine* who we are, we ignore our ontological freedom and the continuing potential of being—who we choose to be and whom we choose to become. This is a fundamental freedom within existentialist thinking. So an essentialist view of human being would imply a very determinist view of who we are: our actions, behaviors, attitudes being determined by our birth, our heredity, upbringing, class, and so on.

To challenge this is not necessarily to take an individualist, neoliberal view of the world. Such factors Sartre (2002) notes as being our 'facticity'—those objective facts concerning our location in the world which are unchangeable. Of course they are influential but not necessarily deterministic unless we choose to believe them to be so. In every situation we have freedom: even in the most restrictive circumstance we have some freedom in terms of how we choose to respond to it. Sartre provides the example of the mountain walker who tires and wonders when to stop and rest. While physical capabilities and limitations obviously restrict what a person can do or achieve, the walker is free to choose when and if to stop and rest. Even the most pressing of human needs can *in extremis* be chosen against as evidenced by the choice of death in many different situations (e.g., hunger strikers, that is, they have chosen not to let their growing hunger determine how they behave). In Sartre's experience of restrictive life in Nazi-occupied France he asserted he was never freer. He and others were constantly faced with challenges and choices so that at an extreme they might decide that it was better to choose death than face the alternative consequences. So in this line of thought, we cannot identify our essential aspects and then maintain we are free. If we are deemed to have any essence it can only be identified retrospectively through looking at what we have chosen to do, when our life's project is at an end. Any other approach would be to restrict our possibilities and potentialities.

Facticity provides the context and influence but does not determine who we become. We have the potential to transcend our facticity, indeed to transcend our present selves and become whom we choose. In short we have the potential, the ability, to reach beyond objective conditions rather than be entirely bound by them. In some cases we may, perversely, seek refuge in our facticity and refuse to accept the possibilities of our situation and of our potential. To believe we are entirely determined by our facticity is to be acting in bad faith according to Sartre (2002). In this case we would be rejecting freedom in our current situation and explaining ourselves and our choices (or lack of them) as being entirely determined by our facticity.

In existentialist thinking choice is fundamental to the human condition and it is unfettered—there is no pre-existing condition or entity to guide our choice. "The subjectivity of choice means that there is nothing to which an individual can point to justify or guarantee a decision" (Hatab, 1999b, 76). Therefore, Hatab argues, to reject choice is to reject the human condition. Anxiety is a constant feature of life and appears as a result of freedom, uncertainty, and constantly choosing our lives. Nor does anxiety end once a choice has been made. In an interesting example contemporary with his times, Kierkegaard uses marriage. The rejection of single living for the broader commitment to spouse and family constitutes a move from the aesthetic to the ethical stage of being. But the choice continues throughout marriage whether to maintain that relationship or change or end it. No one else can make my choice on my behalf and I need continually to make it, as a variety of existentialist writers assert (e.g., Kierkegaard, 1992; Sartre, 2002). This demonstrates clearly the 'existence precedes essence' motif: we have no *a priori* essence but develop our being through the choices we make. In order to consider how such concepts might aid our analysis of social work organizations, the next section summarizes the development of social work and highlights current issues which are themselves amenable to analysis using existentialist concepts.

SOCIAL WORK AS A DEVELOPING PROFESSION

Social work is a relatively new profession in relation to the traditional professions. From its earlier nineteenth century philanthropic predecessors it came into being in the twentieth century during perhaps *the* time modernity. The classical approach of modernity and its influence on the development of social work organization and practice is charted by Howe. He notes that in this period, rationality was seen to be dominant and the people could "stand outside nature" and "proceed by *rationally* investigating objects and events in terms of their internal properties, their essential character, nature's universal laws" (Howe, 1994, 515). This is a period which allows people to be free in that, through knowledge and rationality, they can come to new understandings of the world "natural and social worlds can be *controlled* and then *improved*" (516). Social work became established during such an era of modernity. However, Howe, recognizes that within welfare, such an objectivist ontology does not present clarity in every respect and that contemporary and subsequent discourses "systematically form the objects of which they speak" (517), and in the case of social work, those discourses gradually defined both social worker and client, as was the term used to describe those who used social work services. Leonard (1997) argues similarly that people become service users because of the ideas and actions of social workers. As social work struggled to develop a professional legitimacy, there was the effort to demonstrate a fixed and concrete body of professional knowledge, itself important in determining professional and practice. The ultimate manifestation of this is the development of the generic social worker—a professional service sufficiently competent and developed to apply its standard knowledge and skills across a wide range of 'social problems'—family dysfunction, mental health issues, childhood delinquency, care of the elderly and handicapped, and so on.

However, within both professional practice and social work academia, there is a respected history of challenge to, if not rebellion against, orthodox belief and one might argue this is an important aspect of the foundation of social work as a practice (it certainly applies to the radical social work movement of the 1970s [Bailey and Brake, 1975]), and which continues to the current day. As part of that questioning of the status quo of social work knowledge and organization, the increasing interest in alternative perspectives for examining practice, as presented by developments in cultural studies, is reflected in social work. Howe notes this in his comments on the growing interest in considering social work using postmodern perspectives. Howe argues that this interest recognized the concepts of *being* and *becoming* in social work. The modernist assumes it is possible to pass from becoming to being but being as a static entire entity. The developing critical views recognize the importance of *becoming*. Howe and other writers (e.g., Parton 1994) note that when exposed to extensive positivist examination, social issues did not and do not become fully comprehensible and evade universal explanations: "modernity's promise to deliver order, certainty and security has remained unfulfilled" (Howe, 1994, 520). Parton similarly points to the continuing complexities of social problems which modernity sought to understand and resolve. There is within social work an enduring concern with, and focus on meaning in people's lives. This is obviously not the exclusive preserve of the profession but remains an important aspect which informs practice values. This aspect of human life together with the recognition of the limitations of modernist approaches to human difficulties, led Howe to conclude that "meaning is a perpetual state of interpretation and therefore the human self . . . can have no universal or essential properties" (1994, 521). It is here that this line of argument most closely resonates with existentialist thinking.

The acceptance that perhaps social work does not constitute a cohesive and unitary profession has grown since the 1980s. Thus there are areas of practice and intervention which take a particularly structural and class-based view of the nature of social problems while others in other areas of social problems, take an individual pathological view to inform practice. There is the acceptance today that that universal truths of social work do not apply and that practice differs according to the situation and the aims of any particular service. This acknowledgement of social work as a pluralist range of activities and interventions is reflected in legislation and other developments influencing social work practice. The abandonment of the search for universal truths in social work leads to the argument that there needs to be full participation in decisions which affect people if they are to have any 'truth' for them. In this respect 'truth' is the result of 'collaborative authorship' (Connor, 1989, 5; Howe, 1994, 525]. Meaning is generated in and through the context in which people are situated "understanding is no longer a mode of knowing but a dialogical activity" (Klemm, 1986, 38; Howe, 1994, 525). Dialogue is an important concept in this context, to which we shall return in due course.

However "much of the talk about participation, empowerment and choice has come from neoconservative ideas about the rights and freedoms of individuals in both their personal life and in the marketplace" (Howe, ibid., 525).

CHOICE IN PUBLIC SERVICES

In some respects, issues such as the search for meaning in our lives would appear to be unnecessarily esoteric in the context of discussions on management and organization. However, in relation to public service such a discussion is indeed justified. The issue of meaning in and of life is a fundamental daily issue in many such services, which are regularly face with life-saving, life-ending, and life-regulating activities. To that extent, the consideration of meaning in life is not academic decadence, it is a prime and continuing concern. Existentialist views of meaning are applicable in this context. We are witness to a considerable shift in public service provision over past two decades and more which has seen the role of the target of those services being redefined and reconstituted, as are the services themselves. Within health and social care for example, we have seen a renaming of those who use services—patients and clients have become service users or customers in many respects as a result of a more consumerist model of public service which sees users as having greater involvement in service design and evaluation. The user now is seen as having certain power on the basis of individual demand for services of a particular quality rather than receiving services on the basis on their individual and collective need as defined by more powerful professional and policy groups. Previously, services designed to meet need were seen as being too restrictive, not being sufficiently flexible to cater for individual differences. However, treating users more as 'consumers' of public services may be equally restrictive but for different reasons. This might be particularly the case when the provision of user choice is seen as an end in itself. Consumers in this case are seen as essential beings, among their prime characteristics being the desire to choose between different options of service. Choice here becomes the goal of service design not individual potentiality. Within some services (e.g. social work), there may be significant facticities which restrict capabilities but the service can still present users with opportunities to develop, to become, to exercise freedom even when severely restricted. In the context of public service, there remains a recognition of the importance of individual need (in addition to demand). Services are designed to address need in communities and the processes used to deliver these are constantly being adapted in efforts to deliver them as effectively and efficiently as possible. In addressing the aggregated need within a population there is the predictable view taken of the person who uses the service as being seen largely in mechanistic terms. Variability is not a desirable characteristic of the population as a whole. Users, despite the motivations and intentions of those who attend to their needs, are essentialized. They have traditionally been seen as patients or clients. Despite their now being service users, they are still objectified and categorized in the eyes of service planners in terms of the relatively few aspects of themselves which they have or are deemed to have in common with others with similar needs or in similar situations. This is not especially unusual in that in market orientated commercial contexts, such classifications are not uncommon; for example in the context of product innovation, consumers are categorized as belonging to certain categories on the basis of their characteristics in relation to a model of different take-up rates in the consumer population (Rogers, 2003).

The current incorporation of choice in public service delivery might be seen as recognition of individual difference between users—recognition of individuality. Thus choice is seen as providing the potential to manifest that individuality through the freedom of personal choice. At the same time though, the move away from a 'patient' with 'needs' to a consumer' with 'demand' who can exercise choice might be seen simply as the replacement of one essentialized being with another. Yes, some freedom is acknowledged but the user as consumer is simply seen as someone who exercises choice in the public service arena—ignoring the situation where the user might well wish not to exercise choice—to choose not to choose but to defer to the recommendations of experienced and informed professionals with a fuller comprehension of the complexities and technicalities of the situation. This is in addition to the very real difference between choice in a voluntaristic and open market and choice in a context where the user ideally might choose not to use the service at all (e.g., when they voluntarily opt for treatment for a condition they would rather not have) or, more importantly, when they are receiving the service through some element of coercion or threat (e.g., in some mental health conditions or child protection issues). Thus they do not comfortably fit the role of consumer in the market sense. There are some (e.g., elderly) who are excluded from services as they are deemed to be ineligible for services they would value. Users of social work services fall into categories which consumerist models do not adequately account for including both reluctant users and reluctant nonusers. So the choice agenda is paradoxical: it provides choice in a very restricted area, while ignoring the existential freedom and choice which people always and already have.

Such developments in social welfare and in social work in particular, reflect changes in attitudes adopted by both the left and right in politics. In each case the way this is reflected in practice is similar—a focus on individual choice and empowerment in welfare. From the liberal right there is the imperative from the free market, that services are best delivered through the free and open market, meeting consumer demand. This both meets demand directly, drives up quality standards in response to consumer feedback and developing demand, and provides an efficient means of delivery in that only organizations proficient in delivering effective services survive and prosper. From the left, there is a concern with the unpopularity and dominance of the state and the bureaucratic and inflexible ways in which resources are allocated and services delivered. Individualized services and consumer feedback are seen as ways of transferring power to citizens and away from the state (Harris, 1999). The emphasis though from both ends of the political spectrum tended and still tends to be on consumers rather than citizens. However, "the emerging consensus on citizenship is couched in the language of participation and choice, obscuring the fact that the consumer–citizens of state social work are likely to be poor, vulnerable and rarely in a position to shop around or take their custom elsewhere" (Pollitt, 1990; Harris, 1999, 926). Even if this were not the case, Harris argues, many recipients of social work may not have had positive experience in the economic market and a consumerist role in welfare might not be as comfortable for some of them as policy makers might believe. In some respects then policy makers may be viewing service users in an idealized way, which is an aspect of the developments in markets taken up by Miller (1998) in a related but different way.

Miller (1998) notes the growth of markets as being the most enduring and classical model of how demand and supply are best regulated in the consumer's interest. "This is related to the principal of consumer sovereignty, that individuals are the best judges of what is in their own interest" (Miller, 1998, 200). He also points to the abstract version of the consumer in economics which he refers to as the 'virtual consumer.' General patterns of response are identified by economic research which result in "the creation of the virtual consumer in economic theory, a chimera, the constituent parts of which are utterly daft . . . Indeed neoclassical economists make no claim to represent flesh-and-blood consumers. They claim that their consumers are merely aggregate figures used in modelling . . . these virtual consumers . . . are used to justify forcing actual consumers to behave their virtual counterparts" (201). To apply this argument in social care would thus render the policy objective of individualized services as unachievable: the model service user would be to exemplify that—a model not reflective of real situations and real individual need but which influences service users to behave in ways desirable to service deliverers.

Miller argues that planning for many services is predicated on this notion of the 'virtual consumer'—a stereotype which is the result of aggregated need. He also makes the important point that it is *demand* rather than need which is the driver in free markets and the consumer is the final arbiter of how well demand is met. But the virtual consumer of welfare is precisely that—virtual—and does not exist. The actual user of services is individual and unique and as such needs an individual service, delivered by skilled, sensitive, and flexible professionals with the expertise and experience to adapt their knowledge and skills to the specific requirements of that person at that time. Auditors are purported to act on behalf of customers or users to ensure transparency but in this scenario, this is counterproductive. Indeed as Miller goes on to point out, the auditor acting on behalf of consumers "reduces the ability of citizens to dispute those actions, to protest that there are important criteria other than value for money, supposedly the ultimate consumer good. In sum, policies justified in the name of the consumer citizen become the means to prevent the consumer from becoming a citizen, from determining the priorities of expenditure in the public domain" (187). Here we witness the process of essentializing the service user, on the basis of aggregated need and an ideological model of how resources are best allocated.

If we accept that we are not socially determined individuals, we are faced with choice throughout our existence. Freedom, choice, and responsibility are closely interlinked. Ultimate truths of human existence are to be found, if at all, in nonobjective ways (Kierkegaard, 1992). So developing demonstrable choice in service delivery is a very partial means of acknowledging individual freedom. Kierkegaard argued that truth is experienced subjectively at the three stages of existence (aesthetic, ethical, and religious) and is "not governed by objective criteria that ground decisions in universal truth conditions but by the subjective commitment to choose to live in a certain way" (Hatab, 1999b, 75). Kierkegaard argued against approaches which, even while promoting freedom, sought effectively to suppress the lived subjective experience of existence. The objectification of choice through policy directives, according to this view, serves to mask the difficulties faced in choosing.

FACTICITY AND CHOICE IN THE SOCIAL WORK CONTEXT

Within the practice of certain human services (most notably individuals and families severely restricted by their facticity—their socioeconomic status, their upbringing, etc.) the encouragement of individual potential is a significant element of professional practice. Thus professional workers may encourage people to see the potential of their situation and of themselves, to encourage through support, the development of independent thought and action. In this respect they might be encouraged to 'choose' for themselves—choose how to live their lives, to define the meaning in their lives and to seek fulfilment (Thompson, 1992). This however, is a far cry from choosing the location in which a service is to be delivered (e.g., a hospital operation, or participating in mechanistic decision processes). The institution of choice in this setting essentially shifts responsibility, in part if not entirely, from professional to user. One could argue that an existentialist view would support choice in health and social care provision. And yet, in some cases in this context there might be a strong rational basis for some decisions, where there might be demonstrably a 'best' choice'—of treatment, of facility, of procedure but this is not obviously made clear.

In the context of social work, Hugman (2003) points to the demise of metanarratives—universal explanations of the social world. Thus totalizing theories and prescriptions no longer have the legitimacy of previous eras. The notion of 'human nature', is no longer seen as appropriate as in existentialist thinking. Although there has been a growth in interest in postmodern thinking in relation to social work, he points to the dangers of a reliance on the postmodernist approach within social work in that it can lead to nihilism and solipsism because of is relativity, neither of which prove fruitful for citizens of our society who are in need. Indeed, he argues that this approach might also be seen to undermine the emancipatory agenda of much social work over the past century, because of the absence of any identifiable 'human nature' communally shared.

Hugman gives particular attention to the concept of 'Being for Other,' which he sees as having resonance with postmodern thinking, though noting the existentialist interest in this concept. Hugman uses Levinas as an exponent of this concept. Other existentialist writers also demonstrate such an interest (e.g. Sartre, 2002). We noted earlier how Sartre develops the three abstractions of being in itself, being for itself, and being for others. Sartre's earlier views (Sartre, 1973) on being for others can be rather bleak, focusing on how we become an object in the eyes of others. However he develops these views later to accommodate the concept of other in a more positive way (as do other existentialist writers, e.g., Buber, 2002) in relation to intersubjectivity, to which we shall return later in the chapter. In the social work context, there are important aspects of being for others in relation to empowerment. At one level, following Sartre's earlier position, service users are objectified in the eyes of practitioners and policy makers, and objectified in fairly limited, passive ways—consumers with certain demands. In a more developed notion of being for others we need to acknowledge the power dynamic, at least at a superficial level, in the social work relationship. Professional social workers are in a powerful position in relation to services users. Social workers themselves have a particular situation in the organizational hierarchy within their own employing organizations and so are subject themselves to the power exercised by their managers. Managers take responsibility for managing aspects of the work of their staff. Social workers in turn take responsibility for delivering a service to users. Social workers become concerned with users' interests and at times speak on behalf of users to other agencies within the welfare context. There is the danger of being concerned with, caring for, speaking for, becoming 'power over' that other party, in this the case, the service user, and working in the interests of the care provider, not the recipient. Krentz and Malloy (2005) use Heidegger's distinction between 'leaping in' for people—caring for them but in effect controlling and acting for them—and the more authentic 'leaping ahead,' which recognizes individual potential and focuses on freeing individuals to make their own choices. The stated intentions therefore of 'empowering' service users can be seen as 'leaping in' for others, and taking responsibility for (and from) them. Developing shared empowerment would present an approach which is 'leaping ahead' in allowing potentialities to develop. Empowerment, if this means the individual making their own informed choices which are then given a positive and resourced reception by service providers, can then been seen as a positive development, literally a move away from the possibility of power over the recipient. One then has to ask though about the extent to which 'empowerment' is serving the interests of the provider. If it is to operate as a set of audited, legitimizing practices, as Miller would argue, it becomes an end in itself, not a means to the development of the service user. In this case, the organization is legitimated as it has a set of transparent practices—*regardless of whether those practices have a positive effect*. In which case we are bound to ask: what are services users being empowered for? Taking all this into consideration we can argue that empowerment is not here focusing on potential and developing a more fulfilling life but, as Pease (2002) would argue, empowerment is a means of developing users into becoming better consumers.

There is an important tension here in considering the roles of manager and social worker. The manager may wish to 'empower' social work staff to make decisions within a restricted arena but there is primary interest in the interests of the organization. To that extent the manager's role vis-à-vis the social worker is difficult to describe as 'being for others' in the way it is for the social worker and service relationship. In this latter case the social worker is taking some responsibility for and with the user. The social worker has a focus on the welfare of that particular user at that particular time. In this situation the humanist foundation of social work is evident. The social worker is taking a moral stance in a way which the manager is not. The following quotation from Bauman demonstrates this and also demonstrates the humanist strand of much existentialist thinking: "To take a moral stance means to take responsibility for the Other; to act on the assumption that the well-being of the Other is a precious thing calling for my effort to preserve and enhance it, that whatever I do or do not do affects it . . . it does not depend on what the Other is or does" (Bauman, 1994, 19, cited in Hugman, 2003, 1027).

As noted previously, i

is a continuing trend towards contractual and procedural bases for social welfare provision. Services are provided in the mixed economy of care by a variety of agencies on a contractual basis. Service delivery is monitored and, as noted earlier, audited to ensure contractual standards are maintained. It is difficult to envisage how the concepts of choice and empowerment can be promoted without this being seen as primarily within the interests of service deliverers rather than users unless some empha-sis is placed on the relational aspects of service delivery, again bearing in mind the very personal nature of the service, relying as it often does on the quality of the professional–service user relationship. This can never be adequately accounted for by contracts and procedures. One might argue that empowerment then, is what social work has always stood for. From a critical perspective, universal principles of empowerment and choice or uni-versal procedures to ensure empowerment are rejected. Bauman, in relation to ethics in the work setting, points out the restrictions of systematizing morals because of the ways in which they lose the requisite flexibility and become dogma in the "stiff armour of . . . artificially constructed ethical codes" (Bauman, op cit., in Hugman, 2003, 1028). In the same way we can see how inflexible and restrictive codes of practice relating to empower-ment and choice might well become.

Within the context of contractually based services, there is an increas-ing focus now on tasks—that which is demonstrable and quantifiable and therefore auditable—in estimating service effectiveness. However, a rela-tionship based service needs to be validated by those involved—in this case service users. The question is raised by Hugman (2003) though, of who is making assessments of whether the needs of service users are being inter-preted 'correctly' and whether the complex nature of social work services is amenable to market estimations of effectiveness. When a service user is knowledgeable and articulate and most importantly, is engaged in the relationship voluntarily their views may be entirely appropriate but "when the reluctant or downright unwilling client is considered, whose idea of 'correct' is to be used?" (Hugman 2003, 1034).

It is within this context of a relationship rather than a contract that the concepts of intersubjectivity and dialogue become important. If empow-erment—either of social work staff or of service users—is to be anything more than a policy aspiration monitored by auditable targets—if it is to be a meaningful concept—a full appreciation of the world view of the differ-ent participants is necessary. This appreciation of the being of others is, from an existentialist perspective, made possible through dialogue and the acknowledgement of intersubjectivity. Sartre argues the need to recognize our own subjectivity and that of those with whom we interact, whom we see in an objective light. To us, the other "is a freedom which confronts mine and which cannot think or will without doing so either for or against me. Thus at once we find ourselves in a world which is, let us say, that of 'intersubjectivity'" (Sartre, 1973, 45). This appears to be a somewhat bleak view, as noted earlier, if we see the other simply as being a threat in some way to our own freedom. Later Sartre clarifies the potential of intersubjective freedom: "through the Other I am enriched in a new dimension of Being: through the Other I come to exist in the dimension of Being, through the other I become an object. And this is in no way a threat or fall *in itself.* This comes about only if the Other refuses to see a freedom in me *too.* But if, on the contrary he makes me exist as an existing freedom as well as a *Being/object*, if he makes this autonomous moment exist and thematizes this contingency that I perpetually surpass, he enriches the world and me, he *gives a meaning* to my existence *in addition* to the subjective meaning I myself give it" (Sartre, 2000, 326, italics in original). The implications of this are considerable. To recognize others as having their own subjective and objective freedom means the recognition of a true 'empowerment' where those in the relationship are involved in an intersubjective, sense-making dialogue. This in turn demands interpersonal engagement, not ignoring but acknowledging and negotiating differences in status and power—in facticities.

Buber (2002) distinguishes three types of dialogue: "genuine dialogue . . . where each of the participants really has in mind the other or others in their present and particular being and turns to them with the intention of establishing a living mutual relation between himself and them. There is technical dialogue, which is prompted solely by the need of objective understanding. And there is monologue disguised as dialogue in which two or more men (sic), meeting in space, speak each within himself in strangely tortuous and circuitous ways and yet imagine they have escaped the torment of being thrown back on their own resources" (Buber, 2002, 22). The danger with the current initiatives of choice and empowerment is that they are discussed and practiced as technical dialogue or indeed as professional monologue.

According to Buber, genuine dialogue is enabled through going beyond the onlooker and observer roles in relation to others, that is, seeing 'the other' in different ways. The *observer* identifies certain characteristics of the other and classifies that person on the basis of those characteristics. The *onlooker* is a more involved and empathic role where the other is seen in a more rounded, individual, and contextualized way but both roles objectify the other. Buber argues though that there is an entirely different perspective, when the other 'says something' to a person which cannot be grasped in an objective way. It is in this relationship where meaningful dialogue occurs, when someone becomes 'aware' of the potentialities. Arnett and Arneson (1999, 128) note the potential for personal development, of existentialist growth, as occurring in *the between*; that is, between person and person, again intersubjectively: "life is 'best' lived between persons" (1999, 129) and it is in this space that genuine dialogue takes place. Dialogue involves maintaining one's own existential position and accepting that of the other.

Dialogue acts: "as the existentialist and ontological reality in which the self comes into being and through which it fulfils and authenticates itself" (Buber, 2002, xv). Thus the potential for empowerment exists in meaningful intersubjective relations where both parties are open to benefit rather than viewing empowerment as one party bestowing power on another.

There is a need to encourage genuine dialogue between managers and professionals and between professionals and service users to enable empowerment, that is, the opportunity to recognize one's own freedom and one's own potential. In this way the relationship of professional and service user is recognized for having the potential that it does and that, unlike commodity exchanges, it is dependent on interpersonal qualities and the context and not on procedures and contractual obligations in the legal sense. The quality of interpersonal relationship is the main way in which to resolve the paradox of managers of services being required to 'empower' their staff and their staff in turn to 'empower' service users, while both groups operate in an increasing managerial context, where the degree of discretion both managers and professional each have, is increasingly restricted and monitored.

REFERENCES

Arnett, R.C. and P. Arneson. 1999. *Dialogic civility in a cynical age: Community, hope and interpersonal relationships.* Albany, NY: State University of New York Press.

Bailey, R. and M. Brake. 1975. *Radical social work.* London: Edward Arnold.

Barrett, W. 1990. *Irrational man: A study in existential philosophy.* New York: Anchor Books.

Bauman, Z. 1994. *Alone again: Ethics after certainty.* London: Demos.

Blackham, H.J. 1961. *Six existentialist thinkers.* London: Routledge and Kegan Paul.

Bolden, R., J. Gosling, A. Marturano, and P. Dennison. 2003. *A review of leadership theory and competency frameworks.* Edited version of a Report for Chase Consulting and the Management Standards Centre. Centre for Leadership Studies: University of Exeter. http://www.fcsh.unl.pt/docentes/luisrodrigues/textos/Lideran%C3%A7a.pdf (accessed January 2, 2008).

Buber, M. 2002. *Between man and man.* New York: Routledge.

Burrell, G. and G. Morgan. 1979. *Sociological paradigms and organizational analysis.* London: Heinemann Educational.

Connor, S. 1989. *Postmodernist culture: An introduction to theories of the contemporary.* Oxford, UK: Blackwell

Cooper, D.E. 1999. *Existentialism: A reconstruction, 2nd edition.* Oxford, UK: Blackwell.

Eyre, R. 2002. Preface to J-P Sartre, *Being and nothingness: An essay on phenomenological ontology,* trans. H.E. Barnes. London: Routledge.

Friedman, M., ed. 1991. *The worlds of existentialism: A critical reader.* Atlantic Highlands, NJ: Humanities Press International.

Grint, K. 2000. *The arts of leadership.* Oxford, UK: Oxford University Press.

Harris, J. 1999. State social work and social citizenship: From Clientism to consumerism. *British Journal of Social Work* 29(3): 915–937.

Hatab, L.J. 1999a. Freedom. In *Dictionary of Existentialism,* ed. H. Gordon, 161. Westport, CT: Greenwood Press.

Hatab, L.J. 1999b. Choice. In *Dictionary of Existentialism*, ed. H. Gordon, 74–76. Westport, CT: Greenwood Press.

Heidegger, M. 1977. *On time and being*. Trans. J. Stanbaugh. London: Harper and Row.

Howe, D. 1994. Modernity, postmodernity and social work. *British Journal of Social Work* 24: 513–532.

Hugman, R. 2003. Professional values and ethics in social work: Reconsidering postmodernism. *British Journal of Social Work* 33: 1025–1041.

Kierkegaard, S. 1992. *Concluding unscientific postscript to philosophical fragments, volume 1*, trans H.V. and E.H. Hong. Princeton NJ: Princeton University Press.

Klemm, D.E. 1986. *Hermeneutical enquiry, vol. 1: The interpretation of texts*. Atlanta GA: Scholar's Press.

Krentz, A. and D.C. Malloy. 2005. Opening people to possibilities: A Heideggerian Approach to Leadership. *Philosophy of Management* 5(1): 25–44.

Leonard, P. 1997. *Postmodern welfare: Reconstructing an emancipatory project*. London: Sage.

Martinot, S. 2006. *Forms in the abyss: A philosophical bridge between Sartre and Derrida*. Philadelphia, PA: Temple University Press.

Miller, D. 1998. Conclusion: A Theory of Virtualism. In *Virtualism: A New Political Economy*, eds. J.G. Carrier and D. Miller, 187–216. Oxford, UK: Berg Publishers.

Mintzberg, H. 1973. *The nature of managerial work*. New York: Harper & Row.

Parton, N. 1994. Problematics of government: (Post) modernity and social work. *British Journal of Social Work* 24(1): 9–32.

Pease, B. 2002. Rethinking empowerment: A postmodern re-appraisal for emancipatory practice. *British Journal of Social Work* 32(2): 135–47.

Pollitt, C. 1990. *Managerialism and the public services*. Oxford, UK: Blackwell.

Reynolds, J. 2005. *Understanding existentialism* (Understanding movements in modern thought series). Stocksfield, UK: Acumen Publishing.

Rogers, E.M. 2003. *Diffusion of innovations*. New York: Free Press.

Sartre, J-P. 1953. *Existential psychoanalysis*. Trans. H. Barnes. New York: Philosophical Library.

Sartre, J-P. 2002. *Being and nothingness: An essay on phenomenological ontology*. Trans. H.E. Barnes. London: Routledge Classics.

Solomon, R.C. 1972. *From rationalism to existentialism*. New York: Harper and Row.

Starkey, K. 1998. What can we learn from the learning organization? *Human Relations* 51(4): 531–545.

Thompson, N. 1992. *Existentialism and social work*. Aldershot, UK: Avebury.

15 Adding Value to Critical Public Services Management

Craig Prichard

Academic babble was a force, powerful but ephemeral, was noise, rumour and gossip, something that circulated orally. Ministerial machinations harassed it, transformed it, made it substantial and put it to work (from Clark, 2006)

PREAMBLE

At the end of 1997, about the time I submitted a PhD thesis to the University of Nottingham with the title "Making Managers in UK Further and Higher Education,"[1] I had lunch with some Nottingham colleagues including Michael 'Mick' Rowlinson. Mick is probably best known for his critical historical analysis of Cadburys (Smith et al., 1990). Over lunch he listened politely to what was probably an overly glowing description of a PhD by an overly committed PhD student. When I finished the description he turned to me and asked: "Did you find any managers?"

The simplest questions are often the hard ones to answer. This one disarmed me. The unsatisfactory reply is "yes and no." "Yes," the empirical analysis shows that despite their internal and interpersonal struggles with doing so, many senior post holders in universities and colleges were taking up active positions in managing others' work, controlling expenditure and shaping organizational direction. And "no," as Prichard and Willmott note, many continued to be "subject to existing discursive regimes and localized practices which have a strong mediating effect on the reception and articulation of 'management' disciplines" (1997, 311).

But Mick's question wasn't looking for such an 'either/or' response and neither was he particularly interested in the reception of management disciplines. He wasn't interested in terms like 'discursive regimes' and 'subjectivities' and neither was he concerned with differences between public and private sectors. His question was much more direct. It expressed a form of critical organizational analysis concerned with how managers are implicated in relations of value; how they are involved in efforts to extend, intensify, and speed up the work of others and to raise the rate of exploitation of labor. For Mick, talk of subjectivities and discursive practices simply begged the question of whether anything more than flows of language, symbols, and practices were going on in public sector organizations.

Since 1997 a good deal of my academic work has been an effort to answer Mick's question. In this chapter I present some of that work. The chapter has two aims: to offer those engaged in critical analysis of public services management a means of considering the value dynamics of their particular topic, area, or subject, and to contribute to a broad re-engagement with value and value processes among critically inclined management researchers (e.g., Arvidsson, 2005; Levy, 2008).

INTRODUCTION

As a research enterprise, Critical Management Studies (CMS) has tended to advance by addressing two broad problematics: challenging established and orthodox formations of management knowledge, and questioning how human identity/subjectivity is shaped by the political and cultural dynamics of *organizational* knowledge and practice (see, for example, Alvesson and Willmott, 1992; Grey and Willmott, 2005). In the process this emerging field has tended to be concerned with how we become particular kinds of organizational subjects (such as a manager or professional) rather than with *relations of exploitation* (how surplus value is realized and distributed). The CMS research community's attention to relations of power, and particularly the politics of subjectivity and identity, can be explained as an effect of the political and historical circumstances that surround the field's emergence (see Rowlinson, Hogan, and Hassard, 2001; Rowlinson and Hassard, 2000; Prichard, 2007, 2008).

This chapter presents an approach that sets a critical analysis of *value relations* in organizations (e.g. relations of exploitation) *alongside* relations of power and relations of meaning. The particular approach draws broadly on the work of the economists Steve Resnick and Richard Wolff (1987; 1992; 2003a,b, 2005; Cullenberg, 1994). In what follows I introduce some features of Resnick and Wolff's work and illustrate this with the analysis of a diary entry by the teaching leader in an academic department.

The diary entry deals with the introduction of a teaching review process. The aim is to show how the particular analytical approach works as a means of critically unravelling attempts to lead or manage public service organizations. The analysis of the diary entry is simply an illustration of the approach. The chapter concludes with a discussion of the implications of the approach for research/practice and development of critical public services management.

ADDING VALUE TO CRITICAL PUBLIC SERVICES MANAGEMENT

The editors of this volume wrote in the proposal for this collection that the book would explore "ways to think about managing and organizing public service that are *radically critical* of the current beliefs underpinning 'good management' in public service organizations" (my emphasis). This radical criticality leads them to argue that management and leadership are "intrinsically connected to practices associated with the domination and control of others—public services management is ultimately about the pursuit of power" (Currie et al., 2006, private communication).

The key question this statement raises is why an ultimate, final explanation is needed. One can appreciate the sentiment of the statement, which carries an important political and ethical stance. But is it really *all* about the pursuit of power? Is 'power' the only game in town? While this is unlikely to be the intention of the authors, the statement suggests a limit on the possible range of explanations for the uses of techniques associated with management in public service organizations (e.g., financial arrangements, audit and assessment activities, particular contractual and interpersonal practices) and provokes the question: "What other targets might public services management practice be pursuing?"

It seems reasonable to suggest, on the grounds that it is probably impossible for us to know precisely what the final target of something as multifarious as public services management practice might be, that a range of explanations for such targets is preferable. For instance it seems possible to explain certain aspects of management practice in terms of the *relations of meaning.* For example, some aspects of the work of public services managers could be explained as efforts to produce, form, or solidify the particular meaning of the signifier 'public' among various groups and agencies. Likewise, public services management practice might also be explained in terms of attempts to pursue certain *relations of value.* For example some public services management practices could be explained primarily as efforts to maintain or reduce wage and salary expenditures. And while it is tempting to assume that it is the *relation of power* that is the primary target when efforts are made to control expenditure, the explanation might also run in the opposite direction: That the relation of power (control of expenditure) is one mechanism in pursuit of a particular relation of value (i.e., a certain quantity or quality of effort realized from labor in the midst of particular service activities, e.g., education, health).

What I am suggesting is that we put aside the quest for ultimate explanations and, taking what Bob Jessop (2001) identifies as a 'institutional turn' of the methodological variety, make an *analytical* distinction between power and other possible explanations for public service management practices. Such an approach is inevitably more modest than a singular explanation. It perhaps loses some of the political edge in the process. But it may, potentially, offer a richer and more inclusive explanatory and political platform for critical studies of public services management.

THE MULTIPLE TARGETS OF PUBLIC
SERVICES MANAGEMENT

How might we unravel these various kinds of relations—relations of power, meaning, and value? The first analytical move is to assume that *management practice* (e.g., budgeting, strategizing, work allocating, etc.) establishes particular positions and relations that people may be called upon to occupy as senior post-holders, professionals, staff, and so on. A practice can be understood as an available set of defined and repeatable actions. In this approach a 'manager' is not a person. A 'manager' is a position in a set of relations established through multiple practices. These practices are complex and overdetermine each other (Resnick and Wolff, 1987). Each practice includes features that we would seek to explain as expressing relations of power, value, and meaning (and other relations). While the particular explanation of a practice (or complex formation of practices) might suggest that one or other of these relations is prioritized at certain moments (e.g., the practice of increasing staff–student ratios in education institutions might emphasize relations of value over relations of power and meaning) the analytical presumption is that all practices include features that articulate such relations. Likewise this approach assumes no definitive list of possible concepts that might be used to analyze the relations embedded in practice. Before discussing how we might further unravel such relations let me offer a brief example of how such an analytical approach might play out.

The management practice of distributing work to others, for example, allocating a certain number of students or courses to a teacher or lecturer in a college or university, can be understood as simultaneously the pursuit of a particular relation of power (between the manager and the lecturer), a particular relation of meaning (the ascription of the signifier 'lecturer/teacher' and 'manager' to oneself and the other) and the attempt to establish a particular relation of value—the expectation of the performance of a certain amount of necessary labor, to cover the costs of that labor and related expenses, and surplus labor.

Surplus labor, or what neo-classically informed management researchers call 'rent' (Coff, 1999); can be regarded as the value or labor beyond that which is required to maintain a work process. All work processes consume a certain amounts of necessary effort. Some of that effort might, for instance, be the result of the work done by those positioned as managers (Armstrong, 1989). A key issue for critical analysis of value processes is in exploring the tensions between practices that locate some people in positions as producers of rent/surplus labor, and some in positions as receivers or consumers of the rent/surplus labor produced. It may be that in some settings particular practices are applied that return surplus value/rent to those that produce it either individually or collectively. For example institutions might develop and apply distributive practice that treats all students, regardless of their origin, as recipients of any surplus labor realized from teaching and research activities.

What we tend to find, of course, is that the particular distributive practices applied in further and higher education is consumed in ways that favor the 'tastes' of the institution's dominant coalition. In some institutions surpluses tend to be spent on buildings, in others expensive specialized scientific equipment has a strong call on surplus funds, and in other locations surpluses are spent on swelling the ranks of academic related staff. Of course, in order to grasp how such surpluses are distributed we *must* include, alongside our discussion of value relations found in particular practices, the power and meaning dimensions of such practices. Many distributive practices (those that organize value relations) are imbued with meanings that suggest fairness and democratic processes are followed. A governance practice that distributes surpluses away from the producers of value to the construction of buildings, the purchase of equipment, or even to the payments for cars, trips, and houses as part of remuneration packages of senior managers, is likely to be achieved, to some degree, in publicly funded institutions at least, by mobilizing some notion of 'democratic due process.' There are clearly a number of practices that might support the claim to democratic due process. The governing councils of universities and colleges, for example, tend to include, unlike privately held organizations, students, staff, and community representatives. In some institutions this may be entirely symbolic and disconnected from the power and value relations embedded in the routines of practices that make up a college or university.

SOURCING CONCEPTS FOR CRITICAL ANALYSIS

The multi-threaded critical institutional analysis (Cullenberg, 1994) suggested by the approach just outlined leaves open the particular selection of concepts that might be used to unravel the value, power, and meaning relations found in public services management practice. It would seem possible that the value concepts of recent variants of Marxian analysis (Resnick and Wolff, 2006; Cleaver, 1979; Negri, 1991), symbolic concepts from recent forms of Freudian analysis (Arnaud, 2002) and concepts from Foucault's work on power (Marsden, 1999) might have a certain currency in some setting and not others where already homogenized vocabularies are preferred. For example, Paula Jarzabkowski's recent analysis of the symbolic power and value dimensions of strategic management practice in three UK universities (2008) draws on Giddens' presentation of these relations. In this approach, the concepts of signification, domination, and legitimation which, as she notes, "are inseparable in practice" (2008, 623) reference relations of meaning, value, and power. The concept of 'domination' is used to signal both the "institutionalized distribution of material resources," and the "institutionalized authority relations . . . which are reflected in the way that the interests of different groups are represented with the social system" (ibid.). This presentation of the institutionalized practices that articulate value, power, and meaning processes appears to have benefited significantly from the institutionalization of Giddens' work in North Atlantic sociology and from there into management and organization studies (Barley and Torbert, 1997; Orlikowski, 1996). Of course, the concepts we draw into this critical multi-threaded analysis inevitably come with various commitment and priorities. For some audiences such signification may undermine the legitimacy of such a multi-threaded critical analysis. Academic work is largely a community exercise and some communities are more open to this kind of analysis than other.

CMS continues to have a rather polygamous approach to theory and methodology. It includes a range of divergent approaches including strands of poststructuralism, critical theory, feminism, labor process analysis, and, most recently, postcolonial readings of management knowledge and practice (see Alvesson and Willmott [1992, 1996 and 2003], Fournier and Grey [(2000], Zald [2002], *Organization* [2002], Prasad [2003]). While there have been some disputes over the grounding assumptions that underwrite some of these various traditions of work (the struggle between critical realist and post structural analysis), what unites these various frameworks is their ability to guide critical management education practice that challenges orthodox managerialist knowledge and practice.

What is proposed here, as a contribution to critical studies of public services management, is a form of *critical analysis* that draws on various strands of analysis in order to unravel the different relations (value, power, meaning, and others). Such an approach isn't looking to combines theoretical traditions. It isn't looking to join Foucault and Marx in a critical realist marriage as Richard Marsden outlines (1999). Rather it is seeking, via an analytical distinction between value, power, and meaning processes, a means of revaluing the value dimension of organizational practice alongside the analysis of power and meaning processes—which have been the staple of CMS analysis to date. In order to illustrate this approach the remainder of this chapter provides an analysis of a diary entry written by the teaching leader in an academic department. The diary entry is followed by analysis of the practices it reports using the approach outlined.

DIARY ENTRY: 'GEORGE'S' REACTION TO TEACHING REVIEW COMMITTEE TERMS OF REFERENCE

Teaching Leader: The draft terms of reference for the new review committee went out last week and I really thought people had ignored them, taken them as a summary of the discussion from the meeting, or simply put them aside until the committee meets next week. How wrong I was! George, who for some reason didn't even attend the scoping meeting (it was open invitation), sent me (and everyone else in the department) a reply to my request for any further suggestions that would improve the (terms of reference) document . . . hmm! His response was not a list of suggestions for improvements, but a seemed to be an attempt to derail the whole process! He argued that the review process as proposed would impair professional judgement and decision making and was 'unacceptable and most unwise'. George called for full debate on the document before the first meeting. The hoped for debate did not materialize in email form at least—not a squeak from anyone else after George's epistle. While George's comments were contradictory and confusing he was clearly expressing a reaction to the review process and something to bear in mind regardless of how collegial we attempted to be in order to make the process work.

My response to George by email via the department's email list was to reply very quickly and not to tackle his comments head on (I did not want to engage in an argument about the review process in other words). I replied with clarification of some points that George had confused, and welcomed more debate on the topic. I was trying to position myself to the side as more the facilitator of the process. I also drew attention to something that we were doing to improve our engagement with clients.

ANALYSING DIARY ENTRY

We begin analysis of this diary entry by identifying the particular practices involved. In the incident reported in the diary there are, however, two practices. The first is the distribution of the terms of reference which is part of an the attempt to establish a committee responsible for overseeing the review of teaching (the committee would not actually carry out that review but would provide input into and oversight of the review's process) and the second is George's reaction. These two practices are no doubt familiar to many teachers in further and higher education.

The first temptation in analyzing these two practices is to regard the first as an attempt to extend and intensify the power relation between the department (as representative of the university) and those charged with teaching. The temptation is then to regard the value relations in this practice as inevitably subsumed to the relations of power. The *relation of value* embedded in this first practice appears to be simply a call for a certain amount of time and effort to be contributed to a committee process.

Given that teaching is the primary activity for realizing surplus labor, and this is largely a function of the number of students enrolled (and not the quality of the work done), then the contribution of time and effort by academics to the committee aimed at attempting to change the quality of the teaching effort would likely be regarded as unproductive labor (non-surplus generating). Of course committee work may improve the coherence, consistency, and possibly the quality of teaching and learning practice but surpluses are realized through the quantity of teaching labor rather than its quality and as such efforts to improve the quality of that labor must be simply absorbing as unproductive effort.

What then are the value relations of the second practice—George's denunciation of the review process? What we find is the expression of a different set of relations of value and from this can identify some of the tensions between the value relations of managerially and professionally orchestrated work.

George's challenge to the teaching review process brings to light (and itself enacts) the value relations of professional work. It is tempting to regard George's challenge to the review process in power terms only—as simply an effort to resist the application an extension of relations of power between the managers and academics involved in teaching. The problem is that if we simply interpret the two practices from a power perspective we miss the value relations George is articulating (both speaking about and enacting). From a value perspective George is not only defending the control academics have over their teaching labor, more importantly he is promoting practices that involve significantly different ways of realizing and appropriating surplus value.

The value relations of professional work found in George's reaction to the review process revolve around the performance of 'debate' between professionals. George in effect calls on other academics to perform a debate on the topic of teaching review (and probably more generally on the nature of teaching activity). George suggests that this debate take place outside and prior to proposed committee meeting. In making such a claim he is not simply resisting the controlling aspects of the managerial or bureaucratic committee, he also is promoting a practice that involves value relations where those that create value also consume the value of the work done. Particularly the value relations here are to be found in the quality and quantity of debate—in effect in the value that such debate produces.

The qualitative dimension of value relations can be regarded as the quality of the performance of particular kinds of work, and the distribution and consumption by others of that qualitative performance. The quality of the 'debate' that George is calling for might be found in its eloquence, ferocity, learnedness, or political cunning. The analytical question here is how the necessary and surplus value from this debate is realized and to whom it is distributed. In putting this practice in this form we can suggest that the surplus labor of this professional work of 'debate' will be largely consumed by those taking part—which clearly assumes the support of academics by the state and families (student fees). And here in lies the tension between the value relations of the committee and the manager, on the one hand, and the value relations of the 'debate' and the collective and autonomous professional that George is calling to work on the other.

Open debate, a defining practice of professional academic work, can be very time consuming. If George's call to debate had been successful then such a focus could last some weeks, consume huge quantities of time and effort, and potentially interrupt teaching and research commitments. The key point is that 'debate' is a practice that involves time and intellectual energy that is *consumed* by those taking part. In a sense, such a debate could amount to a kind of intellectual 'feast,' a kind of intellectual potlatch. The academic debate that George calls for could potentially extend over some weeks as academics prepare arguments, check sources, polish papers, and improve their delivery. Potentially, such a 'debate' might consume all available academic labor for some weeks—labor that might otherwise been distributed to students, professional societies, and academic journal publishers. Of course some of the debate's surpluses might not simply add to the performances of others involved or be consumed by the debaters themselves. It might be uplifted by observers (potentially students). But even observers would need to expend significant time and effort to grasp the debate as it develops.

By comparison, the committee process, as outlined in the suggested review of teaching, would, in value terms, set strict temporal and spatial limitations on the performance of academic debate. Only a few fragments of the kind of 'debate' that George envisages would be possible. It is here that we can see how the relations of value found in the practices of professional organizing intersects with its relations of power. George suggests in his note that academics that have fully engaged the work of the 'debate' that he calls for—and which have few temporal or spatial boundaries—may well, as a result, be better prepared to review their own work and as such there may be little need for the ongoing departmental review of teaching work. In other words, 'debate' is not simply an open-ended intellectual 'feast.' It also establishes important relations of power between the academic and his or her own work.

As such 'debate' is not only a device for professional workers to produce and consume their own labor, it is also a pedagogical device for conditioning, organizing, and reproducing the character of the labor that academics do. George's argument is that the quality of teaching labor is not to be found in the practice of teaching review, which we might suggest would quickly descend into the formation of an auditable list of practices to be achieved, but in the practice and quality of debate. In this sense, George's reaction to the review process is a working example of the kind of work he is calling on his professional colleagues to perform.

This brief analysis of the two practices found in the diary entry (the review process and George's reaction) shows not simply a struggle over the control of teaching labor between those positioned as managers and the producers of that labor but also the competing relations of value creation and distribution embedded in such practices. These differences are further confirmed in the ascription of certain meanings (relation of meaning) to the various positions involved. The image of the producer of teaching labor George evokes is one of the autonomous professional whose self-discipline provides the basis for the continuous development of courses and teaching programs. This image is one where the subject has been schooled in the 'feast' of the debate and, we might suggest, does not consequently require supervisory labor in order to monitor and develop teaching activities and practice.

How might the diary author have responded to George's challenge (which is really a third challenge)? One response she might have had to George's call for debate would have been to simply respond in kind—to contribute some professional work, and possibly some qualitative value, to the debate of the issue of teaching review. At a stroke this would have likely affirmed for George a commitment to the value, meaning, and power relations of the professional academic as he had expressed them. Choosing not to engage in debate was, in respect, a response to two features. Firstly she assumed that such a debate would not occur. This was a political judgement based on experience of previous calls for debate that had also failed to illicit the kind of general response that George was calling for. In other words, the lack of previous examples of the practice of 'debate' suggested that the proposed intellectual 'feast' would likely have been an intimate dinner for two.

But, importantly, she justified the lack of direct engagement with George's proposed debate in relation to the managerial dimensions of her positioning as departmental teaching leader. The teaching leader's primary responsibilities was to facilitate the work of others (including review work) rather than engage in it oneself. Here we find another expression of the tension between competing relations of value and their associated relations of power and meaning. The value relations embedded in the practices of the university manager (the teaching leader in this case) take a subsumed form (they do not directly contribute to the creation of surplus value). This difference is reinforced by the power and meaning relations embedded in related practices—such as the manager's employment contract, job description, and pattern of socialization with other managers.

DISCUSSION

Most critical analyses of the struggle between managerial and professional staff in public services organizations regards the tension between these groups as an effect of a power struggle over control of profession labor. Such analysis is not wrong, per se, but it tends to neglect the tensions between the different practices of managers and academics in terms of the embedded relations of value. The core practices of professional academic labor involve debate, detailed scrutiny, criticism, analysis, development of counter-argument, experimentation, and so on. These carry with them and project both quantitative and qualitative relations of value. These differ markedly from those embedded in the familiar managerial practices of work planning, allocation, and review.

Whereas the value of professional labor is drawn from the level of commitment, engagement, and contribution to the practices of 'debate' (over knowledge, issues, and methodology), and the distribution of the value created to those involved, the value relations of managerial practices are located in efforts to increase, extend and/or intensify the value realizing labor of academics (primarily teaching) and to draw a income from that work.

The implication here is that antagonism or tension between managers and professionals is not simply part of a power struggle between managers and professionals over work, but an effect of the tension between different sets of practices with quite different relations of value. Of course such tensions do not always boil over into antagonism. Academic professionals may find that the value relations of the 'debate' (formally we might identify this as the struggle over knowledge and perhaps 'truth') is their primary activity as they engage with students—postgraduate and research students in particular. Others may find however that the value, power, and meaning relations of their professional work maps not to those of the 'debate,' but resembles much more directly the practice of industrial education. Here the value relations map closely to those of managers and workers in commodity and service based businesses. In such instances, the practice of teaching is primarily a relation of value based on a commodity (a course or qualification), and not on the contribution to, and value realized from academic debate (and its surrounding practices depending on the discipline concerned). Commodity-based education is of course organized by those positioned as managers. The aim here is to increase the surplus realized from academic's work. In such settings the core means of raising the rate of return is not to invite more academics to join the debate. Rather it is to increase the numbers of students enrolled in courses (enrollment rather than completion being the point of sale) and thus improve the rate of exploitation of academic labor.

CONCLUSION

I began this chapter with a brief preamble that identified a critical question that Mick Rowlinson put to me some years ago. That question asked if my earlier work had 'found any managers.' This chapter has been an attempt to tackle that question in such a way that some of the commitments found in the earlier work are retained but the discussion of the relations of value, and managers' role in the process of exploitation of labor, are explored. The result and perhaps one of the implications of this work is that critical analysis of managerial work might adopt a critical institutional framework that includes not simply analysis of the way power relations and relations of meaning are played out in the practices of managing, but also how value relations—the creation, realization, and distribution of necessary and surplus labor—is also embedded in practice. The implication of such a move would be that those interested in the critical analysis of public services management practice might consider expanding their conceptual repertoires beyond power and meaning so that analysis of such management practice/s brings to light the many differs dimensions of such repeated activity, including the creation and distribution of value.

NOTES

1. The thesis makes the assumption that 'management,' as a particular formation of knowledge and practice, has come to suffuse, to varying degrees, the UK public sector and higher and further education more particularly. The work explores how those drawn, pushed, or maneuvered into senior position in colleges and universities came to take up such positions. In the years since the work was published (see Prichard and Willmott, 1997; Prichard and Deem, 1999; Prichard, 2000) it appears to have made a small contribution to the higher education literature and continues to be regularly referenced as representative of critical analysis of management and managers in these sectors.

REFERENCES

Alvesson, M., and H. Willmott. 1992. *Critical management studies.* London: Sage.

Alvesson, M., and H. Willmott./ 1996. *Making sense of management: A critical introduction.* London: Sage.

Alvesson, M., and H. Willmott. 2003. *Studying management critically.* London: Sage.

Armstrong, P. 1989. Management, labour process and agency. *Work, Employment and Society* 3(3): 307–322.

Arnaud, G. 2002. The Organization and the Symbolic: Organizational Dynamics Viewed from A Lacanian Perspective. *Human Relations* 55(6): 691–716.

Arvidsson, A. 2005. Brands: A critical perspective. *Journal of Consumer Culture* 5(2): 235–258.

Barley, S.R. and P.S. Tolbert. 1997. Institutionalization and structuration: Studying the links between action and institution. *Organization Studies* 31: 78–109

Clark, W. *Academic charisma and the origins of the research university.* Chicago, IL: University of Chicago. 339.

Cleaver, H. 1979. *Reading capital politically.* Austin, TX: University Of Texas Press.

Coff, R. 1999. When competitive advantage doesn't lead to performance: The resource-based view and stakeholder bargaining power. *Organization Science* 10(2): 119–133.

Cullenberg S. 1994. Overdetermination, totality, and institutions: A genealogy of a Marxist institutionalist economics. *Journal of Economic Issues* 33(4): 801–815.

Currie, G., J. Ford, N. Harding, and M. Learmonth. 2007. *Making public services management critical*. New York: Routledge.

Fournier, V., and C. Grey. 2000. At a critical moment: Conditions and prospects for critical management studies. *Human Relations* 53(1): 7–32.

Grey, C. and H. Willmott. 2005. *Critical management studies: A reader* (Oxford Management Readers). London: Oxford.

Jarzabkowski, P. 2008. Shaping strategy as a structuration process. *Academy of Management Journal* 51(4): 621–650.

Jessop, B. 2001. Institutional re(turns) and the strategic relational approach. *Environment and Planning* A, 33: 1213–1235.

Levy, D. 2008. Political contestation in global production networks. *Academy of Management Review* 33(4): 943–963.

Marsden, R. 1999. *Marx After Foucault*. London: Routledge.

Negri, A. 1991. *Marx beyond Marx: Lessons on the Grundrisse*. New York: Autonomedia.

Organization. 2002. Special Issue on Critical Management Studies. *Organization* 9(3): 363–452.

Orlikowski, W. 1996. 'Improvising Organizational Transformation Overtime. A Situated Change Perspective'. *Information Systems Research* 7(1): 63–92.

Prasad, A. 2003. *Postcolonial theory and organizational analysis*. New York: Palgrave.

Prichard, C. 2000. *Making managers in colleges and universities*. Buckingham, UK: Open University Press.

Prichard, C. 2007. Responding to class theft: Theoretical and empirical links to critical management studies. *Rethinking Marxism* 19(3): 409–421.

Prichard, C. 2008. Class, management and music: Re-engaging class in critical management studies. Paper presented at the Academy of Management Conference, Anahiem, Los Angeles, CA, August 11.

Prichard, C. and R. Deem. 1999. Wo-managing further education: Gender and the construction of the manager in the corporate colleges of England. *Gender and Education* 11(3): 323–342.

Prichard, C., and H. Willmott. 1997. Just how managed is the McUniversity? *Organization Studies* 18(2): 287–316.

Resnick, S., and R. Wolff. 1987. *Knowledge and class*. Chicago, IL: University of Chicago Press.

Resnick, S., and R. Wolff. 1992. Radical economics: A tradition of theoretical differences. In *Radical economics*, eds. B. Roberts and S. Deiner, 15–43. Boston: Klumer.

Resnick, S., and R. Wolff. 2003a. The diversity of class analyses: A critique of Erik Olin Wright and beyond. *Critical Sociology* 29(1): 7–27.

Resnick, S., and R. Wolff. 2003b. Exploitation, consumption, and the uniqueness of US capitalism. *Historical Materialism* 11(4): 209–226.

Resnick, S., and R. Wolff. 2005. The point and purpose of Marx's notion of class. *Rethinking Marxism* 17(1): 33–37.

Resnick, S. and R. Wolff. 2006. *New departures in Marxian theory*. London: Taylor and Francis.

Rowlinson, M., and J. Hassard. 2000. Marxist political economy, revolutionary politics and labour process analysis. *International Studies in Management and Organizations* 30(4): 85–111.

Rowlinson, M., J. Hogan, and J. Hassard. 2001. From labour process theory to critical management studies. *Administrative Theory and Praxis* 23(3): 339–362.

Smith, C., J. Child, and M. Rowlinson. 1990. *Reshaping work: The Cadbury Experience*. Cambridge, UK: Cambridge University Press.

Zald, M.N. 2002. Spinning disciplines: Critical management studies in the context of the transformation of management education. *Organization* 9(3): 365–85

Conclusion
What is to Be Done? On the Merits of Micro-Revolutions

Jackie Ford and Nancy Harding

The chapters in this book provide a comprehensive critique of management in public sector organizations. Readers who have been struggling to find reasons for why they have been feeling unsettled about aspects of their work in the public sector should have found a language that allows them to identify those previously unnamed feelings. Others may have had their views confirmed, while others will find some aspects of the chapters reasonable but disagree with other aspects. Most people who have read some or all of the chapters in this book will have done so from a sense of a need for change. But what sort of change is required and how can it be brought about? In the words of Lenin, usefully appropriated for our discussion: what is to be done? Lenin advocated revolution, a project that has singularly failed and we are not advocating that we follow his lead. However, poststructuralist theories have often been attacked for providing critique without a program of change, so we cannot finish this book without pointing to the potential for each reader to start to change the places in which they work through changing the ways in which they interact with others. We are suggesting that postmodern Marxism's advocacy of micro-revolutions is apposite for public sector organizations, and that the ways in which managers and professional staff can bring about micro-revolutions is through developing the habit of dialogic interactions as part of their everyday worlds. Rather than reducing colleagues to the status of appendages in an organizational machine, such dialogic micro-revolutions would support the very humanity of each and every member of staff.

MICRO-REVOLUTIONS

The concept of micro-revolutions arises from the work of J.K. Gibson-Graham, two feminist postmodern Marxists, J. Gibson and K. Graham, who write as one person. In their 1996 text, *The End of Capitalism (As We Knew It): A Feminist Critique of Political Economy*, they deconstruct the very concept of capitalism, critique the possibility of there ever being a Marxist revolution, and point a way forward, one that we are adapting here.

They begin their discussion as follows: "The performativity of social representations—in other words, the ways in which they are implicated in the worlds they ostensibly represent . . ." (ix). They are thus exploring 'social representations as *constitutive* of the world.' They argue that when theorists:

> depict patriarchy, or racism, or compulsory heterosexuality, or capitalist hegemony they are not only delineating a formation they hope to see destabilized or replaced. They are also generating a representation of the social world and endowing it with performative force. To the extent that this representation becomes influential it may contribute to the hegemony of a "hegemonic formation" and it will undoubtedly influence people's ideas about the possibilities of difference and change, including the potential for successful political interventions (x).

From this, they are able to argue that we can "understand capitalist hegemony as a (dominant) discourse rather than as a social articulation or structure" (xi). That is, rather than seeing capitalism as a social structure we can understand it as also *discursive*, and as a discourse which renders subjugated discourses relatively 'invisible.' It follows that:

> the project of understanding the beast (of capitalism) has itself produced a beast, or even a bestiary, and the process of producing knowledge in service to politics has estranged rather than united understanding and action (1).

Capitalism has been turned into a gargantuan beast because of the ways in which we have discussed it and written about it and theorized it. We have thus made it too big to challenge. It is the way capitalism has been 'thought,' they suggest, that makes it so difficult to imagine its supersession (4).

What happens then is that other forms of economy (not to mention noneconomic aspects of social life) are often understood primarily with reference to capitalism: as being fundamentally the same as (or modelled upon) capitalism, or as being deficient or substandard imitations; as being opposite to capitalism; as being the complement of capitalism; as existing in capitalism's space or orbit. *And thus everything is rendered, through the way we discuss things, as aspects of or inferior to capitalism.*

They go further. Drawing upon Laclau and Mouffe, they show how we erect identities so that they can have only one meaning, that that meaning is constraining, but the refusal of any identity to conform to narrow definitions means identities are always unstable. For example, the term 'woman' has a very different meaning when it is articulated with 'private life' and 'marriage' than when it is set in the context of 'feminism' or 'lesbian.' The latter pair of terms destabilizes the concepts of male prerogative associated with the former. The inference of this, important to our arguments, is that we can become more politically aware if we explore how a concept is deployed.

Now this is important, because often when we (as academics, as policy makers, as managers, as professional workers) talk about a concept we tend to imagine it as if it is one narrow thing. So, the government talks about *the* NHS, or boards of directors talk about *the* organization, or vice-chancellors talk about *the* University. If we take these entities in the way they are defined by those with most power we give up our power (Foucault argued power is everywhere, waiting to be brought into being and thus used at all levels). If we resist those definitions in some way then we can use our power to change our lives and the lives of those around us. So, if the manager refuses to accept the definition of the manager as someone who 'gets things done through other people,' and instead defines the manager as someone who 'works with others to get things done,' removing the status and the hierarchy from the definition, then that manager is taking one small step to changing the ways in which public sector organizations treat their members.

This point is demonstrated in Gibson-Graham's discussion of Althusser's work (28, et passim). They see in Althusser's work the origins of ideas that are now central to poststructuralism and postmodern Marxism. Althusser invented the category of 'overdetermination':

> In the summary terms of a post-Althusserian conception of overde-termination, every entity or event exists at the nexus of a bewildering complexity of natural and social processes, constituting it as a site of contradiction, tension, difference, and instability (Resnick and Wolff, 1987, quoted in Gibson-Graham, 1996, p.29 ff.).

Each overdetermined site or process participates in constituting all others; every cause is an effect, every relationship is a process of (inter) change and mutuality. The analysis of such complexities requires the adoption of an "entry point" that betrays the concerns of the analyst but cannot secure ontological priority or privilege. To understand this, think about the concept 'class' (here we are drawing upon Laclau and Mouffe's [2001] influential work). We bundle millions of people into different 'classes' but do they really add up to a (homogeneous) 'working class' or a (homogeneous) 'middle class'? What we've done, in our theorizing, is to impose a *post hoc* identity upon these millions of people. Once we've imposed that identity, we, the people who supposedly form these classes, start to make ourselves into people who represent that class, or feel somehow traitorous or negative if we fail to live up to those ideals. The relevance of this to people working in public sector organizations, as professional staff, managers, administrators, manual workers, or whatever, is that we tend to see not the real people we are working with, but the label that is applied to the category to which we have allocated those people. So managers and doctors may not get along because they see not a person but a manager or a doctor, a label rather than an individual (Harding and Lee, in review). Rather than seeing someone who breathes and eats, has family responsibilities and hobbies, they see a cardboard cut-out, single-dimensional, stereotypical 'doctor' or 'manager.'

This is one example of how the ways in which we use language can be destructive of others, and of mutual interactions. The ways in which language can intensify the negative aspects of organizational life is shown in Gibson-Graham's discussion of Sharon Marcus' work on rape. The very necessary corrective brought about feminist activists in getting rape treated as the serious crime it is has had the effect of making women scared to go out alone.

Sharon Marcus, they write, is led to explore the construction of rape as a linguistic artifact and:

> to ask how the violence of rape is enabled by narratives, complexes and institutions which derive their strength not from outright, immutable, unbeatable force but rather from their power to structure our lives as . . . cultural scripts' (1992, 388–389).

The term 'cultural scripts' is important here. It is cultural scripts that lead us to regard the doctor or the manager as an ogre. In Marcus's terms, language shapes the rape script—"the verbal and physical interactions of a woman and her would-be assailant"—permitting the would-be rapist to constitute feelings of power and causing the woman to experience corresponding feelings of terror and paralysis. This does not mean that rapist and victim play out fixed roles (124). Rather, they participate in "a series of steps and signals"—whose course and ending is not set. Her notion of a script involves the continual making and remaking of social roles by soliciting responses and responding to cues, and in this sense she highlights the self-contradictory nature of any script and the ways in which it can be challenged from within. Applied to organizations, this means that when managers and staff meet, they play out a script that arises from organizational hierarchies and not from the individuals who are meeting. Each is reduced, again, to a stereotype.

However, *each becomes the stereotype they are portraying*. This can be seen if we explore Gibson-Graham's further discussion of Marcus' arguments. Drawing upon Marcus they argue (134) that one of the powerful things about rape in our culture is that it represents an important *inscription* of female sexual identity. Marcus argues that we should

> view rape not as the invasion of female inner space, but as the forced *creation* of female sexuality as a violated inner space. The horror of rape is not that it steals something from us but that it *makes* us into

things to be taken . . . The most deep-rooted upheaval of rape culture would revise the idea of female sexuality as an object, as property, and as inner space.

This emphasizes the power of language and of discourse. Gibson-Graham suggests we can challenge hegemonic representations through exploring how language sustains those representations, and thus we can start to work to achieve much-desired changes. To do this we should participate in redefining how we interact (264).

This moves revolution to the individual level, to the organizational arena where staff and managers interact. One-to-one interactions are fundamental to every organization and its management. By changing the definitions of those interactions we can bring about small but meaningful local-level changes.

We are thus borrowing Gibson-Graham's arguments and applying them in a somewhat different way in our work. We are suggesting that when people working in organizations meet, they should become aware of the scripts that limit their potential for action and that predispose people to making certain presumptions about the other. This requires reflexivity—or knowing who's pulling our own strings.

Secondly, we are suggesting that the interactions between managers, professional staff, and others are the foundations of the organization—they bring the organization into existence (Ford and Harding, 2004). So changing the ways in which these individuals interact with each other, through the development of dialogic encounters, will bring about micro-level revolutions in that each participant can feel less a cog in the machine and more of an individual making a contribution to the public sector workplace.

We are thus advocating two interrelated actions. Firstly, getting to understand how the organizations in which we work limit the ways in which we can think and speak. Secondly, changing the ways in which those of us with power and authority interact with others so that we contribute to their flourishing, rather than their reduction to cogs in an organizational machine. This can be achieved through dialogic interaction. Reflexivity and dialogic interaction together amount to micro-revolutions. We will discuss each of these two aspects of micro-revolutions in turn.

ON REFLEXIVITY: KNOWING WHO ONE IS SO AS TO UNDERSTAND WHO THE OTHER IS

Notions regarding reflexivity can be traced to Gadamer's work. He argued in 1975 that critical reason requires an on-going self-critical process in which we look at the historical, social, and moral contexts in which we are located. To Gadamer's list we must add the organizational context. Reflexivity is therefore concerned with knowing ourselves; when we have a better understanding of ourselves we gain an understanding of how our own processes of approaching and interacting with others influences how they interact with us, and also how our ways of seeing the world interfere with our seeing the person who is in front of us. We tend otherwise to see others as extensions of ourselves, as people who make us happy or sad, who make our lives more or less difficult, who bolster our egos or demolish our sense of who we are. When we understand that we see others as a reflection of ourselves, we can move beyond that and try to see them in a more honest way, as different from us. We see them as separate selves rather than a projection of our own imaginations. To take one very simple example, if we have grown up as the oldest child in a large family, we will tend to take on responsibilities for others when we are adults, because we have learned to see others as in some ways child-like and needing support. Because that is how we have learned to behave in the world we, all unknowingly, may disempower others. Rather than other people being weak, it is our strength that renders them as appearing to be weak. When we are at work, the label we are given may influence how we see ourselves and others. For example, if we are 'leaders' we see ourselves as somewhat superior beings (or inferior beings who cannot live up to the label) and others (followers) as inferior and lacking desirable attributes (Ford, Harding and Learmonth, 2008).

Through such a process of critical reflexivity we can see individuals as themselves, we can better understand how the world appears to them, and we can begin to explore the 'nitty-gritty of real life' (Bourdieu and Wacquant, 1992, 199). This is one of the reasons why reflexivity has become so widely recommended in management studies (Cunliffe, 2002; Hardy et al., 2001; Perriton, 2000; Alvesson and Wilmott, 1996). As Bourdieu and Wacquant argue:

> When you apply reflexive sociology to yourself, you open up the possibility of identifying true sites of freedom, and thus of building small-scale, modest, practical morals in keeping with the scope of human freedom which, in my opinion, is not that large (1992, 199).

This reflexivity therefore has three aspects:

- intrasubjective approaches, in which we gain self-understanding through focusing on how we came to be the people we are, and what triggers influence the ways in which we interact with others (Benjamin, 1995);
- intersubjective, relational approaches, in which we explore the impact we have upon others and the impact others have upon us (Benjamin, 1995);
- organizational approaches, in which we explore the subtle ways in which the organization influences how we feel about ourselves and how we interrelate with others.

Such an approach involves participants trying to understand their past actions and to give more consideration to some of the constraints and opportunities that may be buried in many of these accounts. This goes beyond the reflective practitioner approach advocated by Schon and others (Schon, 1983; Ghaye and Lillyman, 1996), which essentially adopts a functionalist approach to reflection. The functionalist approach asks participants to make connections and test understanding through seeking patterns, logic, and order in their experiences. This approach lacks the facility to gain critical insights that will allow more open and equal encounters untrammelled by organizational demands.

Through understanding ourselves, getting to know the ways in which others affect how we behave, and identifying how organizations influence the ways we behave with others, we are better equipped to ensure we do not cause any harm to others, and indeed help them flourish. This knowledge can then be used in dialogic encounters with others.

DIALOGIC ENCOUNTERS: MICRO-REVOLUTIONS IN PRACTICE

By 'dialogical' is meant, literally, dialogue. As the earlier discussion about reflexivity has shown, any dialogue between two people involves a range of influences upon each self, some consciously recognized but some unconscious. The chapters in this book show how interactions can often be harmful to the parties involved. Dialogic encounters based on a reflexive self-understanding should reduce, and ideally, remove some of the harm.

We have explored elsewhere (Ford and Harding, 2007; Ford and Lawler, 2007) the practicalities of engaging in reflexive dialogic encounters. We show in Ford and Lawler (2007) the merits of using a narrative 360-degree approach to interactions in organizations. These help colleagues develop an understanding of the impact on both themselves and others. That process involves the reflexive account discussed previously. However, the reflexive account is arrived at through thinking oneself about one's self. The dialogic encounter involves each party being fully cognizant of the other as an individual with their own history, their own subordination to organizational norms, their own triggers and responses. Constructive dissent is encouraged (Grint, 2005), and prejudices, stereotypes and clinging to past are challenged.

Further, a reflexive dialogic encounter requires a strong awareness of the power that is involved in the interaction. The higher up the organizational hierarchy one climbs, the more power one has over others. This power is often used without understanding of its potential destructive powers, or even awareness that it exists as power. Parties to a dialogic encounter should be aware of any power dynamics in the interactions.

A micro-revolutionary dialogical approach would be critical, reflexive, and intersubjective, recognizing embodiment and the investment of emotion

(Collinson, 2005; Elliot and Reynolds, 2002; Gold et al., 2002; Rumens, 2005; Sauko, 2002). It would involve not only understanding of each self in the encounter, but, crucially, the ways in which the organization is influencing the encounter. How organizations remove respect and dignity that should be accorded to each and every human being is at the heart of these encounters. The aim should be to allow participants to flourish, as equals, free of hierarchy or expectations of contribution to the organization. If the organization benefits then that would be a bonus—the aim of this approach is to bring about local level revolutions in the ways in which people are treated.

Participants should go beyond their roles as managers, professionals, administrators, or employees so as to explore how these prescribed roles are enacted jointly. The aim is development of a shared view of activities which goes beyond what is currently so constrained by the organization so as to examine what might be created collectively.

The active encouragement of reflexive and dialogical space enables managers to become more aware of how they constitute, maintain, and thereby retain control over their and other's realities and identities, and the ways in which this inhibits the development of others. Where engagement in a critical, relational, and reflexive dialogical approach has been advocated as encouraging managers and staff alike to a deeper critique and questioning of how they account for their experiences (Cunliffe, 2002; Finlay, 2002; Hardy et al., 2001; Perriton, 2000; Reynolds, 1997, 1999), we go beyond that call to argue interactions should be micro-revolutionary. The 'intersubjective reflection' (Finlay, 2002, 215) of such an encounter is aimed at changing the organization and the organization's effect on selves. The aim is not that of the organization, but of the people who 'make up' the organization.

The aim, in short, is to remove the almost unnoticed shackles that organizations place on us. The hierarchical interactions between participants are used by organizations to impose a highly restricted and damaging order, one that limits the potentials for the constructions of identities and selves. Such impositions, such restrictions upon identities and selves, are taken-for-granted, regarded as the 'reality' of organizational life. Building on the chapters in this book, we conclude by advocating micro-revolutions achieved through reflexive, dialogic interactions designed to remove the organizational imposition of constrained identities.

REFERENCES

Alvesson, M. and H. Wilmott. 1996. *Making sense of management: A critical introduction.* London: Sage.

Benjamin, J. 1995. *Like subjects, love objects. Essays on recognition and sexual difference.* New Haven, CT: Yale University Press.

Bourdieu, P. and L.J.D. Wacquant. 1992. *An invitation to reflexive sociology.* Chicago, IL: University of Chicago Press.

Collinson, D. 2005. Dialectics of leadership. *Human Relations* 58(11): 1419–1442.

Cunliffe, A. 2002. Reflexive dialogical practice in management learning. *Management Learning* 33(1): 33–61.

Elliot, C. and M. Reynolds. 2002. Manager–educator relations from a critical perspective. *Journal of Management Education* 26(5): 512–526.

Finlay, C. 2002. Negotiating the swamp: The opportunity and challenge of reflexivity in research practice. *Qualitative Research* 2(2): 209–230.

Ford, J and N. Harding. 2004. We went looking for an organisation but could find only the metaphysics of its presence. *Sociology* 38(4): 815–830.

Ford, J. and N. Harding. 2007. Move over management: We are all leaders now? *Management Learning* 38(5) 475–493.

Ford, J., N. Harding, and M. Learmonth. 2008. *Leadership as identity: Constructions and deconstructions.* London: Palgrave Macmillan.

Ford, J. and J. Lawler. 2007. Blending existentialist and constructionist approaches to leadership studies: An exploratory account. *Leadership and Organisational Development Journal* 28(5) 409–425.

Gadamer, H.-G. 1975. *Truth and Method.* London: Sheed and Ward.

Ghaye, T. and S. Lillyman. 1996. *Learning journals and critical incidents: Reflective practice for healthcare professionals.* London: Mark Allen.

Gibson-Graham, J.K. 1996. *The end of capitalism (as we knew it): A feminist critique of political economy.* Malden, MA: Blackwell.

Gold, J., D. Holman, and R. Thorpe. 2002. The role of argument analysis and story telling in facilitating critical thinking. *Management Learning* 33(3): 371–388.

Grint, K. 2005. *Leadership: Limits and possibilities.* Hampshire, UK: Palgrave Macmillan.

Harding, N. and H. Lee. In review. Can anyone speak? Epistemological violence in organisations.

Hardy, C., N. Phillips, and S. Clegg. 2001. Reflexivity in organisation and management theory: A study of the production of the research subject. *Human Relations* 54(5): 531–560.

Laclau, E. and C. Mouffe. 2001. *Hegemony and socialist strategy: Towards a radical democratic politics.* London: Verso Books.

Marcus, S. 1992. Fighting bodies, fighting words: A theory and politics of rape prevention. In *Feminists theorize the political*, eds., J. Butler and J.W. Scott, 385–404. New York: Routledge.

Perriton, L. 2000. A reflection of what exactly? A provocation regarding the use of critical reflection in critical management education. Paper presented at the *Second Connecting Learning and Critique Conference*, Lancaster University, July 2000.

Reynolds, M. 1997. Towards a critical management pedagogy. In *Management Learning: Integrating perspectives in theory and practice*, eds. J. Burgoyne and M. Reynolds, 312–328. London: Sage.

Reynolds, M. 1999. Critical reflection and management education: Rehabilitating less hierarchical approaches. *Journal of Management Education* 23(5): 537–553.

Rumens, N. 2005. Extended review: Emotion in work organizations. *Management Learning* 36(1): 117–128.

Sauko, P. 2002. Studying the self: From the subjective and the social to personal and political dialogues. *Qualitative Research* 2(2): 244–263.

Schon, D.A. 1983. *The reflective practitioner: How professionals think in action.* New York: Basic Books.

Contributors

Graeme Currie is Professor of Public Services Management at Nottingham University Business School. He is also Director of one of the NIHR funded Collaborations for Leadership in Applied Health Research and Care (CLAHRC). His main areas of research critically focus on policy-promoted panaceas for organizational ills of leadership, knowledge management, and reconfiguration of professional roles and relationships.

Robert Dingwall is Professor and Director of the Institute for Science and Society at the University of Nottingham. After graduating from Cambridge in 1971 with a degree in social and political sciences, he received a PhD in medical sociology from the University of Aberdeen in 1974 and worked at the Centre for Socio-Legal Studies at the University of Oxford before moving to Nottingham in 1990. Since 1997, he has been directing the Institute for Science and Society, a research and graduate center for the study of the social, legal, cultural, and ethical implications of science and technology. His doctoral thesis was a case study of professional socialization and he has continued irregular contributions to the sociology of the professions for the last thirty-five years. Most of these are collected in *Essays on Professions* (2008).

Patricia A.L. Ehrensal, Ed.D., is an Assistant Professor of Educational Administration at the George Washington University, Washington, DC. The major focus of her research is the critical analysis of public (state) school organizations. Her publications in include articles in *Educational Administration Quarterly*, *Journal of Curriculum Theorizing* and *The Handbook of the Politics of Education*.

Finola Farrant is a Senior Lecturer in Criminology at Roehampton University London, where her research interests include prisoners' life stories and critical penological theory. She previously worked for a number of non-governmental organizations and prison campaign groups in a range of policy and research roles. Her publications include the first national survey of volunteering and citizenship in prisons in England and Wales, the largest investigation into the resettlement needs and pathways towards desistance for young adult male prisoners, a review of the mental health needs of children and young people in prison, and guidance for youth justice practitioners working with young offenders who use substances.

Jackie Ford is Professor of Leadership and Organization Studies at Bradford University School of Management. Current research explores leadership as a discursive and performative phenomenon, examining contemporary discourses of leadership and their complex inter-relations with gender and identity for managers. She is committed to identifying the human effects of managerial and organizational changes approached from feminist, poststructural, and psychoanalytic theoretical perspectives. She has coauthored *Leadership as Identity: Constructions and Deconstructions* and has published in a range of journals including *Journal of Management Studies,Leadership, Management Learning, Organization, Sociology.*

Marianna Fotaki is Senior Lecturer (Associate Professor) of health policy and organization studies in Manchester Business School and holds degrees in medicine and health economics, and a PhD in public policy from London School of Economics and Political Science. Before joining academia, Marianna has worked as a medical doctor for humanitarian organizations and as the EU resident senior adviser on health and social policy and economic restructuring to the governments of the Russian Federation, Armenia, Georgia, Bulgaria, Slovakia, and Tunisia. Her publications have appeared in *Human Relations, Public Administration, Journal of Organizational Change Management, Policy & Politics* and *Social Science and Medicine.* Marianna uses her diverse work experience and her experience in psychoanalysis and psychodynamic group relations to theorize on issues of public policy formation, gender and 'otherness' in organizations and society. She has co-organized a psychoanalytic symposium supported by Organization and Management Theory Division and Critical Management Studies Interest Group (CMS IG) at the annual meeting of the Academy of Management (AoM) in Philadelphia 2007, the stream on psychoanalysis at the International Critical Management Conference, July 2007 and a two-day pre-conference research workshop on 'Psychoanalysis and organizational theory' supported by CMS IG in AoM annual meeting in Anaheim in 2008. She is also convening a stream on 'love and hate for knowledge' in EGOS Conference in Barcelona 2009.

Nancy Harding works at Bradford School of Management teaching organization studies and directing the School's DBA programme. She has published books on *The Social Construction of Dementia* (1997); *The Social Construction of Management* (2003, Routledge); and, with Jackie

Ford and Mark Learmonth, *Leadership as Identity* (2008). She is currently working on a book to be called *On Being at Work*, which will be published by Routledge in 2010. Her papers have appeared in journals including *Organization Studies*, *Organization*, *Journal of Management Studies*, *Sociology*, etc. She is editor of *Journal of Health Organization and Management*.

Michael Humphreys is Professor of Organization Studies at Nottingham University Business School. After spending twenty-eight years in and around further education he joined Nottingham University in 2001. His research involves three main areas of inquiry: empirical studies of organizational identity and change; public sector management and research methodology (including autoethnographic and reflexive approaches to organizational analysis). He has published in a range of journals, including *Human Relations*, *Journal of Management Studies*, *Organization Studies*, *Organization*, *Journal of Organizational Change Management*, *Journal of Applied Behavioral Science*, *Education Studies* and *Qualitative Inquiry*.

Martin Kitchener MBA PhD is Professor of Healthcare Management and Policy at Cardiff Business School. From his research studies, Martin has published widely in the fields of organization theory, public management, health policy, and research methods. Recent papers appear in leading journals including: *Organization Studies*, *Organization*, *Health Services Research*, *Medical Care Research and Review*, *Healthcare Management Science*, *Health Affairs*, *Inquiry*, and *Journal of Health and Social Behavior*. *Martin* is the co-editor of a special edition of the *Journal of Aging and Social Policy* concerning personal care (2007), and is co-author of *Managing Residential Children's Care: A Managed Service* (2005).

John Lawler started his career in local authority social work. His interest in the development of management in that sector led him into research and into academia. His interest in management and leadership development within and beyond public services continues. He has a long-standing interest in existential thinking and is currently exploring ways of analyzing management and leadership from this perspective.

Mark Learmonth teaches qualitative research methods and public sector management at Nottingham University Business School. He worked in the UK NHS for almost seventeen years and still writes mainly about this sector—though with increasingly regular forays elsewhere.

Hugh Lee is a lecturer in Organization Behaviour and Business Ethics in Bradford University School of Management. Prior to this he taught at the Institute of Health Sciences within Leeds University Medical School. His current research interests are in the fields of identity, diversity, and relationships at work.

Graham P. Martin is a Research Fellow at the Institute for Science and Society, University of Nottingham. His research has covered wide-ranging aspects of the management and delivery of health and social care services. His recently completed doctoral thesis is a study of service user involvement in a program of pilot cancer-genetics in the National Health Service. Graham's work on public participation and other issues has been published in journals such as *Journal of Public Administration Research & Theory, Social Science & Medicine* and *Sociology of Health & Illness.*

Darryn Mitussis is a graduate of Murdoch University, University of London, and Oxford University. He has published in the *European Journal of Marketing, Journal of Marketing Management, Journal of Strategic Marketing, Advances in Consumer Research* and the *Journal of Consumer Behaviour.* He is a lecturer in marketing at Nottingham University.

Mona Moufahim is a Lecturer in Marketing at Nottingham University Business School. Her ongoing research is concerned with political marketing, consumption and identity. Her research interests lie in critical marketing, Asian marketing, and discursive research methods.

Craig Prichard is employed by Massey University in Aotearoa/New Zealand to support distance learners taking courses in organizational change. His primary research project is the development of a form of critical institutional analysis. Recent empirical topics include academic journal publishing, computer visualization, and private finance companies. He is associate editor for the journals *Management Learning* and *Organization* and main program chair for the Academy of Management's Critical Management Studies Division in 2009. Recent work has appeared in the journals *Rethinking Marxism, Social Epistemology, New Zealand Sociology* and *Ephemera.*

Patrick Reedy lectures in organizational behaviour at Nottingham University Business School. His research interests include alternative and radical organizations, particularly their history, and the political and ethical implications of managerialism.

Frank E. Scott is Associate Professor of Public Administration at California State University, East Bay. His public service experience includes work as a family and child therapist, a clinical director, and a children's mental health agency executive director. He currently teaches organization theory, public management, and ethics, and his work has appeared in *Administrative Theory & Praxis,* and *American Review of Public Administration.*

Justin Waring is Associate Professor with Nottingham University Business School. His work draws on medical and organizational sociology together with public policy and management. His work endeavours to explore the impact of health care reforms on the work, culture, and management of medicine and for the last decade this has centered on issues of clinical quality, risk, and patient safety. As well as continuing his work in the area of safety, he is currently investigating the changes in health care organization and management associated with the introduction of Indepedent Sector Treatment Centres.

Index